Portuguese

phrasebooks
and
Robert Landon

Portuguese phrasebook
2nd edition – March 2006

Published by
Lonely Planet Publications Pty Ltd ABN 36 005 607 983
90 Maribyrnong St, Footscray, Victoria 3011, Australia

Lonely Planet Offices
Australia Locked Bag 1, Footscray, Victoria 3011
USA 150 Linden St, Oakland CA 94607
UK 2nd fl, 186 City Rd, London, EC1V 2NT

Cover illustration
Saudades de Portugal by Yukiyoshi Kamimura

ISBN 1 74059 213 1

text © Lonely Planet Publications Pty Ltd 2006
cover illustration © Lonely Planet Publications Pty Ltd 2006

10 9 8 7 6 5 4

Printed through the Bookmaker International Ltd
Printed in China

acknowledgments

Editor Vanessa Battersby would like to acknowledge the following people for their contributions to this phrasebook:

Robert Landon, who has written for Lonely Planet, the *San Jose Mercury-News*, Bloomberg.com, an early iteration of Travelocity, and countless other business and travel websites (most now defunct). Special thanks go to Anabela de Azevedo Teixeira Sobrinho, translator, teacher and writer, for proofreading and providing cultural insight and additional translations.

Robert would like to thank Ben Handicott for entrusting him with the project and remaining remarkably tolerant when things did not proceed exactly as planned. Manuel Beja deserves special mention for the help he provided at the project's outset. João Maia e Silva and Tiago Romero Magalhães helped with translations and cultural information and exceeded all expectations – it was a real pleasure to work with both of them. He is also indebted to Paulo Bellot, who provided technical, linguistic and culinary expertise at critical junctures. For moral support, he thanks both Carlos Ponce (once again) and his 7am coffee klatch. Marianne's hang-gliding metaphor was particularly apt, as she knows.

Thanks also to Yukiyoshi Kamimura for the inside illustrations.

Lonely Planet Language Products

Publishing Manager: Chris Rennie
Commissioning Editor: Ben Handicott
Editor: Vanessa Battersby
Assisting Editors: Jodie Martire & Branislava Vladisavljevic
Layout Designer: Michael Ruff
Cartographer: Wayne Murphy

Managing Editor & Project Manager: Annelies Mertens
Managing Layout Designer: Celia Wood
Layout Manager: Adriana Mammarella
Series Designer: Yukiyoshi Kamimura
Production Manager: Jo Vraca

make the most of this phrasebook ...

Anyone can speak another language! It's all about confidence. Don't worry if you can't remember your school language lessons or if you've never learnt a language before. Even if you learn the very basics (on the inside covers of this book), your travel experience will be the better for it. You have nothing to lose and everything to gain when the locals hear you making an effort.

finding things in this book

For easy navigation, this book is in sections. The Tools chapters are the ones you'll thumb through time and again. The Practical section covers basic travel situations like catching transport and finding a bed. The Social section gives you conversational phrases, pick-up lines, the ability to express opinions – so you can get to know people. Food has a section all of its own: gourmets and vegetarians are covered and local dishes feature. Safe Travel equips you with health and police phrases, just in case. Remember the colours of each section and you'll find everything easily; or use the comprehensive Index and Finder. Otherwise, check the two-way traveller's Dictionary for the word you need.

being understood

Throughout this book you'll see coloured phrases on each page. They're phonetic guides to help you pronounce the language. You don't even need to look at the language itself, but you'll get used to the way we've represented particular sounds. The pronunciation chapter in Tools will explain more, but you can feel confident that if you read the coloured phrase slowly, you'll be understood.

communication tips

Body language, ways of doing things, sense of humour – all have a role to play in every culture. 'Local talk' boxes show you common ways of saying things, or everyday language to drop into conversation. 'Listen for ...' boxes supply the phrases you may hear. They start with the language (so local people can point out what they want to say to you) and then lead in to the phonetic guide and the English translation.

introduction 8

tools 11

practical 45

CONTENTS

5

CONTENTS

portuguese

ATLANTIC OCEAN

Viana do Castelo
Minho
Braga
Bragança
Trás-os-Montes
Porto
Douro
Vila Real
Embalse de Almendra
Aveiro
Viseu
Beira Alta
Beira Litoral
Guarda
Coimbra
Leiria
Beira Baixa
PORTUGAL
Castelo Branco
Embalse de Alcântara
Estremadura
Rio Tejo
Santarém
Lisboa (Lisbon)
Ribatejo
Portalegre
Alto Alentejo
Setúbal
Évora
Spain
Baixo Alentejo
Beja
Algarve
Faro

0 ——— 50 km
0 ——— 30 miles

official language
For more details, see the **introduction**.

Portuguese is a Romance language closely related to Spanish, French and Italian (to name just a few). Descended from the colloquial Latin spoken by Roman soldiers, Portuguese is now used by over 200 million people in Europe, Africa, Asia, Oceania and the Americas.

Linguists believe that before the Roman invasion of the Iberian Peninsula in 218 BC, the locals of modern-day Portugal spoke a Celtic language. Under the Romans' 500-year rule of the province of Lusitania (present-day Portugal and Spanish Galicia) that local language was supplanted by the vernacular form of Latin (sometimes called 'Romance') spoken by the occupying forces. During this period, Portuguese also absorbed elements of the languages of invading Germanic tribes. The greatest influence on today's Portuguese, however, was a result of the Moorish invasion of the peninsula in AD 711. Arabic was imposed as the official language of the region until the expulsion of the Moors in 1249, and although Romance was still spoken by the masses, the Moorish language left its mark with words such as *alcatifa* aal·ka·*tee*·fa (carpet) and *alcatrão* aal·ka·*trowng* (tar). From the 16th century on, there were only minor changes to the language, mostly caused by Portugal's proximity to France and Spain. The Portuguese used in 1572 by Luís de Camões

at a glance ...

language name:
Portuguese

name in language:
português poor·too·*gesh*

language family:
Romance

approximate number of speakers: 200 million worldwide

close relatives: Italian, Spanish

donations to English:
albino, auto-da-fé, brocade, commando, dodo, fandango, lingo, molasses, port

introduction

(author of the first great Portuguese classic, *Os Lusíadas*) was already identifiable as the language of José Saramago's Nobel Prize-winning works in the 20th century.

The global distribution of the Portuguese language began during *Os Descobrimentos* (the Discoveries), the golden era of Portugal's colonial expansion into Africa, Asia and South America. In the 15th and 16th centuries, the peninsular nation was a world power and had enormous economic, cultural and political influence, but its dominance subsequently waned. The empire's reach can be seen today in the number of countries besides Portugal itself where Portuguese still has the status of an official language – see the map below for details. There's also a significant population of Portuguese speakers in the USA, and small pockets in the Goa region of India, parts of Africa which were previously ruled by Portugal, and Australia, mainly in Sydney.

While there are many differences between European Portuguese and the Portuguese spoken elsewhere, you shouldn't have too many problems making yourself understood in any of the Portuguese-speaking countries. Local knowledge, new relationships and a sense of satisfaction are on the tip of your tongue, so don't just stand there, say something!

abbreviations used in this book

a	adjective	m	masculine	pol	polite
f	feminine	n	noun	sg	singular
inf	informal	pl	plural	v	verb
lit	literal				

Azores Islands (Portugal)   **Portugal**
North Atlantic Ocean   Madeira (Portugal)
Cape Verde   **Guinea-Bissau**   Macau (China)
São Tomé & Príncipe
Brazil   **Angola**   Indian Ocean   East Timor
South Atlantic Ocean   **Mozambique**

pronúncia

The coloured pronunciation guides in this book are based on the Portuguese spoken in Portugal. There are some variations in pronunciation throughout the country, but they don't cause much difficulty in communication. You'll also generally be understood in other countries where Portuguese is spoken.

vowel sounds

The vowel sounds in Portuguese are quite similar to those found in English, so you should be able to get talking with confidence. There are some differences of course. Most vowel sounds in Portuguese also have a nasal version with an effect similar to the silent '-ng' ending in English, such as *amanhã* aa·ma·*nyang* (tomorrow), for example. The letter 'n' or 'm' at the end of a syllable or a tilde (~) in written Portuguese indicate that the vowel is nasal (also see **consonant sounds**).

symbol	english equivalent	portuguese example	transliteration
a	among	*maçã*	ma·*sang*
aa	father	*tomate*	too·*maa*·te
ai	aisle	*pai*	pai
ay	play	*lei*	lay
e	ten	*cedo*	*se*·doo
ee	feet	*fino*	*fee*·noo
o	lot	*sobre*	*so*·bre
oh	oh!	*couve*	*koh*·ve
oo	book	*gato*	*ga*·too
ow	cow	*Austrália*	ow·*shtraa*·lya
oy	boy	*noite*	*noy*·te

consonant sounds

Most of the consonant sounds in Portuguese are also found in
English, and even *r* (rr), which doesn't exist in standard English,
will be familiar to many people (it's similar to the French 'r').

symbol	english equivalent	portuguese example	transliteration
b	bed	*beber*	be·ber
d	dog	*dedo*	de·doo
f	fit	*faca*	faa·ka
g	gap	*gasolina*	ga·zoo·lee·na
k	kit	*cama*	ka·ma
l	let	*lixo*	lee·shoo
ly	million	*muralhas*	moo·raa·lyash
m	mat	*macaco*	ma·kaa·koo
n	no	*nada*	naa·da
ng	sing (indicates the nasalisation of the preceding vowel)	*ambos* *uns* *amanhã*	ang·boosh oongsh aa·ma·nyang
ny	canyon	*linha*	lee·nya
p	pin	*padre*	paa·dre
r	like 'tt' in 'butter' said fast	*hora*	o·ra
rr	as in French 'croissant'	*relva*	rrel·va
s	sad	*criança*	kree·ang·sa
sh	shut	*chave*	shaa·ve
t	top	*tacho*	taa·shoo
v	very	*vago*	vaa·goo
w	water	*água*	aa·gwa
y	yes	*edifício*	ee·dee·fee·syoo
z	zoo	*camisa*	ka·mee·za
zh	pleasure	*cerveja*	serr·ve·zha

Some consonant sounds can change depending on where they appear in a word. For example, an 's' at the beginning of the word is pronounced like the s in 'sea' – eg *sal* saal (salt). When 's' comes at the end of the word, or at the end of a syllable which is followed by a consonant, as in *está* shtaa (are), it's pronounced sh, but if it's surrounded on both sides by vowels (as in *camisa* ka·*mee*·za), it's pronounced z. Follow the coloured pronunciation guides and you won't have any trouble.

word stress

Stress (ie the emphasis on one syllable over another) generally occurs on the second-to-last syllable of a word, though there are exceptions. If a written vowel has a circumflex (^) or an acute (´) or grave (`) accent marked on it, this cancels the general rule and the stress falls on that syllable.

fino	*fee*·no	**fine**
português	poor·too·*gesh*	**Portuguese**
cajú	ka·*zhoo*	**cashew**

Also, if you're reading Portuguese words for yourself, it's handy to know these other exceptions: when a word ends in a written *i*, *im*, *l*, *r*, *u*, *um* or *z*, or is pronounced with a nasalised vowel, the stress falls on the last syllable.

beber	be·*ber*	**to drink**
calor	ka·*lor*	**heat**
actuação	a·too·a·*sowng*	**performance**

Don't worry too much about it when using phrases from this book though – if you follow the coloured pronunciation guides you can't go wrong.

You'll notice in conversation with Portuguese speakers that as in English, when certain syllables are given more stress, others are practically unpronounced. For example, unless the final syllable is stressed, the vowel is pronounced very lightly and in conversation may disappear altogether – so *antes* is technically pronounced *aang*·tesh but in practice sounds more like ants. Again, we've always given the correct pronunciation in our coloured guides.

reading & writing

Portuguese is written with the Latin alphabet. For spelling purposes (eg if you need to spell your name to book into a hotel), the pronunciation of each letter is provided below.

alphabet					
A a aa	*B b* be	*C c* se	*D d* de	*E e* e	*F f* e·fe
G g je	*H h* a·*gaah*	*I i* ee	*J j* *jo*·ta	*K k* ka·pa	*L l* e·le
M m e·me	*N n* e·ne	*O o* o	*P p* pe	*Q q* ke	*R r* e·rre
S s e·se	*T t* te	*U u* oo	*V v* ve	*W w* *da*·blyoo	*X x* sheesh
Y y *eeps*·lon	*Z z* ze				

You'll notice that some letters, usually vowels, have accent marks. The acute (´) and grave (`) accents and the circumflex (ˆ) indicate stress, and the tilde (~) indicates nasalisation. You'll also see the cedilla sometimes used at the bottom of the letter 'c' – ç is pronounced as s rather than k (*criança* kree·*ang*·sa).

contents

The index below shows which grammatical structures you need to say what you want. Look under each function – in alphabetical order – for information on how to build your own phrases. For example, to tell the taxi driver where your hotel is, look for **giving instructions** below and you'll be directed to information on **personal pronouns**, **prepositions**, etc. A glossary of grammatical terms is included at the end of this chapter to help you.

adjectives & adverbs

describing people/things

Adjectives are generally placed after the noun. They change form depending on the gender and number of the noun they describe (see also **gender**):

the handsome boy
o menino bonito   oo me·*nee*·noo boo·*nee*·too
(lit: the boy handsome)

the handsome boys
os meninos bonitos   oosh me·*nee*·noosh boo·*nee*·toosh
(lit: the boys handsome)

the pretty girl
a menina bonita   a me·*nee*·na boo·*nee*·ta
(lit: the girl pretty)

the pretty girls
as meninas bonitas   ash me·*nee*·nash boo·*nee*·tash
(lit: the girls pretty)

Adverbs are normally formed by adding *-mente* meng·te to the end of the feminine form of the adjective.

adjective			adverb		
clear	*clara* f	*klaa*·ra	clearly	*claramente*	klaa·ra·*meng*·te
slow	*lenta* f	*leng*·ta	slowly	*lentamente*	leng·ta·*meng*·te

articles

describing people/things • naming people/things

The Portuguese words *um* oong and *uma* oo·ma correspond to the English article 'a/an'. If what you're referring to is masculine you use *um*, if it's feminine you use *uma*. The plurals *uns* oongsh and *umas* oo·mash correspond to the English 'some'.

masculine	sg	*um café* oong *ka*·fe	a coffee
	pl	*uns cafés* oongsh *ka*·fesh	some coffees
feminine	sg	*uma sandes* oo·ma*sang*·desh	a sandwich
	pl	*umas sandes* oo·mash *sang*·desh	some sandwiches

There are four words that correspond to the English article 'the'. The form you use is determined by the gender and number of the noun the article is used with:

masculine	sg	*o comboio* oo kong·*boy*·oo	the train
	pl	*os comboios* oosh kong·*boy*·oosh	the trains
feminine	sg	*a mochila* a moo·*shee*·la	the backpack
	pl	*as mochilas* ash moo·*shee*·lash	the backpacks

See also **gender** and **plurals**.

be

describing people/things • doing things • indicating location • making statements • pointing things out

Portuguese has two words which can be translated as 'be' in English: *ser* ser and *estar* shtaar. They're both irregular verbs (just like 'be' in English) so you need to learn by heart the various forms they take. Learning to use them perfectly will take some time and effort, but the basic difference in their usage isn't too difficult to grasp.

The verb *ser* refers to states that have a degree of permanency or durability about them.

I	am	*eu*	e·oo	*sou*	soh
you sg inf	are	*tu*	too	*és*	esh
you sg pol	are	*você*	vo·se	*é*	e
he/she	is	*ele/ela*	e·le/e·la	*é*	e
we	are	*nós*	nosh	*somos*	so·moosh
you pl inf	are	*vocês*	vo·sesh	*são*	sowng
you pl pol	are	*vós*	vosh	*sois*	soysh
they m/f	are	*eles/elas*	e·lesh/ e·lash	*são*	sowng

You also use *ser* to point something out in Portuguese. Just start your phrase with *É … e …* (lit: it-is …) as in the example below. See also **demonstratives** and **there is/are**.

That's a beautiful building.
  É um edifício lindo.   e oong ee·dee·fee·syoo *leeng*·do
  (lit: it-is a building beautiful)

The verb *estar* generally refers to events which are temporary in nature. It's also used to talk about the location of things that are moveable.

I	am	*eu*	e·oo	*estou*	shtoh
you sg inf	are	*tu*	too	*estás*	shtaash
you sg pol	are	*você*	vo·se	*está*	shtaa
he/she	is	*ele/ela*	e·le/e·la	*está*	shtaa
we	are	*nós*	nos	*estamos*	shta·moosh
you pl inf	are	*vocês*	vo·sesh	*estão*	shtowng
you pl pol	are	*vós*	vosh	*estais*	shtaish
they m/f	are	*eles/elas*	e·lesh/ e·lash	*estão*	shtowng

demonstratives

describing people/things • indicating location • naming people/things • pointing things out

To refer to or point at a person or object, use one of the following words before the noun, depending on whether the person or object you're referring to is close or further away, masculine or feminine, and singular or plural:

	singular		plural	
	masculine	feminine	masculine	feminine
close	*este* esh·te	*esta* esh·ta	*estes* esh·tesh	*estas* esh·tash
away	*aquele* a·ke·le	*aquela* a·ke·la	*aqueles* a·ke·lesh	*aquelas* a·ke·lash

Is this seat free?
> *Este lugar está livre?*   esh·te loo·gaar shtaa *lee*·vre
> (lit: this place is free)

These words can also be used on their own without an accompanying noun – meaning 'this (one)', 'that (one)', 'these' and 'those'.

Those are Portuguese.
> *Aqueles são*   a·ke·lesh sowng
> *portugueses.*   poor·too·ge·zesh
> (lit: those are Portuguese)

gender

describing people/things • naming people/things

All Portuguese nouns are either masculine m or feminine f. This determines the endings on any adjectives you use to describe them, as well as which forms of the Portuguese equivalents of the articles 'a/an' and 'the' are used.

The gender that a given noun takes is often arbitrary: there's no reason why, for example, the noun *sol* sol (sun) is masculine while *praia* prai·a (beach) is feminine. The dictionaries and word lists in this book give all nouns with their gender, but here are some guidelines for taking a guess at gender if you need to:

often masculine	often feminine
nouns referring to male persons (or male animals)	nouns referring to female persons (or female animals)
nouns ending in *-o*	nouns ending in *-a*
nouns ending in *-ema* and *-oma*	nouns ending with *-dade*

See also **articles** and **adjectives & adverbs**.

have

making statements · possessing

An easy way to indicate possession is to use the verb *ter* ter (have), which has different forms for each person.

I have a flight at 6pm.
Eu tenho um voo   e·oo ta·nyoo oong vo·o
às seis da tarde.   aash saysh da taar·de
(lit: I have a flight at six in-the afternooon)

	have				
I	have	*eu*	e·oo	*tenho*	ta·nyoo
you sg inf	have	*tu*	too	*tens*	tengsh
you sg pol	have	*você*	vo·se	*tem*	teng
he/she	has	*ele/ela*	e·le/e·la	*tem*	teng
we	have	*nós*	nosh	*temos*	te·moosh
you pl inf	have	*vocês*	vo·sesh	*têm*	teng·eng
you pl pol	have	*vós*	vosh	*tendes*	teng·desh
they	have	*eles/elas*	e·lesh/ e·lash	*têm*	teng·eng

negatives

To make a sentence negative, just add the word *não* nowng
(no) before the main verb – in the example below, this is *vejo*
ve·zhoo (see).

I see the market.
  Vejo o mercado.   ve·zhoo oo mer·*kaa*·doo
  (lit: I-see the market)

I don't see the market.
  Não vejo o   nowng ve·zhoo oo
  mercado.   mer·*kaa*·doo
  (lit: no I-see the market)

In Portuguese, the double negative is not only acceptable, but
correct:

I can't see anything.
  Não vejo nada.   nowng ve·zhoo *naa*·da
  (lit: no I-see nothing)

negative words		
never	*nunca*	*noong*·ka
no/not	*não*	nowng
nobody	*ninguém*	neeng·*geng*
none sg m/f	*nenhum/nenhuma*	neng·*yoong*/neng·*yoo*·ma
nor	*nem*	neng

See also **there is/are**.

personal pronouns

Subject pronouns corresponding to 'I', 'you', and so on (listed
in the first box below) are often left out in Portuguese, as the
verb endings make it clear who the subject is. You only need
to use them if you want to emphasise who or what is doing
the action. You'll notice that there are polite and informal
versions of 'you' (marked with **pol** and **inf**). The polite version,
combined with a verb in the third person singular (he/she), is
used with people older than you or that you don't know very
well. In this book we've used the form that best suits the con-
text – generally this means the polite form unless it's marked
otherwise in the chapter – so you don't need to worry about it
(see also the box on page 120).

singular			plural		
I	eu	e·oo	we	nós	nosh
you inf	tu	too	you inf	vocês	vo·sesh
you pol	você	vo·se	you pol	vós	vosh
he	ele	e·le	they m or m&f	eles	e·lesh
she	ela	e·la	they f	elas	e·lash

The direct object pronouns corresponding to 'me', 'you' and so
on are listed below.

singular			plural		
me	me	me	us	nos	noosh
you inf	te	te	you inf	vos	voosh
you pol m/f	o/a	oo/a	you pol m/f	os/as	oosh/ash
him	o	oo	them m or m&f	os	oosh
her	a	a	them f	as	ash

a–z phrasebuilder

23

plurals

You can make a noun ending in a vowel plural by simply adding -s sh:

singular		plural	
book	*livro* m lee·vroo	books	*livros* m pl lee·vroosh
bed	*cama* f ka·ma	beds	*camas* f pl ka·mash
city	*cidade* f see·*daa*·de	qualities	*cidades* f pl see·*daa*·desh

If the noun ends in -s, -z or -r and the final syllable is stressed, then the plural is formed by adding -es esh:

singular		plural	
Portuguese	*português* poor·too·*gesh*	Portuguese	*portugueses* poor·too·ge·zesh
nose	*nariz* na·*reesh*	noses	*narizes* na·*ree*·zesh
flower	*flor* flor	flowers	*flores* *flo*·resh

Don't forget, you have to change any articles and adjectives you use with a plural noun to their plural forms too.

There are some exceptions and additional rules for making nouns plural – if you'd like to find out more, you could consult a comprehensive grammar of Portuguese.

See also **articles**, **adjectives & adverbs** and **gender**.

possessives

describing people/things • naming people/things • possessing

There are various ways to indicate possession in Portuguese. One easy way is by using the verb ter ter (have). Simplest of all is to use the preposition *de* de (of), followed by the name of the person who owns the object.

It's Carla's backpack.

É a mochila da Carla.   e a moo·*shee*·la da *caar*·la
(lit: it-is the backpack of Carla)

Also, as you do in English, you can indicate possession using pronouns. The table below lists the equivalents for the English possessive pronouns 'my', 'your' and 'our'. Put them between an article and the noun they describe, and make them agree in number (singular or plural) and gender (masculine or feminine) with the noun.

It's my ticket.

É o meu bilhete.   e oo *me*·oo bee·*lye*·te
(lit: it-is the my ticket)

	singular		plural	
	masculine	feminine	masculine	feminine
my	meu me·oo	minha mee·nya	meus me·oosh	minhas mee·nyash
your sg inf	teu te·oo	tua too·a	teus te·oosh	tuas too·ash
your sg pol	seu se·oo	sua soo·a	seus se·oosh	suas soo·ash
our	nosso no·soo	nossa no·sa	nossos no·soosh	nossas no·sash
your pl inf	vosso vo·soo	vossa vo·sa	vossos vo·soos	vossas vo·sash

For the equivalents of 'his', 'her' and 'their' (overleaf), it's a bit different. The pronoun goes after the noun, and the gender and number don't match the noun, they match the owner – eg 'her book' is *o livro dela* oo lee·vroo de·la (lit: the book her).

his	*dele*	de·le	**their** m or m&f	*deles*	de·lesh
her	*dela*	de·la	**their** f	*delas*	de·lash

See also **have**, **gender** and **articles**.

prepositions

giving instructions · indicating location · pointing things out

Prepositions in Portuguese can be placed before the noun, as in *com leite* kong lay·te (with milk), or after verbs. Here are some common prepositions:

between	*entre*	eng·tre	over	*por cima de*	poor see·ma de
to/for	*para*	pa·ra	under	*debaixo de*	de·bai·shoo de
until	*até*	a·te	with	*com*	kong

Some other prepositions have a standard form but when they come before an article they combine with the article (which agrees in gender and number with the noun it goes with). 'In the rooms', for example, is *nos quartos* noosh kwaar·toosh – *nos* is a combination of *em* eng (in) and *os* oosh (the m pl).

	standard form	combined with an article			
		m sg	f sg	m pl	f pl
by/for	*por* por	*pelo* pe·loo	*pela* pe·la	*pelos* pe·loosh	*pelas* pe·lash
in/on	*em* eng	*no* noo	*na* na	*nos* noosh	*nas* nash
of/from	*de* de	*do* doo	*da* da	*dos* doosh	*das* dash
to	*a* a	*ao* ow	*à* aa	*aos* owsh	*às* aash

See also **articles** and **gender**.

questions

To ask a question, simply make a statement but raise your voice inquisitively at the end of the sentence, as you would in English.

Do you speak Portuguese?
Fala português?   faa·la poor·too·*gesh*
(lit: you-speak portuguese)

You can also use one of the question words below, which go at the beginning of the sentence as they do in English.

how?	como	ko·moo
how much?	quanto	kwang·too
how many?	quantos/ quantas m/f	kwang·toosh/ kwang·tash
what?	quê	ke
what/which?	qual	kwaal
where?	onde	ong·de
who?	quem	keng
why?	porquê	poor·ke

To make a request, start your sentence with *Podia* … poo·*dee*·a … (lit: could-you …).

Could you take a photo of me, please?
Podia tirar-me uma   poo·*dee*·a tee·*raar*·me *oo*·ma
fotografia, por favor?   foo·too·gra·*fee*·a poor fa·*vor*
(lit: could-you-**sg-pol** take-me a photo please)

there is/are

To say 'there is' or 'there are' in Portuguese, use *há* aa (lit: it-has).
Add *não* nowng (no) before *há* to make a negative sentence.

There's a seat available.
> *Há um lugar vago.*   aa oong loo-*gaar vaa*-goo
> (lit: it-has a seat free)

There aren't any seats available.
> *Não há lugares vagos.*   nowng aa loo-*gaa*-resh *vaa*-goosh
> (lit: no it-has seat free)

See also **be**.

verbs

Portuguese has three types of verbs: those ending in *-ar* aar
(*morar* mor-*aar*, 'live'), those ending in *-er* er (*comer* koo-*mer*,
'eat') and those ending in *-ir* eer (*partir* par-*teer*, 'leave'). The
present tense verb endings for each person ('I', 'you', 'we' etc)
are very similar for all three, so you can recognise them easily:

	-ar	-er	-ir
I	*-o* oo	*-o* oo	*-o* oo
you sg inf	*-as* ash	*-es* esh	*-es* esh
you sg pol	*-a* a	*-e* e	*-e* e
he/she	*-a* a	*-e* e	*-e* e
we	*-amos* a-moosh	*-emos* e-moosh	*-imos* ee-moosh
you pl pol	*-ais* aish	*-eis* aysh	*-is* eesh
you pl inf	*-am* owng	*-em* eng	*-em* eng
they	*-am* owng	*-em* eng	*-em* eng

As in any language, some Portuguese verbs are irregular. The most important ones are *ser* ser (be), *estar* shtaar (be) and *ter* ter (have). For more details see **be** and **have**.

word order

doing things • giving instructions • making requests • making statements

Generally, the order of words in a sentence is the same as in English (subject–verb–object).

I'd like a room.
   Eu queria um quarto.   e·oo ke·*ree*·a oong *kwaar*·too
   (lit: I would-like a room)

ladies & gentlemen, boys & girls

Many of the words listed in this book have different masculine and feminine forms, marked with m or f. If the word is an adjective that goes with a noun (eg 'blue tile'), use the form that matches the gender of the noun. When you say a phrase like 'It's **beautiful**' or 'I'm a **doctor**', use the version of 'beautiful' and 'doctor' that match the gender of whatever you're talking about – in the second phrase, yourself! The same applies to saying thank you – use the gender that matches your own. If you're male, say *Obrigado* (o·bree·*gaa*·doo), if you're female, say *Obrigada* (o·bree·*gaa*·da).

glossary

adjective	a word that describes something – 'the bull looked **fierce**'
adverb	a word that explains how an action is done – 'the horse moved **quickly**'
article	the words 'a', 'an' and 'the'
demonstrative	a word that means 'this' or 'that'
gender	Portuguese nouns and pronouns are categorised as masculine or feminine, and adjectives and articles must match the gender of the noun they belong to
noun	a thing, person or idea – 'the **crowd**'
number	whether a word is singular or plural – 'the horseman had planted three **barbs** in the bull's neck'
object	the thing or person in the sentence that has the action directed to it – 'The crowd praised **him**'
personal pronoun	a word that means 'I', 'you', 'me', etc
possessive pronoun	a word that means 'my', 'mine', 'yours', etc
preposition	a word like 'for' or 'before' in English
present tense	the verb tense which tells what's happening now – 'the crowd **roars**'
proper nouns	names of people, places and things which would be capitalised in English
subject	the thing or person in the sentence that does the action – '**the foot soldiers** enter the ring'
transliteration	pronunciation guide for words and phrases of a foreign language
verb	the word that tells you what action happened – 'the foot soldiers **wrestle** the bull'
verb ending	the part of a verb which changes to show number, person or tense – 'he twist**s** the bull's tail' and 'they kill**ed** the bull'

language difficulties
dificuldades com a língua

Do you speak (English)?
Fala (inglês)? · faa·la (eeng·glesh)

Does anyone speak (English)?
Alguém aqui fala (inglês)? · aal·geng a·kee faa·la (eeng·glesh)

Do you understand (me)?
Entende(-me)? · eng·teng·de(·me)

Yes, I understand.
Sim, entendo. · seeng eng·teng·doo

No, I don't understand.
Não, não entendo. · nowng nowng eng·teng·doo

I (don't) understand.
(Não) entendo. · (nowng) eng·teng·doo

Pardon?
Desculpe? · desh·kool·pe

I speak (English).
Falo (inglês). · faa·loo (eeng·glesh)

I don't speak (Portuguese).
Não falo (português). · nowng faa·loo (poor·too·gesh)

I speak a little.
Falo um pouco. · faa·loo oong poh·koo

I would like to practise (Portuguese).
Gostava de praticar (português). · goosh·taa·va de pra·tee·kaar (poor·too·gesh)

Let's speak (Portuguese).
Vamos falar (português). · vaa·moosh fa·laar (poor·too·gesh)

What does (bem-vindo) mean?
O que quer dizer (bem-vindo)? · oo ke ker dee·zer (beng·veeng·doo)

language difficulties

31

How do you ...?	*Como é que se ...?*	ko·moo e ke se ...
pronounce	*pronuncia*	proo·noong·*see*·a
this	*isto*	*eesh*·too
write (*ajuda*)	*escreve (ajuda)*	shkre·ve (a·*zhoo*·da)

Could you	*Podia ...*	poo·*dee*·a ...
please ...?	*por favor?*	poor fa·*vor*
repeat that	*repetir isto*	rre·pe·*teer eesh*·too
speak more	*falar mais*	fa·*laar* maish
slowly	*devagar*	de·va·*gaar*
write it down	*escrever isso*	shkre·*ver ee*·soo

tongue torture

Think you've got a bit of a handle on Portuguese? Amuse the locals by reciting one of these little beauties.

Um prato de trigo para três tigres tristes.
oong *praa*·too de *tree*·goo *pa*·ra tresh *tee*·gresh *treesh*·tesh
A plate of wheat for three sad tigers.

Se cá nevasse fazia-se cá esqui.
se kaa ne·*vaa*·se fa·*zee*·a·se kaa shkee
If it snowed here you could ski.

O rato roeu a rolha do garrafão do rei da Rússia.
oo *rraa*·too rroo·e·oo a *rro*·lya doo ga·rra·*fowng*
doo rray da *rru*·sya
The mouse nibbled the cork of the large wickerwork bottle of the king from Russia.

cardinal numbers

números cardinais

As in English, the numbers in Portuguese have to be memorised up to 20, but follow a fairly simple pattern after that – for '21' just join the words for '20' and '1' with e e (and), '22' literally is '20 and 2', and so on.

0	zero	ze·roo
1	um	oong
2	dois	doysh
3	três	tresh
4	quatro	kwaa·troo
5	cinco	seeng·koo
6	seis	saysh
7	sete	se·te
8	oito	oy·too
9	nove	no·ve
10	dez	desh
11	onze	ong·ze
12	doze	do·ze
13	treze	tre·ze
14	catorze	ka·tor·ze
15	quinze	keeng·ze
16	dezasseis	de·za·saysh
17	dezassete	de·za·se·te
18	dezoito	de·zoy·too
19	dezanove	de·za·no·ve
20	vinte	veeng·te
21	vinte e um	veeng·te e oong
22	vinte e dois	veeng·te e doysh
30	trinta	treeng·ta

40	*quarenta*	kwa·*reng*·ta
50	*cinquenta*	seeng·*kweng*·ta
60	*sessenta*	se·*seng*·ta
70	*setenta*	se·*teng*·ta
80	*oitenta*	oy·*teng*·ta
90	*noventa*	no·*veng*·ta
100	*cem*	seng
125	*cento e*	*seng*·too e
	vinte e cinco	*veeng*·te e *seng*·koo
200	*duzentos*	doo·*zeng*·toosh
300	*trezentos*	tre·*zeng*·toosh
400	*quatrocentos*	kwa·troo·*seng*·toosh
500	*quinhentos*	keeng·*yeng*·toosh
600	*seiscentos*	say·*seng*·toosh
700	*setecentos*	se·te·*seng*·toosh
800	*oitocentos*	oy·too·*seng*·toosh
900	*novecentos*	no·ve·*seng*·toosh
1000	*mil*	meel
1,000,000	*um milhão*	oong mee·*lyowng*

ordinal numbers

Ordinal numbers are written with a degree sign in Portuguese –
1st is written '1º', 10th is '10º', and so on.

1st	*primeiro/primeira* m/f	pree·*may*·roo/pree·*may*·ra
2nd	*segundo/segunda* m/f	se·*goong*·doo/se·*goong*·da
3rd	*terceiro/terceira* m/f	ter·*say*·roo/ter·*say*·ra
4th	*quarto/quarta* m/f	*kwaar*·too/*kwaar*·ta
5th	*quinto/quinta* m/f	*keeng*·too/*keeng*·ta
6th	*sexto/sexta* m/f	*sesh*·too/*sesh*·ta
7th	*sétimo/sétima* m/f	se·*tee*·moo/se·*tee*·ma
8th	*oitavo/oitava* m/f	oy·*taa*·voo/oy·*taa*·va
9th	*nono/nona* m/f	*no*·noo/*no*·na
10th	*décimo/décima* m/f	de·*see*·moo/de·*see*·ma

fractions & decimals

a quarter	um quarto	oong kwaar·too
a third	um terço	oong ter·soo
a half	a metade	a me·taa·de
three-quarters	três quartos	tresh kwaar·toosh
all	todo m	to·doo
	toda f	to·da
none	nenhum m	neng·yoong
	nenhuma f	neng·yoo·ma

In Portugal, decimals are written – and pronounced – as in English, except that the period is replaced by a comma (*vírgula veer·goo·*la).

3.14	três vírgula catorze (3,14)	tresh veer·goo·la ka·tor·ze
4.2	quatro vírgula dois (4,2)	kwaa·troo veer·goo·la doysh
5.1	cinco vírgula um (5,1)	seeng·koo veer·goo·la oong

this goes with that

Many of the words listed in this book have different masculine and feminine forms, marked with m or f. If the word is an adjective that goes with a noun (eg 'blue tile'), use the form that matches the gender of the noun. When you say a phrase like 'It's **beautiful**' or 'I'm a **doctor**', use the version of 'beautiful' and 'doctor' that match the gender of whatever you're talking about – in the second phrase, yourself!

useful amounts

How much?	Quanto?	kwang·too
How many?	Quantos? m	kwang·toosh
	Quantas? f	kwang·tash

Please give me ...	Por favor dê-me ...	poor fa·vor de·me ...
(100) grams	(cem) gramas	(seng) graa·mash
half a dozen	meia dúzia	may·a doo·zya
half a kilo	meio quilo	may·oo kee·loo
a kilo	um quilo	oong kee·loo
a bottle	uma garrafa	oo·ma ga·rraa·fa
a jar	um frasco	oong fraash·koo
a packet	um pacote	oong pa·ko·te
a slice	uma fatia	oo·ma fa·tee·a
a tin (can)	uma lata	oo·ma laa·ta
a few	uns poucos m	oongsh poh·koosh
	umas poucas f	oo·mash poh·kash
less	menos	me·noosh
(just) a little	(só) um bocadinho	(so) oong boo·ka·dee·nyoo
a lot	muito	mweeng·too
many	muitos m	mweeng·toosh
	muitas f	mweeng·tash
more	mais	maish
some	uns m	oongsh
	umas f	oo·mash

For more amounts, see **self-catering**, page 161.

telling the time

Generally, the 12-hour clock is used for telling the time in Portuguese, though the 24-hour clock is often what you'll see written down.

To tell the time, use *são* sowng (the plural form of the verb ser ser, 'be'), except in the case of 1 o'clock, when you use *é* e. For minutes past the hour or before the next hour, it's pretty straightforward. Up to the half-hour, say the hour plus *e* e (and) and the number of minutes. For 'half-past' add *e meia* e *may*·a (and a half) instead. Past the half-hour, give the number of minutes plus *para as pa*·ra ash (before) and the following hour. You can add *da manhã* da ma·*nyang* (in the morning), *da tarde* da *taar*·de (in the afternoon) or *da noite* da *noy*·te (in the evening – ie 8pm onward) to specify the time of day.

What time is it?	*Que horas são?*	kee *o*·rash sowng
It's (one) o'clock.	*É (uma) hora.*	e (*oo*·ma) *o*·ra
It's (ten) o'clock.	*São (dez) horas.*	sowng (desh) *o*·rash
Five past (ten).	*(Dez) e cinco.*	(desh) e *seeng*·koo
Quarter past (ten).	*(Dez) e quinze.*	(desh) e *keeng*·ze
Half past (ten).	*(Dez) e meia.*	(desh) e *may*·a
Quarter to (eleven).	*Quinze para as (onze).*	*keeng*·ze pa·ra ash (*ong*·ze)
am	*da manhã*	da ma·*nyang*
pm (afternoon)	*da tarde*	da *taar*·de
pm (evening)	*da noite*	da *noy*·te

At what time …?	A que horas …?	a ke o·rash …
At (one).	À (uma).	aa (oo·ma)
At (two).	Às (duas).	aash (doo·ash)
At (five).	Às (cinco).	aash (seeng·koo)
At (7.57pm).	Às (sete e cinquenta e sete da noite).	aash (se·te e seeng·kweng·ta e se·te da noy·te)

the calendar

calendário

days

Monday	segunda-feira	se·goong·da·fay·ra
Tuesday	terça-feira	ter·sa·fay·ra
Wednesday	quarta-feira	kwaar·ta·fay·ra
Thursday	quinta-feira	keeng·ta·fay·ra
Friday	sexta-feira	saysh·ta·fay·ra
Saturday	sábado	saa·ba·doo
Sunday	domingo	doo·meeng·goo

months

January	Janeiro	zha·nay·roo
February	Fevereiro	fe·vray·roo
March	Março	maar·soo
April	Abril	a·breel
May	Maio	maa·yoo
June	Junho	zhoo·nyoo
July	Julho	zhoo·lyoo
August	Agosto	a·gosh·too
September	Setembro	se·teng·broo
October	Outubro	oh·too·broo
November	Novembro	no·veng·broo
December	Dezembro	de·zeng·broo

dates

In Portuguese, use plain (cardinal) numbers to give dates.

What date is it today?
    Qual é a data de hoje?   kwaal e a *daa*·ta de o·zhe

It's (18 October).
    Hoje é dia   o·zhe e *dee*·a
    (dezoito de Outubro).   (de·*zoy*·too de oh·*too*·broo)

seasons

spring	*primavera* f	pree·ma·*ve*·ra
summer	*verão* m	ve·*rowng*
autumn/fall	*outono* m	oh·*to*·noo
winter	*inverno* m	eeng·*ver*·noo
dry season	*estação seca* f	shta·*sowng se*·ka
rainy season	*estação das*	shta·*sowng* dash
	chuvas f	*shoo*·vash

present

now	*agora*	a·*go*·ra
today	*hoje*	o·zhe
tonight	*hoje à noite*	o·zhe aa *noy*·te
this ...		
morning	*esta manhã*	*esh*·ta ma·*nyang*
afternoon	*esta tarde*	*esh*·ta *taar*·de
week	*esta semana*	*esh*·ta se·*ma*·na
month	*este mês*	*esh*·te mesh
year	*este ano*	*esh*·te *a*·noo

While you're in Portugal, you might have the good luck to wander into a town that's taking the day off to celebrate its patron saint (*santo padroeiro sang*·too pa·droo·*ay*·roo) – complete with decorated streets, a procession (*procissão* proo·see·*sowng*), and a street party (*arraial* a·rray·*aal*). Portugal also has the full gamut of religious holidays you'd expect in a Catholic country, along with secular holidays:

New Year's Day
  Dia de Ano Novo   *dee*·a de *a*·noo *no*·voo

Mardi Gras
  Carnaval   kar·na·*vaal*

Good Friday
  Sexta-feira Santa   sesh·ta·*fay*·ra *sang*·ta

Liberation Day (25 April)
  Dia da Liberdade   *dee*·a da lee·ber·*daa*·de

Labour Day (1 May)
  Dia do Trabalhador   *dee*·a doo tra·ba·lya·*dor*

Corpus Christi
  Corpo de Deus   *kor*·poo de de·oosh

Portugal Day (10 June)
  Dia de Portugal   *dee*·a de poor·too·*gaal*

Assumption (15 August)
  Assunção de   aa·soong·*sowng* de
  Nossa Senhora   *no*·sa se·*nyo*·ra

All Saints' Day (1 November)
  Dia de   *dee*·a de
  Todos-os-Santos   to·doosh·oosh·sang·toosh

Immaculate Conception (8 December)
  Imaculada Conceição   ee·ma·koo·*laa*·da kong·say·*sowng*

Republic Day (5 October)
  Implantação   eeng·plang·ta·*sowng*
  da República   da rre·*poo*·blee·ka

Independence Restoration Day (1 December)
Restauração da   resh·tow·ra·*sowng* da
Independência   eeng·de·peng·*deng*·sya

Christmas Day (25 December)
Natal   na·*taal*

For some holiday greetings in Portuguese, see the box on
page 110.

past

passado

day before yesterday	*anteontem*	ang·tee·*ong*·teng
(three days) ago	*há (três dias)*	aa (tresh *dee*·ash)
since (May)	*desde (Maio)*	desh·de (*maa*·yoo)
last ...		
night	*a noite passada*	a *noy*·te pa·*saa*·da
week	*a semana passada*	a se·*ma*·na pa·*saa*·da
month	*o mês passado*	oo mesh pa·*saa*·doo
year	*o ano passado*	oo *a*·noo pa·*saa*·doo
yesterday ...	*ontem ...*	*ong*·teng ...
morning	*de manhã*	de ma·*nyang*
afternoon	*à tarde*	aa *taar*·de
evening	*à noite*	aa *noy*·te

future

futuro

day after tomorrow	*depois de amanhã*	de·*poysh* de aa·ma·*nyang*
in (six days)	*daqui à (seis dias)*	da·*kee* a (saysh *dee*·ash)
until (June)	*até (Junho)*	a·*te* (*zhoo*·nyoo)

next ...		
week	*na próxima*	na pro·see·ma
	semana	se·ma·na
month	*no próximo mês*	noo pro·see·moo mesh
year	*no próximo ano*	noo pro·see·moo a·noo
tomorrow ...	*amanhã ...*	aa·ma·nyang ...
morning	*de manhã*	de ma·nyang
afternoon	*à tarde*	aa taar·de
evening	*à noite*	aa noy·te

during the day

durante o dia

afternoon	*tarde* f	taar·de
dawn	*madrugada* f	ma·droo·gaa·da
day	*dia* m	dee·a
evening	*noite* f	noy·te
midday	*meio dia* m	may·oo dee·a
midnight	*meia noite* f	may·a noy·te
morning	*manhã* f	ma·nyang
night	*noite* f	noy·te
sunrise	*nascer do sol* m	nash·ser doo sol
sunset	*pôr do sol* m	por doo sol

Since 1992, Portugal's national currency has of course been the euro. One *euro* (e·oo·roo) is made up of one hundred cents, but the Portuguese tend to use the word *cêntimos* seng·tee·moosh rather than 'cent'.

How much is it?
Quanto custa?   kwang·too koosh·ta

Can you write down the price?
Pode escrever o preço?   po·de shkre·ver oo pre·soo

Do I have to pay?
Tenho de pagar?   ta·nyoo de pa·gaar

Where's …?	*Onde há …?*	ong·de aa …
an automated teller machine	*um caixa automático*	oong kai·sha ow·too·maa·tee·koo
a foreign exchange office	*um câmbio*	oong kang·byoo

I'd like to …	*Queria …*	ke·ree·a …
cash a cheque	*trocar um cheque*	troo·kaar oong she·ke
change a travellers cheque	*trocar um traveller cheque*	troo·kaar oong tra·ve·ler shek
change money	*trocar dinheiro*	troo·kaar dee·nyay·roo
get a cash advance	*fazer um levantamento adiantado*	fa·zer oong le·vang·ta·meng·too a·dee·ang·taa·doo
get change for this note	*trocar esta nota*	troo·kaar esh·ta no·ta
withdraw money	*levantar dinheiro*	le·vang·taar dee·nyay·roo

What's the ...?	Qual é o ...?	kwaal e oo ...
charge	imposto	eeng·posh·too
exchange rate	câmbio do dia	kang·byoo doo dee·a
Do you accept ...?	Aceitam ...?	a·say·tang ...
credit cards	cartão de crédito	kar·towng de kre·dee·too
debit cards	multibanco	mool·tee·bang·koo
travellers cheques	travellers cheques	tra·ve·ler she·kesh
I'd like (a) ..., please.	Queria ..., por favor.	ke·ree·a ... poor fa·vor
my change	o troco	oo tro·koo
receipt	um recibo	oong rre·see·boo
refund	ser reembolsado/ reembolsada m/f	ser rree·eng·bol·saa·doo/ rree·eng·bol·saa·da
to return this	devolver isto	de·vol·ver eesh·too
How much is it per ...?	Quanto é que é por ...?	kwang·too e ke e poor ...
caravan	caravana	ka·ra·va·na
day	dia	dee·a
game	jogo	zho·goo
hour	hora	o·ra
(five) minutes	(cinco) minutos	(seeng·koo) mee·noo·toosh
night	noite	noy·te
page	página	paa·zhee·na
person	pessoa	pe·so·a
tent	tenda	teng·da
vehicle	veículo	ve·ee·koo·loo
visit	visita	vee·zee·ta
week	semana	se·ma·na
It's ...	É ...	e ...
(12) euros	(doze) euros	(do·ze) e·oo·roosh
free	gratuito	gra·twee·too

For more money-related phrases, see banking, page 89.

getting around

deslocar-se

Which ... goes to (Lisbon)?	Qual é o ... que vai para (Lisboa)?	kwaal e oo ... ke vai pra (leezh·bo·a)
Is this the ... to (Peniche)?	Este é o ... para (Peniche)?	esh·te e oo ... pra (pe·neesh)
boat	barco	baar·koo
bus	autocarro	ow·to·kaa·rroo
train	comboio	kong·boy·oo
tram	eléctrico	e·le·tree·koo

When's the ... (bus)?	Quando é que sai o ... (autocarro)?	kwang·doo e ke sai oo ... (ow·to·kaa·rroo)
first	primeiro	pree·may·roo
last	último	ool·tee·moo
next	próximo	pro·see·moo

Where's (the station)?
Onde é (a estação)? ong·de e (a shta·sowng)

What time does it leave?
A que horas sai? a ke o·rash sai

What time does it get to (Porto)?
A que horas chega ao (Porto)? a ke o·rash she·ga ow (por·too)

How long will it be delayed?
Quanto tempo é que vai chegar atrasado? kwang·too teng·poo e ke vai she·gaar a·tra·zaa·doo

Is this seat available?
Este lugar está vago? esh·te loo·gaar shtaa va·goo

That's my seat.
Este é o meu lugar. esh·te e oo me·oo loo·gaar

Please tell me when we get to (Évora).

Por favor avise-me   poor fa·*vor* a·*vee*·ze·me
quando chegarmos   kwang·doo she·*gaar*·moosh
a (Évora).   a (e·*voo*·ra)

Please stop here.

Por favor pare aqui.   poor fa·*vor* paa·re a·*kee*

How long do we stop here?

Quanto tempo   kwang·too teng·poo
vamos ficar   va·moosh fee·*kaar*
parados aqui?   pa·*raa*·doosh a·*kee*

tickets

bilhetes

Where do I buy a ticket?

Onde é que eu   ong·de e ke e·oo
compro o bilhete?   kong·proo oo bee·*lye*·te

Do I need to book (very far in advance)?

Preciso de fazer   pre·*see*·zoo de fa·*zer*
reserva (muito   rre·zer·va (mweeng·too
antecipada)?   ang·te·see·*paa*·da)

A ... ticket (to Braga).	*Um bilhete de ... (para Braga).*	oong bee·*lye*·te de ... (pra braa·ga)
1st-class	*primeira classe*	pree·*may*·ra klaa·se
2nd-class	*segunda classe*	se·*goong*·da klaa·se
child's	*criança*	kree·*ang*·sa
one-way	*ida*	ee·da
return	*ida e volta*	ee·da ee *vol*·ta
student	*estudante*	shtoo·*dang*·te

I'd like a/an ... seat.	*Queria um lugar ...*	ke·*ree*·a oong loo·*gaar* ...
aisle	*na coxia*	na koo·*shee*·a
nonsmoking	*de não fumadores*	de nowng foo·ma·*do*·resh
smoking	*para fumadores*	pra foo·ma·*do*·resh
window	*à janela*	aa zha·*ne*·la

Is there (a) …?	Tem …?	teng …
air	ar	aar
conditioning	condicionado	kong·dee·syoo·*naa*·doo
blanket	cobertor	koo·ber·*tor*
sick bag	saco para	*saa*·koo pra
	vomitar	voo·mee·*taar*
toilet	casa de banho	*kaa*·za de *ba*·nyoo

I'd like to …	Queria …	ke·*ree*·a …
my ticket,	o bilhete,	oo bee·*lye*·te
please.	por favor.	poor fa·*vor*
cancel	cancelar	kang·se·*laar*
change	trocar	troo·*kaar*
confirm	confirmar	kong·feer·*maar*

listen for …

agente de viagens m&f	a·*zheng*·te de vee·*aa*·zhengsh	travel agent
atrasado/ atrasada m/f	a·tra·*zaa*·doo/ a·tra·*zaa*·da	delayed
bilheteira f	bee·lye·*tay*·ra	ticket window
cancelado/ cancelada m/f	kang·se·*laa*·doo/ kang·se·*laa*·da	cancelled
cheio/cheia m/f	*shay*·oo/*shay*·a	full
greve f	*gre*·ve	strike
horário m	o·*raa*·ryoo	timetable
plataforma f	pla·ta·*for*·ma	platform

How much is it?

 Quanto é?   *kwang*·too e

How long does the trip take?

 Quanto tempo é que   *kwang*·too teng·poo e ke
 leva a viagem?   *le*·va a vee·*aa*·zheng

Is it a direct route?

 É uma rota directa?   e *oo*·ma *rro*·ta dee·*re*·ta

Can I get a stand-by ticket?

 Posso comprar um   *po*·soo kong·*praar* oong
 bilhete de última hora?   bee·*lye*·te de *ool*·tee·ma *o*·ra

Can I get a sleeping berth?
Tem carruagem cama?   teng ka·rroo·*aa*·zheng *ka*·ma

What time should I check in?
A que horas devo fazer   a ke o·rash *de*·voo fa·*zer*
o check-in?   oo *shek*·eeng

luggage

bagagem

Where can I find a/the ...?	*Onde fica ...?*	ong·de *fee*·ka ...
baggage claim	*o balcão de bagagens*	oo bal·*kowng* de ba·*gaa*·zhengsh
lost and found	*o balcão de perdidos e achados*	oo bal·*kowng* de per·*dee*·doosh e a·*shaa*·doosh
luggage locker	*o depósito de bagagens*	oo de·*po*·zee·too de ba·*gaa*·zhengsh
trolley	*um carrinho*	oong ka·*rree*·nyoo

That's (not) mine.
Isto (não) é meu.   *eesh*·too (nowng) e *me*·oo

Can I have some coins/tokens?
Pode-me dar umas   *po*·de·me daar oo·mash
moedas/fichas?   mo·e·dash/*fee*·shash

---

listen for ...

bagagem de cabine f	ba·*gaa*·zheng de kaa·*bee*·ne	carry-on baggage
cartão de embarque m	kar·*towng* de eng·*baar*·ke	boarding pass
excesso de bagagem m	aysh·*se*·soo de ba·*gaa*·zheng	excess baggage
passaporte m	paa·sa·*por*·te	passport
transferência f	trangsh·fe·*reng*·sya	transfer
trânsito m	*trang*·zee·too	transit

My luggage has been ...	A minha bagagem ...	a *mee*·nya ba·*gaa*·zheng ...
damaged	foi danificada	foy da·nee·fee·*kaa*·da
lost	perdeu-se	per·*de*·oo·se
stolen	foi roubada	foy rroh·*baa*·da

plane

avião

Where does flight (TP 615) arrive/depart?
De onde pára/parte o voo (TP seiscentos e quinze)?
de *ong*·de *paa*·ra/*paar*·te oo *vo*·oo (te pe saysh·*seng*·toosh e *keeng*·ze)

Where's (the) ...?	*Onde é ...?*	*ong*·de e ...
airport shuttle	*o autocarro do aeroporto*	oo ow·to·*kaa*·rroo doo a·e·ro·*por*·too
arrivals hall	*a porta de chegada*	a *por*·ta de she·*gaa*·da
departures hall	*a porta de partida*	a *por*·ta de par·*tee*·da
duty-free shop	*a loja duty-free*	a *lo*·zha doo·tee·free
gate (20)	*a porta (vinte)*	a *por*·ta (*veeng*·te)

bus, coach & tram

autocarro, camioneta & eléctrico

Is this a bus/tram stop?
Isto é uma paragem de autocarro/eléctrico?
eesh·too e *oo*·ma pa·*raa*·zheng de ow·to·*kaa*·rroo/e·*le*·tree·koo

How do I get to the (bus terminal)?
Como posso chegar (á rodoviária)?
ko·moo *po*·soo she·*gaar* (aa rroo·doo·vee·*aa*·ree·a)

How often do buses/trams come?

Qual é a frequência
dos autocarros/
eléctricos?

kwaal e a fre·*kweng*·sya
doosh ow·to·*kaa*·rroosh/
e·*le*·tree·koosh

How much is it to (Lagos)?

Quanto custa até
(Lagos)?

kwang·too *koosh*·ta a·*te*
(*laa*·goosh)

Does it stop at (Amarante)?

Pára em (Amarante)?

paa·ra eng (a·ma·*rang*·te)

What's the next stop?

Qual é a próxima
paragem?

kwaal e a *pro*·see·ma
pa·*raa*·zheng

I'd like to get off at (Cascais).

Queria sair
em (Cascais).

ke·*ree*·a sa·*eer*
eng (kash·*kaa*·eesh)

city bus	*autocarro*	ow·to·*kaa*·rroo
	da cidade m	da see·*daa*·de
departure bay	*portão*	poor·*towng*
	de embarque m/f	de eng·*baar*·ke
intercity bus	*autocarro*	ow·to·*kaa*·rroo
	inter-cidades m	eeng·ter·see·*daa*·desh
local bus	*autocarro* m	ow·to·*kaa*·rroo
	local	loo·*kaal*
local bus station	*paragem de*	pa·*raa*·zheng de
	autocarros	ow·to·*kaa*·rroosh
	locais f	loo·*kaish*
long distance station	*rodoviária*	rro·do·vee·*aa*·ree·a
	inter-cidades f	eeng·ter·see·*daa*·desh
shuttle bus (hotel)	*carrinha*	ka·*rree*·nya
	do hotel f	doo o·*tel*
timetable display	*horário*	o·*raa*·ryoo
	de partidas e	de par·*tee*·dash e
	chegadas m	she·*gaa*·dash

For bus numbers, see **numbers & amounts**, page 33.

Bilheteira	bee·lye·*tay*·ra	**Ticket Booth**
Chegadas	she·*gaa*·dash	**Arrivals**
Depósito	de·*po*·zee·too	**Luggage Check-In**
de Bagagens	de ba·*gaa*·zhengsh	
Embarque	eng·*baar*·ke	**Departure**
Gare de	*gaa*·re de	**Boarding Area**
Embarque	eng·*baar*·ke	
Passageiros	pa·sa·*zhay*·roosh	**Passengers**
Sala de Espera	*saa*·la de *shpe*·ra	**Waiting Room**

train

comboio

What station is this?
Qual estação é este? — kwaal shta·*sowng* e *esh*·te

What's the next station?
Qual é a próxima estação? — kwaal e a *pro*·see·ma shta·*sowng*

Does it stop at (Leiria)?
Pára em (Leiria)? — *paa*·ra eng (lay·*ree*·a)

Do I need to change?
Preciso de mudar *pre·see·soo de moo·daar*
de comboio? — de kong·*boy*·oo

Where's the ticket machine?
Onde está a bilheteira — *ong*·de shtaa a bee·lye·*tay*·ra
automática? — ow·too·*maa*·tee·ka

listen for ...

directo	dee·*re*·too	**direct**
expresso	aysh·*pre*·soo	**express (non-stop)**
foguete	foo·*ge*·te	**express (has only one or two stops)**
rápido	*rraa*·pee·doo	**express (stops only in main cities)**

Which carriage is (for) …?	Qual é a carruagem …?	kwaal e a ka·rroo·aa·zheng …
1st class	de primeira classe	de pree·may·ra klaa·se
2nd class	de segunda classe	de se·goong·da klaa·se
dining (Faro)	restaurante para o (Faro)	rresh·tow·rang·te pra oo (fa·roo)

boat

barco

What's the lake/sea like today?
Como está o lago/mar hoje? — ko·moo shtaa oo laa·goo/maar o·zhe

Are there life jackets?
Tem coletes salva-vidas? — teng koo·le·tesh saal·va·vee·dash

What island/beach is this?
Que ilha/praia é esta? — ke ee·lya/prai·a e esh·ta

I feel seasick.
Estou enjoado/enjoada. m/f — shtoh eng·zhoo·aa·doo/eng·zhoo·aa·da

cabin	camarote m	ka·ma·ro·te
captain	capitão m	ka·pee·towng
(car) deck	convés (de automóveis) m	kong·vesh (de ow·too·mo·vaysh)
ferry	ferryboat m	fe·rree·boht
lifeboat	barco salva-vidas m	baar·koo saal·va·vee·dash
yacht	iate m	ee·aat

taxi

I'd like a taxi …	Queria chamar um táxi …	ke·*ree*·a sha·*maar* oong *taak*·see …
at (9am)	*para as (nove da manhã)*	pra ash (*no*·ve da ma·*nyang*)
now	*agora*	a·*go*·ra
tomorrow	*amanhã*	aa·ma·*nyang*

Where's the taxi rank?
Onde é a praça de táxis? — *ong*·de e a *praa*·sa de *taak*·seesh

Is this taxi available?
Este táxi está livre? — *esh*·te *taak*·see shtaa *lee*·vre

How much is it (to Silves)?
Quanto custa (até ao Silves)? — *kwang*·too *koosh*·ta (a·*te* ow *seel*·vesh)

53

How much is the flag fall/hiring charge?

Quanto custa a	kwang·too koosh·ta a
bandeirada base?	bang·day·raa·da baa·ze

Please take me to (this address).

Leve-me para (este	le·ve·me pa·ra (esh·te
endereço), por favor.	eng·de·re·soo) poor fa·vor

Please put the meter on.

Por favor, ligue	poor fa·vor lee·ge
o taxímetro.	oo taak·see·me·troo

I don't want to pay a flat fare.

Eu não quero pagar	e·oo nowng ke·roo pa·gaar
uma tarifa estipulada.	oo·ma ta·ree·fa shtee·poo·laa·da

Please …	*Por favor …*	poor fa·vor …
come back	*volte (às dez*	vol·te (aash desh
at (10am)	*da manhã)*	da ma·nyang)
slow down	*vá mais*	vaa maish
	devagar	de·va·gaar
stop here	*pare aqui*	paa·re a·kee
wait here	*espere aqui*	shpe·re a·kee

For other useful phrases, see **directions**, page 63 and **money**, page 43.

car & motorbike

car & motorbike hire

I'd like to hire	*Queria alugar*	ke·ree·a a·loo·gaar
a/an … car.	*um carro …*	oong kaa·rroo …
4WD	*com tracção*	kong traa·sowng
	às quatro	aash kwaa·troo
	rodas	rro·dash
automatic	*de mudanças*	de moo·dang·sash
	automáticas	ow·too·maa·tee·kash
manual	*de mudanças*	de moo·dang·sash
	manuais	ma·noo·aish

with	com ar	kong aar
air conditioning	condicionado	kong·dee·syoo·naa·doo
with a driver	com motorista	kong moo·too·reesh·ta

How much	Quanto custa	kwang·too koosh·ta
for … hire?	para alugar	pa·ra a·loo·gaar
	por…?	poor …
daily	dia	dee·a
weekly	semana	se·ma·na

I'd like to hire a motorbike.
Queria alugar uma mota. ke·ree·a a·loo·gaar oo·ma mo·ta

Does that include insurance/mileage?
Inclui seguro/ eeng·kloo·ee se·goo·roo/
kilometragem? kee·lo·me·traa·zheng

Do you have a guide to the road rules (in English)?
Tem um guia das regras teng oong gee·a dash rre·grash
de trânsito (em inglês)? de trang·see·too (eng eeng·glesh)

Do you have a road map?
Tem um mapa teng oong maa·pa
de estradas? de shtraa·dash

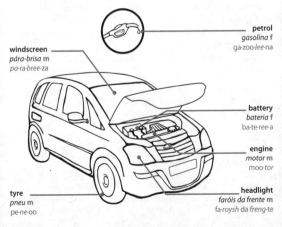

petrol
gasolina f
ga·zoo·lee·na

windscreen
pára-brisa m
pa·ra·bree·za

battery
bateria f
ba·te·ree·a

engine
motor m
moo·tor

tyre
pneu m
pe·ne·oo

headlight
faróis da frente m
fa·roysh da freng·te

carta de condução f	kaar·ta de kong·doo·sowng	drivers licence
grátis m&f	graa·teesh	free
multa f	mool·ta	fine
parquímetro m	par·kee·me·troo	parking meter
portagem f	por·taa·zheng	motorway pass
quilómetros m pl	kee·lo·me·troosh	kilometres

on the road

What's the speed limit?
Qual é o limite de velocidade?
kwaal e oo lee·mee·te de ve·loo·see·daa·de

Is this the road to (Sintra)?
Esta é a estrada para (Sintra)?
esh·ta e a shtraa·da pa·ra (seeng·tra)

Where's a petrol station?
Onde fica um posto de gasolina?
ong·de fee·ka oong posh·too de ga·zoo·lee·na

Please fill it up.
Encha o tanque, por favor.
eng·sha oo tang·ke poor fa·vor

I'd like (25) litres.
Ponha (vinte e cinco) litros.
po·nya (ving·te e seeng·koo) lee·troosh

... petrol/gas	gasolina ...	ga·zoo·lee·na ...
leaded	com chumbo	kong shoong·boo
unleaded	sem chumbo	seng shoong·boo

diesel	diesel m	dee·zel
LPG	gás m	gash

Can you check the ...?	Pode verificar ...?	po·de ve·ree·fee·kaar ...
oil	o óleo	oo o·le·oo
tyre pressure	os pneus	oosh pe·ne·oosh
water	a água	a aa·gwa

(How long) Can I park here?
(Quanto tempo) Posso   *(kwang·too teng·poo) po·soo*
estacionar aqui?   shta·see·oo·*naar* a·*kee*

Do I have to pay?
Tenho que pagar?   ta·nyoo ke pa·*gaar*

problems

I need a mechanic.
Preciso de um   pre·*see*·zoo de oong
mecânico.   me·*kaa*·nee·koo

I've had an accident.
Tive um acidente.   *tee*·ve oong a·see·*deng*·te

(The car) has broken down (at Setúbal).
(O carro) avariou-se   (oo *kaa*·rroo) a·va·ree·*oh*·se
(em Setúbal).   (eng se·*too*·baal)

(The car) won't start.
(O carro) não pega.   (oo *kaa*·rroo) nowng *pe*·ga

I have a flat tyre.
Tenho um furo no pneu.   ta·nyoo oong *foo*·roo noo pe·*ne*·oo

I've lost my car keys.
Perdi a chave do carro.   per·*dee* a *sha*·ve doo *kaa*·rroo

I've locked the keys inside.
Tranquei o carro com   trang·*kay* oo *kaa*·rroo kong
as chaves lá dentro.   ash *sha*·vesh laa *deng*·troo

signs

Entrada	eng·*traa*·da	**Entrance**
Dar Prioridade	daar pree·oo·ree·*daa*·de	**Give Way**
Pare	*paa*·re	**Stop**
Portagem	por·*taa*·zheng	**Toll**
Proibido Entrar	pro·ee·*bee*·doo eng·*traar*	**No Entry**
Sair da	sa·*eer* da	**Freeway**
Autoestrada	ow·to·*shtraa*·da	**Exit**
Sentido Único	seng·*tee*·doo oo·nee·koo	**One-Way**

transport

57

I've run out of petrol.
Estou sem gasolina.   shtoh seng ga·zoo·*lee*·na

Can you fix it (today)?
Pode-se arranjar (hoje)?   *po*·de·se a·rrang·*zhaar* (o·zhe)

How long will it take?
Quanto tempo vai levar?   kwang·too *teng*·poo vai le·*vaar*

bicycle

bicicleta

I'd like ...	*Queria ...*	ke·*ree*·aa ...
my bicycle repaired	*consertar a minha bicicleta*	kong·ser·*taar* a *mee*·nya bee·see·*kle*·ta
to buy a bicycle	*comprar uma bicicleta*	kong·*praar* oo·ma bee·see·*kle*·ta
to hire a bicycle	*alugar uma bicicleta*	a·loo·*gaar* oo·ma bee·see·*kle*·ta

I'd like a ... bike.	*Queria uma bicicleta ...*	ke·*ree*·a oo·ma bee·see·*kle*·ta ...
mountain	*de montanha*	de mong·*taa*·nya
racing	*de corrida*	de koo·*rree*·da
second-hand	*em segunda mão*	eng se·*goong*·da mowng

How much is it per day/hour?
Quanto custa por dia/hora?   kwang·too *koosh*·ta poor *dee*·a/o·ra

Do I need a helmet?
Preciso de usar capacete?   pre·*see*·soo de oo·*zaar* ka·pa·*se*·te

Are there bicycle paths?
Há trilhos para bicicletas?   aa *tree*·lyoosh *pa*·ra bee·see·*kle*·tash

I have a puncture.
Tenho um furo no pneu.   *ta*·nyoo oong *foo*·roo noo pe·*ne*·oo

border crossing

atravessar a fronteira

I'm ...	Estou ...	shtoh ...
in transit	em trânsito	eng *trang*·zee·too
on business	em negócios	eng ne·*go*·syoosh
on holiday	de férias	de *fe*·ree·ash

I'm here for ...	Vou ficar por ...	voh fee·*kaar* poor ...
(10) days	(dez) dias	(desh) *dee*·ash
(three) weeks	(três) semanas	(tresh) se·*ma*·nash
(two) months	(dois) meses	(doysh) *me*·zesh

I'm going to (Elvas).
Vou para (Elvas).
voh *pa*·ra (*el*·vash)

I'm staying at (the Hotel Lisboa).
Estou no (Hotel Lisboa).
shtoh noo (o·*tel* leezh·*bo*·a)

The children are on this passport.
As crianças estão averbadas neste passaporte.
ash kree·*ang*·sash shtowng a·ver·*baa*·dash *nesh*·te paa·sa·*por*·te

Alfândega	aal·*fang*·de·ga	**Customs**
Controlo de Passaportes	kong·*tro*·loo de paa·sa·*por*·tesh	**Passport Control**
Duty-Free	*doo*·tee·free	**Duty-free**
Imigração	ee·mee·gra·*sowng*	**Immigration**
Quarentena	kwa·reng·*te*·na	**Quarantine**

at customs

na alfândega

I have nothing to declare.
Não tenho nada a declarar.
nowng *ta*·nyoo *naa*·da a de·kla·*raar*

I have something to declare.
Tenho algo a declarar.
ta·nyoo *al*·goo a de·kla·*raar*

Do I have to declare this?
Preciso de declarar isto?
pre·*see*·zoo de de·kla·*raar* eesh·too

That's (not) mine.
Isto (não) é meu.
eesh·too (nowng) e *me*·oo

I didn't know I had to declare it.
Não sabia que tinha que declarar isto.
nowng sa·*bee*·a ke *tee*·nya ke de·kla·*raar* eesh·too

Could I please have an (English) interpreter?
Pode-me arranjar um intérprete de (inglês), por favor?
po·de·me a·rrang·*zhaar* oong eeng·*ter*·pre·te de (eeng·*glesh*) poor fa·*vor*

For phrases on payments and receipts, see **money**, page 43.

Do you have this form in (English)?
Tem este formulário   teng *esh*·te foor·moo·*laa*·ree·oo
em (inglês)?   eng (eeng·*glesh*)

name	*nome*	*no*·me
(permanent)	*endereço*	eng·de·*re*·soo
address	*(permanente)*	(per·ma·*neng*·te)
date/place	*data/local*	*daa*·ta/loo·*kaal*
of birth	*de nascimento*	de nash·see·*meng*·too
age	*idade*	ee·*daa*·de
sex	*sexo*	*sek*·soo
nationality	*nacionalidade*	na·syoo·na·lee·*daa*·de
religion	*religião*	rre·lee·zhee·*owng*
occupation/	*ocupação/*	o·koo·pa·*sowng*/
profession	*profissão*	proo·fee·*sowng*
marital status	*estado civil*	*shtaa*·doo see·*veel*
single	*solteiro/*	sol·*tay*·roo/
	solteira m/f	sol·*tay*·ra
divorced	*divorciado/*	dee·vor·see·*aa*·doo/
	divorciada m/f	dee·vor·see·*aa*·da
married	*casado/*	ka·*zaa*·doo/
	casada m/f	ka·*zaa*·da
widower	*viúvo* m	vee·*oo*·voo
widow	*viúva* f	vee·*oo*·va
country of	*país de*	pa·*eesh* de
departure/	*partida/*	par·*tee*·da/
destination	*destino*	desh·*tee*·noo
entry/exit	*data de*	*daa*·ta de
date	*entrada/saída*	eng·*traa*·da/sa·ee·da
purpose	*razão da*	rra·*zowng* daa
of visit	*visita*	vee·*zee*·ta
holiday	*férias*	*fe*·ree·ash
business	*negócios*	ne·*go*·see·oosh
visiting	*visita a*	vee·*zee*·ta a
relatives	*familiares*	fa·mee·lee·*aa*·resh
visiting the	*visita a país*	vee·*zee*·ta a pa·*eesh*
homeland	*de origem*	de o·*ree*·zheng

paperwork

birth certificate	certidão de nascimento	ser·tee·*downg* de nash·see·*meng*·too
drivers licence	carta de condução	*kaar*·ta de kong·doo·*sowng*
identification	identidade	ee·deng·tee·*daa*·de
passport (number)	(número de) passaporte	(*noo*·me·roo de) paa·sa·*por*·te
work/study permit	licença para trabalhar/ estudar	lee·*seng*·sa *pa*·ra tra·ba·*lyaar*/ shtoo·*daar*

Where's (the market)?
Onde é o mercado? — ong·de e oo mer·*kaa*·doo

What's the address?
Qual é o endereço? — kwaal e oo eng·de·*re*·soo

How do I get there?
Como é que eu chego lá? — *ko*·moo e ke *e*·oo *she*·goo laa

How far is it?
A que distância fica? — a ke deesh·*tang*·sya *fee*·ka

Can you show me (on the map)?
Pode-me mostrar (no mapa)? — *po*·de·me moosh·*traar* (noo *maa*·pa)

What (street) is this?
Que (rua) é isto? — ke (*rroo*·a) e *eesh*·too

It's ...	É ...	e ...
behind ...	*atrás de ...*	a·*traash* de ...
close	*perto*	*per*·too
here	*aqui*	a·*kee*
in front of ...	*em frente de ...*	eng *freng*·te de ...
near ...	*perto de ...*	*per*·too de ...
next to ...	*ao lado de ...*	ow *laa*·doo de ...
on the corner	*na esquina*	na *shkee*·na
opposite ...	*do lado oposto ...*	doo *laa*·doo oo·*posh*·too ...
straight ahead	*em frente*	eng *freng*·te
there	*lá*	laa

listen for ...

... metros	... *me*·troosh	... metres
... minutos	... mee·*noo*·toosh	... minutes
... quarteirões	... kwar·tay·*royngsh*	... blocks
... quilómetros	... kee·*lo*·me·troosh	... kilometres

Turn ...	Vire ...	vee·re ...
at the corner	na esquina	na shkee·na
at the traffic	nos	noosh
lights	semáforos	se·maa·foo·roosh
left	à esquerda	aa shker·da
right	à direita	aa dee·ray·ta
by bus	de autocarro	de ow·to·kaa·rroo
by taxi	de táxi	de taak·see
by train	de comboio	de kong·boy·oo
by tram	de tram	de trang
on foot	a pé	a pe
north	norte	nor·te
south	sul	sool
east	leste	lesh·te
west	oeste	o·esh·te

For information on reading Portuguese addresses, see the box **typical addresses** on page 92.

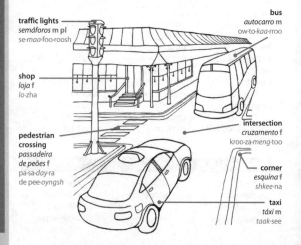

traffic lights
semáforos m pl
se·*maa*·foo·roosh

bus
autocarro m
ow·to·*kaa*·rroo

shop
loja f
lo·zha

intersection
cruzamento f
kroo·za·*meng*·too

pedestrian
crossing
*passadeira
de peões* f
pa·sa·*day*·ra
de pee·*oyngsh*

corner
esquina f
shkee·na

taxi
táxi m
taak·see

finding accommodation

Where's a ...?	Onde é que há ...?	ong·de e ke aa ...
bed and	um turismo	oong too·reezh·moo
breakfast	de habitação	de a·bee·ta·sowng
camping	um parque de	oong paar·ke de
ground	campismo	kang·peezh·moo
guesthouse	uma casa de	oo·ma kaa·za de
	hóspedes	osh·pe·desh
hotel	um hotel	oong o·tel
inn	uma pousada	oo·ma poh·zaa·da
youth hostel	uma pousada	oo·ma poh·zaa·da
	de juventude	de zhoo·veng·too·de

Can you	Pode	po·de
recommend	recomendar	rre·koo·meng·daar
somewhere ...?	algum lugar ...?	aal·goong loo·gaar ...
cheap	barato	ba·raa·too
clean	limpo	leeng·poo
good	bom	bong
luxurious	de luxo	de loo·shoo
nearby	perto daqui	per·too da·kee
romantic	romântico	rroo·mang·tee·koo
safe for women	seguro para	se·goo·ro pa·ra
travellers	viajantes do	vee·a·zhang·tesh doo
	sexo feminino	sek·soo fe·me·nee·noo

local talk

dive	buraco m	boo·raa·koo
rat-nest	ninho de ratos m	nee·nyoo de rraa·toosh
top spot	melhor m	me·lyor

I want something near the …	Eu quero algo perto …	e·oo ke·roo aal·goo per·too …
beach	da praia	da prai·a
city centre	do centro	doo sen·troo
	da cidade	da see·daa·de
shops	de lojas	de lo·zhash
train station	da estação	da shta·sowng
	do comboio	doo kong·boy·oo

What's the address?	Onde é o endereço?	ong·de e oo eng·de·re·soo

For responses, see **directions**, page 63.

booking ahead & checking in

I'd like to book a room, please.

  Eu queria fazer uma   e·oo ke·ree·a fa·zer oo·ma
  reserva, por favor.   rre·zer·va poor fa·vor

I have a reservation.

  Eu tenho uma reserva.   e·oo ta·nyoo oo·ma rre·zer·va

My name's …

  O meu nome é …   oo me·oo no·me e …

For (three) nights/weeks.

  Para (três) noites/   pa·ra (tresh) noy·tesh/
  semanas.   se·ma·nash

From (2 July) to (6 July).

  De (dois de julho) até   de (doysh de zhoo·lyoo) a·te
  (seis de julho).   (saysh de zhoo·lyoo)

Do you have a … room?	Tem um quarto …?	teng oong kwaar·too …
double	de casal	de ka·zaal
single	de solteiro	de sol·tay·roo
twin	duplo	doo·ploo

How much is it per …?	Quanto custa por …?	kwang·too koosh·ta poor …
night	noite	noy·te
person	pessoa	pe·so·a
week	semana	se·ma·na

Can I pay by …?	Posso pagar com …?	po·soo pa·gaar kong …
credit card	cartão de crédito	kar·towng de kre·dee·too
travellers cheque	traveller cheque	tra·ve·ler shek

Do I need to pay upfront?	Tenho que pagar adiantado?	ta·nyoo ke pa·gaar aa·dee·ang·taa·doo
Can I see it?	Posso ver?	po·soo ver
I'll take it.	Fico com ele.	fee·koo kong e·le

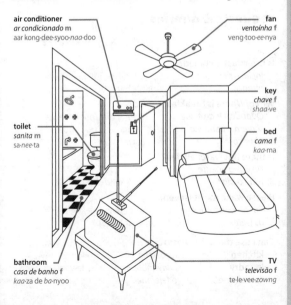

air conditioner
ar condicionado m
aar kong·dee·syoo·naa·doo

fan
ventoinha f
veng·too·ee·nya

key
chave f
shaa·ve

toilet
sanita m
sa·nee·ta

bed
cama f
kaa·ma

bathroom
casa de banho f
kaa·za de ba·nyoo

TV
televisão f
te·le·vee·zowng

listen for ...

chave f	*shaa*·ve	key
identidade	ee·deng·tee·*daa*·de	identification
não há vaga	nowng aa *vaa*·ga	full
passaporte	paa·sa·*por*·te	passport
Quantas noites?	*kwang*·tash *noy*·tesh	How many nights?
recepção f	rre·se·*sowng*	reception

requests & queries

pedidos & perguntas

Is breakfast included?

Inclui o pequeno almoço? — eeng·*kloo*·ee oo pe·*ke*·noo aal·*mo*·soo

When/Where is breakfast served?

Quando/Onde é que servem o pequeno almoço? — *kwang*·doo/*ong*·de e ke *ser*·veng oo pe·*ke*·noo aal·*mo*·soo

Is there hot water all day?

Há água quente todo o dia? — aa *aa*·gwa *keng*·te *to*·doo oo *dee*·a

Please wake me at (seven).

Por favor acorde-me às (sete). — poor fa·*vor* aa·*kor*·de·me aash (*se*·te)

Can I use the ...? — *Posso usar ...?* — *po*·soo oo·*zaar* ...

kitchen	*a cozinha*	a koo·*zee*·nya
laundry	*a lavandaria*	a la·vang·da·*ree*·a
telephone	*o telefone*	oo te·le·*fo*·ne

Do you have a/an ...?	Tem ...?	teng ...
elevator	elevador	e·le·va·dor
laundry service	tratamento de roupas	tra·ta·meng·too de rroh·pash
message board	quadro de recados	kwaa·droo de rre·kaa·doosh
safe	cofre	ko·fre
swimming pool	piscina	pesh·see·na

Do you ... here?	... aqui?	... aa·kee
arrange tours	Organizam passeios	or·ga·nee·zowng pa·say·oosh
change money	Trocam dinheiro	tro·kowng dee·nyay·roo

Could I have ..., please?	Pode-me dar ..., por favor?	po·de·me daar ... poor fa·vor
my key	a minha chave	a mee·nya shaa·ve
a receipt	um recibo	oong rre·see·boo

Is there a message for me?

Há algum recado para mim?
aa aal·goong rre·kaa·doo pa·ra meeng

Can I leave a message for someone?

Posso deixar um recado para alguém?
po·soo day·shaar oong rre·kaa·doo pa·ra aal·geng

I'm locked out of my room.

Fiquei fechado/fechada fora do quarto. m/f
fee·kay fe·shaa·doo/fe·shaa·da fo·ra doo kwaar·too

a knock at the door ...

Who is it?	Quem é?	keng e
Just a moment.	Um minuto.	oong mee·noo·too
Come in.	Pode entrar.	po·de eng·traar
Come back later, please.	Volte mais tarde, por favor.	vol·te maish taar·de poor fa·vor

complaints

It's too ...	É demasiado ...	e de·ma·zee·*aa*·doo ...
bright	claro	*klaa*·roo
cold	frio	*free*·oo
dark	escuro	shkoo·roo
expensive	caro	*kaa*·roo
noisy	barulhento	ba·roo·*lyeng*·too
small	pequeno	pe·*ke*·noo

The ...	... não	... nowng
doesn't work.	funciona.	foong·see·o·na
air	O ar	oo aar
conditioner	condicionado	kong·dee·syoo·*naa*·doo
fan	A ventoínha	a veng·too·*ee*·na
toilet	A sanita	a sa·*nee*·ta

Can I get another (blanket)?
Pode-me dar mais   po·de·me daar maish
um (cobertor)?   oong (koo·ber·*tor*)

This (pillow) isn't clean.
Esta (almofada)   *esh*·ta (aal·moo·*faa*·da)
está suja.   shtaa *soo*·zha

There's no hot water.
Não há água quente.   nowng aa *aa*·gwa *keng*·te

checking out

What time is checkout?
A que horas é a partida?   a ke o·rash e a par·*tee*·da

Can I have a late checkout?
Posso deixar o quarto   *po*·soo day·*shaar* oo *kwaar*·too
mais tarde?   maish *taar*·de

Can you call a taxi for me (for 11am)?
Pode-me chamar um taxi (para as onze da manhã)?
po·de·me sha·*maar* oong *taak*·see (*pa*·ra ash *ong*·ze da ma·*nyang*)

Can I leave my bags here?
Posso deixar as minhas malas aqui?
po·soo day·*shaar* ash *mee*·nyash *maa*·lash a·*kee*

I'm leaving now.
Vou sair agora.
voh sa·*eer* a·*go*·ra

There's a mistake in the bill.
Há um erro na conta.
aa oong e·rroo na *kong*·ta

I had a great stay, thanks.
A estadia foi óptima, obrigado/obrigada. m/f
a shta·*dee*·a foy o·tee·ma o·bree·*gaa*·doo/o·bree·*gaa*·da

I'll recommend it to my friends.
Vou recomendar aos meus amigos.
voh rre·koo·meng·*daar* owsh me·oosh a·*mee*·goosh

Could I have my ..., please?	*Pode-me devolver ..., por favor?*	po·de·me de·vol·*ver* ... poor fa·*vor*
deposit	o depósito	oo de·*po*·zee·too
passport	o passaporte	oo paa·sa·*por*·te
valuables	os objectos de valor	oosh o·be·*zhe*·toosh de va·*lor*

I'll be back ...	*Vou regressar ...*	voh rre·gre·*saar* ...
in (three) days	em (três) dias	eng (tresh) *dee*·ash
on (Tuesday)	na (terça-feira)	na (*ter*·sa *fay*·ra)

camping

acampar

Can I ...?	*Posso ...?*	po·soo ...
camp here	acampar aqui	a·kang·*paar* a·*kee*
park next to my tent	estacionar ao lado da minha tenda	shta·syoo·*naar* ow *laa*·doo da *mee*·nya *teng*·da

Do you have (a) …?	Tem …?	teng …
campsite	um lugar	oong loo·*gaar*
	para acampar	pa·ra a·kang·*paar*
electricity	eletricidade	ee·le·tree·see·*daa*·de
laundry	uma	*oo*·ma
	lavandaria	la·vang·da·*ree*·a
shower facilities	chuveiro	shoo·*vay*·roo
tents for hire	tendas para	*teng*·dash pa·ra
	alugar	a·loo·*gaar*

How much	Quanto custa	kwang·too koosh·ta
is it per …?	por …?	poor …
caravan	caravana	ka·ra·*va*·na
person	pessoa	pe·*so*·a
tent	tenda	*teng*·da
vehicle	veículo	ve·*ee*·koo·loo

Who do I ask to stay here?
*A quem é que peço
para ficar aqui?*
a keng e ke *pe*·soo
pa·ra fee·*kaar* a·*kee*

Is it coin-operated?
*Isto funciona
com moedas?*
eesh·too foong·see·*o*·na
kong moo·e·dash

Is the water drinkable?
A água é potável?
a *aa*·gwa e poo·*taa*·vel

Could I borrow (a lighter)?
*Empresta-me
(um isqueiro)?*
eng·*presh*·ta·me
(oong eesh·*kay*·roo)

renting

Do you have a/an ... for rent?	Tem ... para alugar?	teng ... pa·ra a·loo·gaar
apartment	um apartamento	oong a·par·ta·meng·too
cabin	uma cabana	oo·ma ka·ba·na
house	uma casa	oo·ma kaa·za
room	um quarto	oong kwaar·too
villa	uma casa de campo	oo·ma kaa·za de kang·poo
(partly) furnished	(parcialmente) mobilado/ mobilada m/f	(par·see·al·meng·te) moo·bee·laa·doo/ moo·bee·laa·da
unfurnished	sem mobília	seng moo·bee·lya

I'm here about the ... for rent.

Estou aqui por causa   shtoh a·kee poor kow·za
de ... para alugar.   de ... pa·ra a·loo·gaar

Is there a deposit?

Há depósito?   aa de·po·zee·too

Are bills extra?

As contas são   ash kong·tash sowng
à parte?   aa par·te

staying with locals

ficar em casa de gente local

In general, the Portuguese don't go in for rigid etiquette –
use common courtesy and you'll be fine. If you're invited to
dinner or to stay overnight, a gift of flowers or wine will always be welcome. Offers to help with dishwashing and so
on will also be appreciated, though your hosts will probably
refuse them.

Can I stay at your place?
   Posso ficar na sua casa?   *po·soo fee·kaar na soo·a kaa·za*

Is there anything I can do to help?
   Posso ajudar   *po·soo a·zhoo·daar*
   nalguma coisa?   *naal·goo·ma koy·za*

I have my own ...	*Tenho o meu*	*ta·nyoo o me·oo*
	próprio ...	*pro·pree·oo ...*
mattress	*colchão*	*kol·showng*
sleeping bag	*saco cama*	*saa·koo kaa·ma*

Can I ...?	*Posso ...?*	*po·soo ...*
bring anything	*trazer alguma*	*tra·zer aal·goo·ma*
for the meal	*coisa para a*	*koy·za pa·ra a*
	refeição	*rre·fay·sowng*
do the dishes	*lavar a loiça*	*la·vaar a loy·sa*
set/clear	*por/tirar*	*poor/tee·raar*
the table	*a mesa*	*a me·za*
take out	*deitar o*	*day·taar oo*
the rubbish	*lixo fora*	*lee·shoo fo·ra*

Thanks for your hospitality.
   Obrigado/obrigada   *o·bree·gaa·doo/o·bree·gaa·da*
   pela hospitalidade. m/f   *pe·la osh·pee·ta·lee·daa·de*

To compliment your hosts' cooking, see **eating out**, page 153.

looking for ...

à procura de ...

Where's (a convenience store)?
Onde fica (um   ong·de *fee*·ka (oong
mini-mercado)?   mee·nee·mer·*kaa*·doo)

Where can I buy (a padlock)?
Onde é que posso comprar   ong·de e ke *po*·soo kong·*praar*
(um cadeado)?   (oong ka·de·*aa*·doo)

What hours are the shops open?
Qual é o horário de   kwaal e oo o·*raa*·ryoo de
abertura das lojas?   a·ber·*too*·ra dash *lo*·zhash

Are the shops open on (10 June)?
As lojas estão abertas   ash *lo*·zhash shtowng a·*ber*·tash
no (dia dez de Junho)?   noo (*dee*·a desh de zhoo·nyoo)

For more items and shopping locations, see the **dictionary**.

making a purchase

fazer compras

I'm just looking.
Estou só a ver.   shtoh so a ver

I'd like to buy (an adaptor plug).
Queria comprar   ke·*ree*·a kong·*praar*
(um adaptador).   (oong a·da·pe·ta·*dor*)

How much is it?
Quanto custa?   kwang·too koosh·ta

Can you write down the price?
Pode escrever o preço?   po·de shkre·*ver* oo pre·soo

Do you have any others?
Tem outros?   teng *oh·*troosh

Can I look at it?
Posso ver?   *po·*soo ver

Is this (220) volts?
A corrente é   a koo·*rreng·*te e
(220) volts?   (doo·*zeng·*toosh e *veeng·*te) voltsh

Do you accept ...?	*Aceitam ...?*	a·*say·*tang ...
credit cards	*cartão de*	kar·*towng* de
	crédito	kre·dee·too
debit cards	*multi-banco*	mool·tee·*bang·*koo
travellers	*travellers*	*tra·*ve·ler
cheques	*cheques*	*she·*kesh

Could I have	*Pode-me dar*	*po·*de·me daar
a ..., please?	*um ..., por favor?*	oong ... poor fa·*vor*
bag	*saco*	*saa·*koo
receipt	*recibo*	rre·*see·*boo

I don't need a bag, thanks.
Não preciso de saco,   nowng pre·*see·*zoo de *saa·*koo
obrigado/obrigada. m/f   o·bree·*gaa·*doo/o·bree·*gaa·*da

Could I have it wrapped?
Pode embrulhar?   *po·*de eng·broo·*lyaar*

Does it have a guarantee?
Tem garantia?   teng ga·rang·*tee·*a

Can I have it sent abroad?
Podem enviar para   *po·*deng eng·vee·*aar* pa·ra
o estrangeiro?   oo shtrang·*zhay·*roo

Can you order it for me?
Pode-me encomendá-lo?   *po·*de·me eng·koo·meng·*daa·*lo

Can I pick it up later?
Posso vir buscar   *po·*soo veer boosh·*kaar*
mais tarde?   maish *taar·*de

It's faulty.
Tem defeito.   teng de·*fay·*too

I'd like (a) ..., please.	Queria ..., por favor.	ke·*ree*·a ... poor fa·*vor*
my change	o troco	oo *tro*·koo
receipt	um recibo	oong rre·*see*·boo
refund	ser reembolsado/ reembolsada m/f	ser rre·eng·bol·*saa*·doo/ rre·eng·bol·*saa*·da
to return this	devolver isto	de·vol·*ver* eesh·too

bargaining

That's too expensive.
Está muito caro.   shtaa *mweeng*·too *kaa*·roo

Can you lower the price?
Pode baixar o preço?   po·de bai·*shaar* oo *pre*·soo

Do you have something cheaper?
Tem algo mais barato?   teng *aal*·goo maish ba·*raa*·too

What's your final price?
Qual é o seu   kwaal e oo *se*·oo
último preço?   *ool*·tee·moo *pre*·soo

I'll give you (five euros).
Dou-lhe (cinco euros).   *doh*·lye (*seeng*·koo e·*oo*·roosh)

---

retail therapy

Pondering souvenirs? Portugal's most famous (not to mention enjoyable) export is *porto* por·too (port wine). If you want to support the Portuguese cork (*cortiça* koor·*tee*·sa) industry further, you can pick up cork handicrafts and products in most towns. The famous hand-painted tiles, called *azulejos* a·zoo·*le*·zhoosh, are another distinctively Portuguese option. For something a bit more utilitarian, consider bringing home a leather belt (*cinto de couro* seeng·too de *koh*·roo) or bag (*saco de couro* sa·koo de *koh*·roo), as leather products are good quality in Portugal.

books & reading

Do you have a/an ...?	*Tem ...?*	teng ...
book (by Fernando Pessoa)	*algum livro (do Fernando Pessoa)*	aal·*goong lee*·vroo (doo fer·*nang*·doo pe·*so*·a)
entertainment guide	*um guia de espectáculos*	oong *gee*·a de shpe·*taa*·koo·loosh
Is there an (English-) language ...?	*Há uma ... de língua (inglesa)?*	aa *oo*·ma ... de *leeng*·gwa (eeng·*gle*·za)
bookshop	*livraria*	lee·vra·*ree*·a
section	*secção*	sek·*sowng*
I'd like a ...	*Queria comprar um ...*	ke·*ree*·a kong·*praar* oong ...
dictionary	*dicionário*	dee·see·oo·*naa*·ryoo
newspaper (in English)	*jornal (em inglês)*	zhor·*naal* (eng eeng·*glesh*)
notepad	*bloco de notas*	*blo*·koo de *no*·tash

Can you recommend a book for me?

Recomenda-me algum livro?	rre·koo·*meng*·da·me aal·*goong lee*·vroo

Do you have Lonely Planet guidebooks?

Tem os guias de viagem do Lonely Planet?	teng oosh *gee*·ash de vee·*aa*·zheng doo *loh*·ne·lee *ple*·nat

local talk		
bargain	*pechincha* f	pe·*sheeng*·sha
rip-off	*roubo* m	*rroh*·boo
sale	*saldos* m pl	*saal*·doosh
specials	*preço especial* m	*pre*·soo es·pe·see·*al*

clothes

My size is ...	O meu	oo me·oo
	número é ...	noo·me·roo e ...
(40)	(quarenta)	(kwa·reng·ta)
small	pequeno	pe·ke·noo
medium	médio	me·dyoo
large	grande	grang·de

Can I try it on?
Posso experimentar? po·soo shpree·meng·taar

It doesn't fit.
Não serve. nowng ser·ve

For different types of clothing and colours see the **dictionary**, and for sizes see **numbers & amounts**, page 33.

hairdressing

cabeleireiro

I'd like (a) ...	Queria ...	ke·ree·a ...
colour	pintar	peeng·taar
haircut	cortar o cabelo	koor·taar oo ka·be·loo
my beard	aparar	a·pa·raar
trimmed	a barba	a baar·ba
my hair	lavar/secar	la·vaar/se·kaar
washed/dried	o cabelo	oo ka·be·loo
shave	fazer a barba	fa·zer a baar·ba
trim	aparar	a·pa·raar

| I love it! | Eu adoro! | e·oo a·do·roo |
| I don't like this! | Não gosto! | nowng gosh·too |

Don't cut it too short.
Não corte muito curto. nowng kor·te mweeng·too koor·too

Please use a new blade.
Por favor use uma poor fa·vor oo·ze oo·ma
gilete nova. zhee·le·te no·va

music & DVD

I'd like a ...	Queria comprar um ...	ke·ree·a kong·praar oong ...
CD	CD	se·de
DVD	DVD	de·ve·de
video	vídeo	vee·dee·oo

I'm looking for something by (Amália Rodrigues).
Estou à procura de shtoh aa proo·koo·ra de
qualquer coisa (da kwaal·ker koy·za (da
Amália Rodrigues). a·maa·lya rroo·dree·gesh)

What's his/her best recording?
Qual é o melhor kwaal e oo me·lyor
disco dele/dela? m/f deesh·koo de·le/de·la

Can I listen to this?
Posso ouvir? po·soo oh·veer

Will this work on any DVD player?
Isto funciona em eesh·too foong·syo·na eng
qualquer leitor de DVDs? kwaal·ker lay·tor de de·ve·desh

Is this for a PAL or NTSC system?
Que sistema é este, ke seesh·te·ma e esh·te
PAL ou NTSC? paal oh e·ne te e·se se

video & photography

I need a cable to connect my camera to a computer.
Preciso de um cabo pre·see·zoo de oong kaa·boo
para ligar a minha pa·ra lee·gaar a mee·nya
máquina a um maa·kee·na a oong
computador. kong·poo·ta·dor

I need a cable to recharge this battery.
Preciso de um cabo pre·see·zoo de oong kaa·boo
para carregar esta pilha. pa·ra ka·rre·gaar esh·ta pee·lya

Do you have (a) ... for this camera?	*Tem ... para esta máquina?*	teng ... pa·ra esh·ta maa·kee·na
batteries	*pilhas*	pee·lyash
flash	*flash*	flash
(zoom) lens	*lente (zoom)*	leng·te (zoom)
memory cards	*cartão de memória*	kar·towng de me·mo·ree·a
video cassette	*uma cassete de vídeo*	oo·ma ka·se·te de vee·dee·oo

I need a/an ... film for this camera.	*Preciso de filme ... para esta máquina.*	pre·see·zoo de feel·me ... pa·ra esh·ta maa·kee·na
APS	*sistema APS*	seesh·te·ma aa pe e·se
B&W	*a preto e branco*	a pre·too e brang·koo
colour	*a cores*	a ko·resh
slide	*de dia-positivos*	de dee·a·po·zee·tee·voosh
(200) ASA	*de (duzentos) ASA*	de (doo·zeng·toosh) aa·za

Can you ...?	*Pode ...?*	po·de ...
develop digital photos	*revelar fotos digitais*	rre·ve·laar fo·toosh dee·zhee·taysh
develop this film	*revelar este filme*	rre·ve·laar esh·te feel·me
recharge the battery for my digital camera	*carregar a pilha da minha máquina fotográfica digital*	ka·rre·gaar a pee·lya da mee·nya maa·kee·na foo·too·graa·fee·ka dee·zhee·tal
transfer photos from my camera to CD	*transferir as fotografias da minha máquina para um CD*	trangsh·fe·reer ash foo·too·gra·fee·ash da mee·nya maa·kee·na pa·ra oong se·de

When will it be ready?
    Quando fica pronto?   kwang·doo *fee*·ka *prong*·too

I need a passport photo taken.
    Preciso de tirar fotos   pre·*see*·zoo de tee·*raar* fo·toosh
    para o passaporte.   *pa*·ra oo paa·sa·*por*·te

I'm not happy with these photos.
    Não gostei destas fotos.   nowng gosh·*tay* desh·tash fo·toosh

repairs

Can I have my ... repaired here?
    Vocês consertam ...?   vo·*sesh* kong·*ser*·tang ...

When will my ... be ready?	*Quando é que ...?*	kwang·doo e ke ...
bag	*o saco está pronto*	oo *saa*·koo shtaa *prong*·too
camera	*a câmera está pronta*	*kaa*·me·ra shtaa *prong*·ta
(sun)glasses	*os óculos (de sol) estão prontos*	oosh o·koo·loosh (de sol) shtowng *prong*·toosh
shoes	*os sapatos estão prontos*	oosh sa·*paa*·toosh shtowng *prong*·toosh

---

listen for ...

Posso ajudar? po·soo a·zhoo·*daar*	**Can I help you?**
Mais alguma coisa? maish al·*goo*·ma *koy*·za	**Anything else?**
Não, não temos. nowng nowng te·moosh	**No, we don't have any.**

PRACTICAL

the internet

Where's the local Internet café?
Onde fica um café da   ong·de *fee*·ka oong ka·*fe* da
internet nas   eeng·ter·*net* nash
redondezas?   rre·dong·*de*·zash

I'd like to ...	*Queria ...*	ke·*ree*·a ...
burn a CD	*gravar um CD*	gra·*vaar* oong se·*de*
check my email	*ler o meu email*	ler oo *me*·oo ee·*mayl*
download	*fazer o download*	fa·*zer* oo down·*lohd*
my photos	*das minhas*	dash *mee*·nyash
	fotos	*fo*·toosh
get Internet	*ter acesso à*	ter a·*se*·soo aa
access	*internet*	eeng·ter·*net*
use a printer	*usar uma*	oo·*zaar* oo·ma
	impressora	eeng·pre·*so*·ra
use a scanner	*usar um*	oo·*zaar* oong
	digitalizador	dee·zhee·ta·lee·za·*dor*

Do you have ...?	*Tem ...?*	teng ...
PCs	*PCs*	pe·*sesh*
Macs	*Macs*	maksh
a Zip drive	*um zip drive*	oong zeep draiv

Can I connect	*Posso ligar ...*	*po*·soo lee·gar ...
my ... to this	*a este*	a *esh*·te
computer?	*computador?*	kong·poo·ta·*dor*
camera	*a minha máquina*	a *mee*·nya *maa*·kee·na
media player	*mp3*	e·me·pe·*tresh*
portable	*impulsor*	eeng·*pool*·sor
hard drive	*rígido*	rre·*zhee*·doo
	portátil	por·*taa*·tel
USB flash drive	*flash drive USB*	flash draiv oo·e·se·*be*

How much is it per (hour/page)?

Quanto custa por	kwang·too koosh·ta poor
(hora/página)?	(o·ra/paa·zhee·na)

Please change it to the English-language setting.

Mude o programa para	moo·de oo proo·gra·ma pa·ra
inglês, por favor.	eeng·glesh poor fa·vor

How do I log on?

Como é que eu entro?	ko·moo e ke e·oo eng·troo

Bloody Internet!

Porra para a internet!	po·rra pa·ra a eeng·ter·net

It's crashed.

Desligou-se.	desh·lee·goh·se

I've finished.

Acabei.	a·ka·bay

mobile/cell phone

telemóvel

I'd like a …	*Queria …*	ke·ree·a …
charger for	*comprar uma*	kong·praar oo·ma
my phone	*pilha para o*	pee·lya pa·ra oo
	meu telefone	me·oo te·le·fo·ne
mobile/cell	*alugar um*	a·loo·gaar oong
phone for hire	*telemóvel*	te·le·mo·vel
prepaid mobile/	*comprar um*	kong·praar oong
cell phone	*telemóvel*	te·le·mo·vel
	pré-pago	pre·paa·goo
SIM card for	*cartão SIM*	kar·towng seeng
your network	*para a sua rede*	pa·ra a soo·a rre·de

What are the call rates?

Qual é o valor cobrado?	kwaal e oo va·lor koo·braa·doo

(30c) per (30) seconds.

(Trinta cêntimos) por	(treeng·ta seng·tee·moosh) poor
(trinta) segundos.	(treeng·ta) se·goong·doosh

phone

telefone

What's your phone number?

Qual é o seu número de telefone?   kwaal e oo *se*·oo *noo*·me·roo de te·le·*fo*·ne

The number is …

O número é …   oo *noo*·me·roo e …

Where's the nearest public phone?

Onde fica o telefone público mais perto?   ong·de *fee*·ka o te·le·*fo*·ne poo·blee·koo maish *per*·too

Can I look at a phone book?

Posso usar a lista telefónica?   po·soo oo·*zaar* a *leesh*·ta te·le·*fo*·nee·ka

Can I have some coins/tokens?

Pode-me dar algumas moedas/fichas?   po·de·me daar aal·*goo*·mash moo·e·dash/*fee*·shash

What's the code for (New Zealand)?

Qual é o indicativo para (a Nova Zelândia)?   kwaal e o eeng·dee·ka·*tee*·voo *pa*·ra (a *no*·va ze·*lang*·dee·a)

It's engaged.

Está ocupado.   shtaa o·koo·*paa*·doo

I've been cut off.

Desligaram.   desh·lee·*gaa*·rowng

The connection's bad.

A ligação está má.   a lee·ga·*sowng* shtaa maa

communications

85

I want to …	Quero …	ke·roo …
buy a phonecard	comprar um cartão telefónico	kong·praar oong kar·towng te·le·fo·nee·koo
call (Singapore)	telefonar (para Singapura)	te·le·foo·naar (pa·ra seeng·ga·poo·ra)
make a (local) call	fazer uma chamada (local)	fa·zer oo·ma sha·maa·da (loo·kaal)
reverse the charges	fazer uma chamada a cobrar	fa·zer oo·ma sha·maa·da a koo·braar
speak for (three) minutes	falar por (três) minutos	fa·laar poor (tresh) mee·noo·toosh

How much does … cost?	Quanto custa …?	kwang·too koosh·ta …
a (three)-minute call	uma ligação de (três) minutos	oo·ma lee·ga·sowng de (tresh) mee·noo·toosh
each extra minute	cada minuto extra	kaa·da mee·noo·too aysh·tra

Hello.
Está?   shtaa

It's …
Daqui fala …   da·kee faa·la …

Can I speak to (Pedro)?
Queria falar com (o Pedro)?   ke·ree·a fa·laar kong (oo pe·droo)

Can I leave a message?
Posso deixar um recado?   po·soo day·shaar oong rre·kaa·doo

Please tell him/her I called.
Por favor diga-lhe que eu telefonei.   poor fa·vor dee·ga·lye ke e·oo te·le·foo·nay

My number is …
O meu número é …   oo me·oo noo·me·roo e …

I don't have a contact number.

Eu não tenho um
número de contacto.

e·oo nowng ta·nyoo oong
noo·me·roo de kong·taak·too

I'll call back later.

Volto a telefonar
mais tarde.

vol·too a te·le·foo·naar
maish taar·de

What time should I call?

A que horas devo
telefonar?

a ke o·rash de·voo
te·le·foo·naar

---

listen for ...

Quem fala? keng faa·la	**Who's calling?**
Com quem quer falar? kong keng ker fa·laar	**Who do you want to speak to?**
Só um minuto. so oong mee·noo·too	**One moment.**
Ele/Ela não está. e·le/e·la nowng shtaa	**He/She isn't here.**
Marcou o número errado. mar·koh oo noo·me·roo ee·rraa·doo	**Wrong number.**

---

post office

correios

I want to send a ...	*Quero* *enviar ...*	ke·roo eng·vee·aar ...
fax	*um fax*	oong faks
letter	*uma carta*	oo·ma kaar·ta
parcel	*uma* *encomenda*	oo·ma eng·koo·meng·da
postcard	*um postal*	oong poosh·taal

I want to	Quero	ke·roo
buy a/an ...	comprar um ...	kong·praar oong ...
aerogram	aerograma	aa·e·roo·graa·ma
(padded)	envelope	eng·ve·lo·pe
envelope	(almofadado)	(aal·moo·fa·daa·doo)
stamp	selo	se·loo

customs	declaração de	de·kla·ra·sowng de
declaration	alfândega f	aal·fang·de·ga
domestic	doméstico	doo·mesh·tee·koo
fragile	frágil	fraa·zheel
international	internacional	eeng·ter·na·syoo·naal
mail	correspondência f	koo·rresh·pong·deng·sya
mailbox	marco do	maar·koo doo
	correio m	koo·rray·oo
postcode	código postal m	ko·dee·goo poosh·taal

It contains (souvenirs).

Contém (lembranças).   kong·teng (leng·brang·sash)

Where's the poste restante section?

Onde é a secção de   ong·de e a sek·sowng de
posta restante?   posh·ta rresh·tang·te

Is there any mail for me?

Há alguma   aa aal·goo·ma
correspondência   koo·rresh·pong·deng·sya
para mim?   pa·ra meeng

---

snail mail

air a	via aérea	vee·a a·e·ree·a
express	correio azul	koo·rray·oo a·zool
registered	registado/	rre·zheesh·taa·doo/
	registada m/f	rre·zheesh·taa·da
sea a	via marítima	vee·a ma·ree·tee·ma
surface a	via terrestre	vee·a te·rresh·tre

banking
ir ao banco

What days is the bank open?
Em que dias é que   eng ke *dee*·ash e ke
abre o banco?   *aa*·bre oo *bang*·koo

What times is the bank open?
A que horas é que   a ke *o*·rash e ke
abre o banco?   *aa*·bre oo *bang*·koo

Where can I ...?	*Onde é que posso ...?*	*ong*·de e ke *po*·soo ...
I'd like to ...	*Queria ...*	ke·*ree*·a ...
cash a cheque	*trocar um cheque*	troo·*kaar* oong *she*·ke
change a travellers cheque	*trocar traveller cheque*	troo·*kaar* tra·ve·ler shek
change money	*trocar dinheiro*	troo·*kaar* dee·*nyay*·roo
get a cash advance	*fazer um levantamento adiantado*	fa·*zer* oong le·vang·ta·*meng*·too a·dee·ang·*taa*·doo
get change for this note	*trocar esta nota*	troo·*kaar* esh·ta *no*·ta
withdraw money	*levantar dinheiro*	le·vang·*taar* dee·*nyay*·roo
Where's a/an ...?	*Onde é que há ...?*	*ong*·de e ke aa ...
automated teller machine	*um caixa automático*	oong *kai*·sha ow·too·*maa*·tee·koo
foreign exchange office	*um câmbio*	oong *kang*·byoo

What's the charge for that?

Qual é a taxa aplicável?   kwaal e a *taa*·sha a·plee·*kaa*·vel

What's the exchange rate?

Qual é o câmbio do dia?   kwaal e oo *kang*·byoo doo *dee*·a

The automated teller machine took my card.

O caixa automático   oo *kai*·sha ow·too·*maa*·tee·koo
ficou com o meu cartão.   fee·*koh* kong oo *me*·oo kar·*towng*

I've forgotten my PIN.

Esqueci-me do código.   shke·*see*·me doo ko·dee·goo

Can I use my credit card to withdraw money?

Posso utilizar o   *po*·soo oo·tee·lee·*zaar* oo
cartão de crédito para   kar·*towng* de kre·dee·too *pa*·ra
levantar dinheiro?   le·vang·*taar* dee·*nyay*·roo

Has my money arrived yet?

O meu dinheiro   oo *me*·oo dee·*nyay*·roo
já chegou?   zhaa she·*goh*

How long will it take to arrive?

Quanto tempo vai   *kwang*·too *teng*·poo vai
levar para chegar?   le·*vaar* *pa*·ra she·*gaar*

For other useful phrases, see **money**, page 43.

---

listen for ...

Assine aqui.		
a·*see*·ne a·*kee*		**Sign here.**
Não podemos fazer isso.		
nowng poo·*de*·moosh		**We can't do that.**
fa·*zer* ee·soo		
Não tem mais fundos disponíveis.		
nowng teng maish *foong*·doosh		**You have no**
deesh·poo·*nee*·vaysh		**funds left.**
Temos um problema.		
te·moosh oong pro·*ble*·ma		**There's a problem.**
identificação	ee·deng·tee·fee·ka·*sowng*	**identification**
passaporte	paa·sa·*por*·te	**passport**

I'd like a/an ...	Queria ...	ke·*ree*·a ...
audio set	um aparelho	oong a·pa·*re*·lyoo
	de áudio	de ow·dee·oo
catalogue	um catálogo	oong ka·*taa*·loo·goo
guide	um guia	oong *gee*·a
(person)		
(local) map	um mapa (local)	oong *maa*·pa (loo·*kaal*)
Do you have	Tem	teng
information	informações	eeng·foor·ma·*soyngsh*
on ... sights?	sobre locais ...?	*so*·bre loo·*kaish* ...
cultural	culturais	kool·too·*raish*
historical	históricos	esh·*to*·ree·koosh
religious	religiosos	rre·lee·zhee·o·zoosh

I'd like to see ...
Eu gostava de ver ... e·oo goosh·*taa*·va de ver ...

What's that?
O que é aquilo? oo ke e a·*kee*·loo

Who made it?
Quem é que o construiu? keng e ke oo kong·shtroo·*ee*·oo

How old is it?
Que idade tem? ke ee·*daa*·de teng

Could you take a photo of me/us?
Pode-me/Pode-nos tirar *po*·de·me/*po*·de·noosh tee·*raar*
uma fotografia? oo·ma foo·too·gra·*fee*·a

Can I take a photo (of you)?
Posso(-lhe) tirar *po*·soo(·lye) tee·*raar*
uma fotografia? oo·ma foo·too·gra·*fee*·a

I'll send you the photo.

Eu envio-lhe a	e·oo eng·*vee*·o·lye a
fotografia.	foo·too·gra·*fee*·a

Could you write down your name and address?

Pode escrever o seu	po·de shkre·*ver* oo *se*·oo
nome e o seu endereço?	*no*·me e oo *se*·oo eng·de·re·soo

getting in

What time does it open/close?

A que horas abre/fecha? a ke o·rash *aa*·bre/*fe*·sha

What's the admission charge?

Qual é o preço de entrada? kwaal e oo *pre*·soo de eng·*traa*·da

Is there a	*Tem desconto*	teng desh·*kong*·too
discount for …?	*para …?*	*pa*·ra …
children	*crianças*	kree·*ang*·sash
families	*famílias*	fa·*mee*·lyash
groups	*grupos*	*groo*·poosh
older people	*terceira idade*	ter·*say*·ra ee·*daa*·de
pensioners	*reformados*	rre·for·*maa*·doosh
students	*estudantes*	shtoo·*dang*·tesh

typical addresses

alley	*beco* m	*be*·koo
avenue/boulevard	*avenida (av.)* f	a·ve·*nee*·da
road	*estrada (estd.)* f	esh·*traa*·da
street	*rua (r.)* f	*rroo*·a

Street numbers follow the name of the street. Often apartments are indicated by floor number as well as by the side of the landing on which they're located — *direita* for right, *esquerda* for left. For example, *Rua do Rei, no. 15 – 3º drt.* could be translated '15 King Street, 3rd floor, right side of the landing'.

tours

Can you recommend a …?
Pode recomendar um/uma …? m/f
po·de rre·koo·meng·*daar* oong/*oo*·ma …

When's the next …?
Quando é a próxima/ o próximo …? m/f
kwang·doo e a pro·*see*·ma/ oo pro·*see*·moo …

boat trip	*viagem de barco* f	vee·*aa*·zheng de *baar*·koo
day trip	*passeio* m	pa·*say*·oo
tour	*excursão* f	shkoor·*sowng*

Is … included?	*Inclui …?*	eeng·*kloo*·ee …
accommodation	*hospedagem*	osh·pe·*daa*·zheng
food	*comida*	koo·*mee*·da
transport	*transporte*	trangsh·*por*·te

The guide will pay.
O guia vai pagar.   oo *gee*·a vai pa·*gaar*

How long is the tour?
Quanto tempo dura   kwang·too teng·poo doo·ra
a excursão?   a shkoor·*sowng*

What time should we be back?
A que hora é que devemos   a ke o·ra e ke de·*ve*·moosh
estar de volta?   shtaar de *vol*·ta

I'm with them.
Estou com eles.   shtoh kong e·lesh

I've lost my group.
Perdi o meu grupo.   per·*dee* oo me·oo groo·poo

---

on the nose

Here are three guidelines about pronunciation which can be
helpful when you're reading Portuguese for yourself:

- a vowel followed by 'm' or 'n', or with a tilde (~) above
  it, is usually nasalised – eg *viagem* vee·*aa*·zheng, *avião*
  a·vee·*owng*
- 'o' is often pronounced oo, especially at the end of a word –
  eg *gato* gaa·too
- 'es' at the start of a word and 's' at the end of a word are
  almost always pronounced sh – eg *estômago* shto·ma·goo,
  crianças kree·*ang*·sash

I'm attending a …	Estou a participar …	shtoh a par·tee·see·paar …
conference	numa conferência	noong·ma kong·fe·reng·sya
course	num curso	noong koor·soo
meeting	numa reunião	noo·ma rree·oo·nyowng
trade fair	numa feira de comércio	noo·ma fay·ra de koo·mer·syoo
I'm here for …	Vou ficar aqui por …	voh fee·kaar a·kee poor …
(two) days	(dois) dias	(doysh) dee·ash
(three) weeks	(três) semanas	(tresh) se·ma·nash
I'm with …	Estou com …	shtoh kong …
(Telecel)	(a Telecel)	(a te·le·sel)
colleagues	colegas de trabalho	koo·le·gash de tra·baa·lyoo
(two) others	outros (dois)	oh·troosh (doysh)

I'm alone.
Estou sozinho/sozinha. m/f   shtoh so·zee·nyoo/so·zee·nya

I have an appointment with …
Tenho uma reunião   ta·nyoo oo·ma rree·oo·nyowng
marcada com …   mar·kaa·da kong …

I'm staying at (the Hotel do Rei), room (205).
Estou no (Hotel do Rei),   shtoh noo (o·tel doo rray)
no quarto   noo kwaar·too
(duzentos e cinco).   (doo·zeng·toosh e seeng·koo)

Where's the ...?	Onde é ...?	ong·de e ...
business centre	o centro de negócios	oo seng·troo de ne·go·syoosh
conference	a conferência	a kong·fe·reng·sya
meeting	a reunião	a rree·oo·nyowng

I need ...	Preciso de ...	pre·see·zoo de ...
a computer	um computador	oong kong·poo·ta·dor
an Internet connection	ligação à internet	lee·ga·sowng aa eeng·ter·net
an interpreter	um intérprete	oong eeng·ter·pre·te
to send a fax	enviar um fax	eng·vee·aar oong faks

Here's my ...	Aqui está o meu ...	a·kee shtaa oo me·oo ...
What's your ...?	Qual é o seu ...?	kwaal e oo se·oo ...
(email) address	endereço (de email)	eng·de·re·soo (de ee·mayl)
fax number	número de fax	noo·me·roo de faks
mobile/cell number	número do telemóvel	noo·me·roo doo te·le·mo·vel
pager number	número do pager	noo·me·roo doo pay·zher
work number	número de telefone do trabalho	noo·me·roo de te·le·fo·ne doo tra·baa·lyoo

Can I have your business card?
Pode-me dar o seu cartão de visita? — po·de·me daar oo se·oo kar·towng de vee·zee·ta

Thank you for your time.
Obrigado/Obrigada pela atenção. m/f — o·bree·gaa·doo/o·bree·gaa·da pe·la a·teng·sowng

Shall we go for a ...?	Vocês gostariam de ...?	vo·sesh gosh·ta·ree·ang de ...
drink	tomar alguma coisa	too·maar aal·goo·ma koy·za
meal	jantar	zhang·taar

It's on me. Eu pago. — e·oo paa·goo

senior & disabled travellers
viajantes idosos & com deficiência física

I have a disability.
Eu tenho uma   e·oo ta·nyoo oo·ma
deficiência física.   de·fee·see·eng·sya fee·zee·ka

I need assistance.
Preciso de ajuda.   pre·see·zoo de a·zhoo·da

What services do you have for people with a disability?
Que serviços é que vocês   ke ser·vee·soosh e ke vo·sesh
oferecem para pessoas   o·fe·re·seng pa·ra pe·so·ash
com deficiências   kong de·fee·see·eng·syash
físicas?   fee·zee·kash

Are there disabled toilets?
Tem casa de banho   teng kaa·za de ba·nyoo
para deficientes   pa·ra de·fee·see·eng·tesh
físicos?   fee·zee·koosh

Are there disabled parking spaces?
Tem estacionamento   teng shta·see·oo·na·meng·too
para deficientes   pa·ra de·fee·see·eng·tesh
físicos?   fee·zee·koosh

Is there wheelchair access?
Tem acesso para cadeira   teng a·se·soo pa·ra ka·day·ra
de rodas?   de rro·dash

How wide is the entrance?
Qual é a largura da   kwaal e a lar·goo·ra da
entrada?   eng·traa·da

I'm (deaf).
Sou (surdo/surda). m/f   soh (soor·doo/soor·da)

I have a hearing aid.
Uso aparelho para   oo·zoo a·pa·re·lyoo pa·ra
surdez.   soor·desh

My companion's (blind). (for a man)
O meu companheiro   oo me·oo kong·pa·nyay·roo
é (cego).   e (se·goo)

My companion's (blind). (for a woman)
  A minha companheira   a *mee*·nya kong·pa·*nyay*·ra
  é (cega).   e (*se*·ga)

Are guide dogs permitted?
  É permitida a entrada   e per·mee·*tee*·da a eng·*traa*·da
  de cães-guia?   de kaingsh·*gee*·a

How many steps are there?
  Quantos degraus há ai?   *kwang*·toosh de·*growsh* aa a·*ee*

Is there an elevator?
  Tem elevador?   teng e·le·va·*dor*

Are there rails in the bathroom?
  Tem corrimão na casa   teng koo·rree·*mowng* na *kaa*·za
  de banho?   de *ba*·nyoo

Could you call me a disabled taxi?
  Pode-me chamar um   *po*·de·me sha·*maar* oong
  táxi para deficientes   *taak*·see *pa*·ra de·fee·see·*eng*·tesh
  físicos?   *fee*·zee·koosh

Could you help me cross the street safely?
  Pode-me ajudar a   *po*·de·me a·zhoo·*daar* a
  atravessar a rua   a·tra·ve·*saar* a *rroo*·a
  com segurança?   kong se·goo·*rang*·sa

Is there somewhere I can sit down?
  Há algum lugar onde me   aa aal·*goong* loo·*gaar* ong·de me
  possa sentar?   *po*·sa seng·taar

guide dog	*cão-guia* m	kowng·*gee*·a
older person	*pessoa idosa* f	pe·*so*·a ee·*do*·za
person with	*pessoa com*	pe·*so*·a kong
a disability	*deficiência* f	de·fee·see·*eng*·sya
ramp	*rampa* f	*rrang*·pa
walking frame	*armação*	ar·ma·*sowng*
	para andar f	*pa*·ra ang·*daar*
walking stick	*bengala* f	beng·*gaa*·la
wheelchair	*cadeira de rodas* f	ka·*day*·ra de *rro*·dash

travelling with children

Is there a ...?	*Há ...?*	aa ...
baby change room	*uma sala reservada para bebés*	oo·ma saa·la rre·zer·vaa·da pa·ra be·besh
child-minding service	*serviço de ama*	ser·vee·soo de a·ma
children's menu	*menu para crianças*	me·noo pa·ra kree·ang·sash
crèche	*creche*	kre·she
discount for children	*desconto para crianças*	desh·kong·too pa·ra kree·ang·sash
family ticket	*passagem de família*	pa·saa·zheng de fa·mee·lya
I need a/an ...	*Preciso de ...*	pre·see·zoo de ...
baby seat	*um lugar para bebés*	oong loo·gaar pa·ra be·besh
(English-speaking) babysitter	*uma ama (que fale inglês)*	oo·ma a·ma (ke faa·le eeng·glesh)
booster seat	*assento de elevação*	a·seng·too de ee·le·va·sowng
cot	*cama de grades*	ka·ma de graa·desh
highchair	*uma cadeira para crianças*	oo·ma ka·day·ra pa·ra kree·ang·sash
plastic bag	*um saco de plástico*	oong saa·koo de plaash·tee·koo
potty	*um bacio*	oong ba·see·oo
pram/stroller	*um carrinho de bebé*	oong ka·rree·nyoo de be·be

Where's the nearest ...?	*Onde está ...*	ong·de shtaa ...
	mais próximo/	maish pro·see·moo/
	próxima? m/f	pro·see·ma
park	*o parque*	oo paar·ke
playground	*o parque*	oo paar·ke
	infantil	eeng·fang·teel
swimming pool	*a piscina*	a pesh·see·na
tap	*a torneira*	a tor·nay·ra
theme park	*o parque de*	oo paar·ke de
	diversões	dee·ver·zoyngsh
toyshop	*a loja de*	a lo·zha de
	brinquedos	breeng·ke·doosh

Do you sell ...?	*Vendem ...?*	veng·deng ...
baby wipes	*toalhinhas*	twa·lyee·nyash
	de bebé	de be·be
painkillers for	*analgésicos*	a·naal·zhe·zee·koosh
infants	*infantis*	eeng·fang·teesh
disposable	*fraldas*	fraal·dash
nappies/diapers	*descartáveis*	desh·kar·taa·vaysh
tissues	*lenços de papel*	leng·soosh de pa·pel

Are there any good places to take children around here?

Há algum lugar agradável aa aal·goong loo·gaar a·gra·daa·vel
para levar as crianças pa·ra le·vaar ash kree·ang·sash
por aqui perto? poor a·kee per·too

Are children allowed?

É permitida a entrada e per·mee·tee·da a eng·traa·da
a crianças? a kree·ang·sash

Where can I change a nappy/diaper?

Onde posso mudar ong·de po·soo moo·daar
a fralda? a fraal·da

Do you mind if I breast-feed here?

Importa-se que eu eeng·por·ta·se ke e·oo
amamente aqui? a·ma·meng·te a·kee

Could I have some paper and pencils, please?

Pode-me dar papel po·de·me daar pa·pel
e lápis, por favor? ee laa·peesh poor fa·vor

Is this suitable for … year-old children?

Isto é apropriado	*eesh·too e a·proo·pree·aa·doo*
para crianças de …	*pa·ra kree·ang·sash de …*
anos de idade?	*a·noosh de ee·daa·de*

Do you know a doctor/dentist who is good with children?

Conhece algum médico/	*ko·nye·se aal·goong me·dee·koo/*
dentista bom para	*deng·teesh·ta bong pa·ra*
crianças?	*kree·ang·sash*

If your child is sick, see **health**, page 183.

talking with children

conversar com crianças

What's your name?
Como se chama? · *ko·moo se shaa·ma*

How old are you?
Quantos anos tem? · *kwang·toosh aa·noosh teng*

When's your birthday?
Quando é que fazes anos? · *kwang·doo e ke faa·zesh a·noosh*

Do you go to school?
Vais à escola? · *vaish aa shko·la*

What grade are you in?
Em que ano estás? · *eng ke a·noo shtaash*

Do you like (sport)?
Gostas (de desporto)? · *goosh·tash (de desh·por·too)*

What do you do after school?
O que é que fazes · *o ke e ke faa·zesh*
depois da escola? · *de·poysh da shko·la*

Do you learn (English)?
Aprendes (inglês)? · *a·preng·desh (eeng·glesh)*

talking about children

When's the baby due?
Para quando	pa·ra kwang·doo
está previsto o	shtaa pre·veesh·too oo
nascimento do bebé?	nash·see·meng·too doo be·be

What are you going to call the baby?
Que nome vai dar	ke no·me vai daar
ao bebé?	ow be·be

How many children do you have?
Quantos filhos tem?	kwang·toosh fee·lyoosh teng

What a beautiful child!
Que linda criança!	ke leeng·da kree·ang·sa

Is it a boy or a girl?
É menino ou menina?	e me·nee·noo oh me·nee·na

Is this your first child?
É o seu primeiro filho?	e oo se·oo pree·may·roo fee·lyoo

How old is he/she?
Quantos anos tem?	kwang·toosh a·noosh teng

Does he/she go to school?
Vai à escola?	vai aa shko·la

What's his/her name?
Como se chama?	ko·moo se sha·ma

animal noises

cat	miau	mee·ow
chick	piu-piu	pee·oo·pee·oo
dog (big)	ão-ão	owng·owng
dog (small)	béu-béu	be·oo·be·oo
duck	quá-quá	kwaa·kwaa
horse	ee-ee-ee	ee·ee·ee

basics

conhecimentos básicos

English	Portuguese	Pronunciation
Yes.	*Sim.*	seeng
No.	*Não.*	nowng
Please.	*Por favor.*	poor fa·*vor*
Thank you (very much).	*(Muito) Obrigado/ Obrigada.* m/f	(*mweeng*·too) o·bree·*gaa*·doo/ o·bree·*gaa*·da
You're welcome.	*De nada.*	de *naa*·da
Excuse me. (to get attention)	*Faz favor!*	faash fa·*vor*
Excuse me. (to get past)	*Com licença.*	kong lee·*seng*·sa
Sorry.	*Desculpe.*	desh·*kool*·pe

greetings & goodbyes

saudações & despedidas

English	Portuguese	Pronunciation
Hello/Hi.	*Olá.*	o·*laa*
Good morning/day.	*Bom dia.*	bong *dee*·a
Good afternoon.	*Boa tarde.*	bo·a *taar*·de
Good evening.	*Boa noite.*	bo·a *noy*·te
How are you?	*Como está?*	ko·moo shtaa
Fine. And you?	*Bem, e você?*	beng e vo·*se*

English	Portuguese	Pronunciation
What's your name?	*Qual é o seu nome?*	kwaal e oo *se*·oo *no*·me
My name is ...	*O meu nome é ...*	oo *me*·oo *no*·me e ...
I'd like to introduce you to ...	*Eu gostava de te apresentar ...*	*e*·oo goosh·*taa*·va de te a·pre·zeng·*taar* ...
Luís	*ao Luís*	ow loo·*eesh*
Maria	*à Maria*	aa ma·*ree*·a
This is my ...	*Este é o meu ...* m *Esta é a minha ...* f	*esh*·te e oo *me*·oo ... *esh*·ta e a *mee*·nya ...
child	*filho/filha* m/f	*fee*·lyoo/*fee*·lya
colleague	*colega* m&f	koo·*le*·ga
friend	*amigo/amiga* m/f	a·*mee*·goo/a·*mee*·ga
husband	*marido*	ma·*ree*·doo
partner (intimate)	*companheiro/ companheira* m/f	kong·pa·*nyay*·roo/ kong·pa·*nyay*·ra
wife	*esposa*	*shpo*·za

I'm pleased to meet you.
Prazer em conhecê-lo/ conhecê-la. m/f
pra·*zer* eng koo·nye·*se*·lo/ koo·nye·*se*·la

See you later.
Até logo.
a·*te* lo·goo

Goodbye.
Adeus.
a·*de*·oosh

Good night.
Boa noite.
bo·a *noy*·te

Bon voyage!
Boa viagem!
bo·a vee·*aa*·zheng

addressing people

If you're talking to people who are older than you or that you don't know very well, it's polite to use their name or title. You might address a male doctor, for example, as *Senyor Doutor* se·*nyor* doh·*tor*. See the box on page 120 for more on formality and informality.

Mr	Senhor	se·nyor
Sir	Cavalheiro	ka·va·lyay·roo
Mrs/Ms	Senhora	se·nyo·ra
Miss	Menina	me·nee·na
Madam	Senhora Dona	se·nyo·ra do·na

making conversation

What a beautiful day!
   Que lindo dia!   ke *leeng*·doo *dee*·a

Nice/Awful weather, isn't it?
   Que tempo
   fantástico/terrível!   ke *teng*·poo
   fang·*taash*·tee·koo/te·*rree*·vel

That's (beautiful), isn't it!
   Isto é (lindo),   *eesh*·too e (*leeng*·doo)
   não acha?   nowng *aa*·sha

What's this called?
   Como se chama isto?   ko·moo se *sha*·ma *eesh*·too

Do you live here?
   Mora aqui?   mo·ra a·*kee*

Where are you going?
   Onde vai?   *ong*·de vai

What are you doing?
   O que é que está a fazer?   oo ke e ke shtaa a fa·*zer*

Can I take a photo (of you)?
 Posso(-lhe) tirar   po·soo(·lye) tee·*raar*
 uma fotografia?   oo·ma foo·too·gra·*fee*·a

I'll send you the photo.
 Mando-lhe a   *mang*·do·lye a
 fotografia.   foo·too·gra·*fee*·a

Do you like it here?
 Gosta daqui?   goosh·ta da·*kee*

I love it here.
 Eu adoro.   e·oo a·*do*·roo

How long are you here for?
 Quanto tempo   kwang·too *teng*·poo
 vai cá ficar?   vai kaa fee·*kaar*

Are you here on holiday?
 Está aqui de férias?   shtaa a·*kee* de fe·ree·ash

I'm here for	*Fico cá*	*fee*·koo kaa
(four) ...	*(quatro) ...*	*(kwaa*·troo) ...
days	*dias*	*dee*·ash
weeks	*semanas*	se·*ma*·nash

I'm here ...	*Estou aqui ...*	shtoh a·*kee* ...
for a holiday	*de férias*	de fe·ree·ash
on business	*em negócios*	eng ne·*go*·syoosh
to study	*a estudar*	a shtoo·*daar*

---

local talk

Hey!	*Ei!*	ay
Great!	*Óptimo!*	*o*·tee·moo
Sure.	*É claro.*	e *klaa*·roo
Maybe.	*Talvez.*	taal·*vesh*
No way!	*De maneira*	de ma·*nay*·ra
	nenhuma!	neeng·*yoo*·ma
Just a minute.	*Só um minuto.*	so oong mee·*noo*·too
Just joking.	*Estou a brincar.*	shtoh a breeng·*kaar*
It's OK.	*Está bem.*	shtaa beng
No problem.	*Não há problema.*	nowng aa pro·*ble*·ma

nationalities

Where are you from?	*De onde é?*	*dong·de e*
I'm from ...	*Eu sou ...*	*e·oo soh ...*
Australia	*da Austrália*	da owsh·*traa*·lya
Canada	*do Canadá*	doo ka·na·*daa*
Singapore	*de Singapura*	de seeng·ga·*poo*·ra
USA	*dos Estados Unidos*	doosh *shtaa*·doosh oo·*nee*·doosh

For more countries, see the **dictionary**.

age

idade

How old ...?	*Quantos anos ...?*	*kwang*·toosh *a*·noosh ...
are you	*tem*	teng
is your daughter	*tem a sua filha*	teng a *soo*·a *fee*·lya
is your son	*tem o seu filho*	teng oo *se*·oo *fee*·lyoo

I'm ... years old.
Tenho ... anos.   *ta*·nyoo ... *a*·noosh

He/She is ... years old.
Ele/Ela tem ... anos.   *e*·le/*e*·la teng ... *a*·noosh

Too old!
Demasiado velho/velha! m/f   de·ma·zee·*aa*·doo ve·lyoo/ve·lya

I'm younger than I look.
Sou mais novo/nova   soh maish *no*·voo/*no*·va
do que pareço. m/f   doo ke pa·*re*·soo

I'm older than I look.
Sou mais velho/velha   soh maish *ve*·lyoo/*ve*·lya
do que pareço. m/f   doo ke pa·*re*·soo

For your age, see **numbers & amounts**, page 33.

meeting people

occupations & studies

What's your occupation?	Qual é a sua profissão?	kwaal e a *soo*·a proo·fee·*sowng*
I'm a ...	Sou ...	soh ...
chef	cozinheiro chefe/ cozinheira chefe m/f	koo·zee·*nyay*·roo *she*·fe/ koo·zee·*nyay*·ra *she*·fe
journalist	jornalista m&f	zhoor·na·*leesh*·ta
teacher	professor/ professora m/f	proo·fe·*sor*/ proo·fe·*so*·ra
I work in ...	Trabalho em ...	tra·*baa*·lyoo eng ...
health	saúde	sa·*oo*·de
sales and marketing	vendas e marketing	*veng*·dash ee *mar*·ke·teeng

I'm retired.
Eu estou reformado/ reformada m/f
e·oo shtoh rre·for·*maa*·doo/ rre·for·*maa*·da

I'm self-employed.
Eu sou empregado/ empregada por conta própria. m/f
e·oo soh eng·pre·*gaa*·doo/ eng·pre·*gaa*·da poor *kong*·ta *pro*·pree·a

I'm unemployed.
Eu estou desempregado/ desempregada. m/f
e·oo shtoh de·zeng·pre·*gaa*·doo/ de·zeng·pre·*gaa*·da

What are you studying?
O que é que está a estudar?
oo ke e ke shtaa a shtoo·*daar*

I'm studying ...	Estudo ...	shtoo·doo ...
humanities	humanísticas	oo·ma·*neesh*·tee·kash
Portuguese	português	poor·too·*gesh*
science	ciências	see·*eng*·see·ash

family

Do you have a …?	*Tem …?*	teng …
I (don't) have a …	*Eu (não)*	e·oo (nowng)
	tenho …	ta·nyoo …
brother	*um irmão*	oong eer·*mowng*
daughter	*uma filha*	oo·ma *fee*·lya
father	*pai*	pai
granddaughter	*neta*	ne·ta
grandfather	*avô*	a·*voh*
grandmother	*avó*	a·*vo*
grandson	*neto*	ne·too
husband	*marido*	ma·*ree*·doo
mother	*mãe*	maing
partner	*companheiro/*	kong·pa·*nyay*·roo/
(intimate)	*companheira* m/f	kong·pa·*nyay*·ra
sister	*uma irmã*	oo·ma eer·*mang*
son	*um filho*	oong *fee*·lyoo
wife	*esposa*	*shpo*·za
I'm …	*Eu sou …*	e·oo soh …
divorced	*divorciado/*	dee·vor·see·*aa*·doo/
	divorciada m/f	dee·vor·see·*aa*·da
married	*casado/*	ka·*zaa*·doo/
	casada m/f	ka·*zaa*·da
single	*solteiro/*	sol·*tay*·roo/
	solteira m/f	sol·*tay*·ra

Are you married?
É casado/casada? m/f   e ka·*zaa*·doo/ka·*zaa*·da

I'm separated.
Eu estou separado/   e·oo se·pa·*raa*·doo/
separada m/f   se·pa·*raa*·da

I live with someone. (with a man)
Vivo com o meu   *vee*·voo kong oo *me*·oo
namorado. m   na·moo·*raa*·doo

I live with someone. (with a woman)
Vivo com a minha   *vee*·voo kong a *mee*·nya
namorada. f   na·moo·*raa*·da

farewells

Tomorrow is my last day here.
Amanhã é o meu
último dia aqui.
aa·ma·*nyang* e oo me·oo
ool·tee·moo dee·a a·*kee*

If you come to (Scotland) you can stay with me.
Se vier à (Escócia) pode
ficar em minha casa.
se vee·*er* aa (*shko*·sya) po·de
fee·*kar* eng mee·nya *kaa*·za

Keep in touch!
Mantenha-se em
contacto!
mang·*te*·nya·se eng
kong·*taak*·too

It's been great meeting you.
Foi fantástico
conhecê-lo/conhecê-la. m/f
foy fang·*taash*·tee·koo
koo·nye·*se*·loo/koo·nye·*se*·la

Here's my ...	*Aqui está o meu ...*	a·*kee* shtaa oo me·oo ...
What's your ...?	*Qual é o seu ...?*	kwaal e oo se·oo ...
address	*endereço*	eng·de·*re*·soo
email address	*email*	ee·*mayl*
phone	*número de*	noo·me·roo de
number	*telefone*	te·le·*fo*·ne

well-wishing

Bless you!	*Deus o*	de·ooz oo
	abençoe!	a·beng·*so*·e
Congratulations!	*Parabéns!*	pa·ra·*bengzh*
Good luck!	*Boa sorte!*	bo·a *sor*·te
Happy Birthday!	*Feliz*	fe·*leesh*
	aniversário!	a·nee·ver·*saa*·ree·oo
Happy New Year!	*Feliz Ano Novo!*	fe·*leesh* a·noo *no*·voo
Happy Easter!	*Páscoa Feliz!*	*paash*·kwa fe·*leesh*
Merry Christmas!	*Feliz Natal!*	fe·*leesh* na·*taal*

common interests

interesses comuns

What do you do in your spare time?
O que faz nos seus   oo ke fazh noosh *se·*oosh
tempos livres?   *teng·*poosh *lee·*vresh

Do you like …?   *Gosta de …?*   *gosh·*ta de …
I (don't) like …   *Eu (não)*   *e·*oo (nowng)
    gosto de …   *gosh·*too de …

bullfighting	*touradas*	toh·*raa·*dash
computer games	*jogos de computador*	*zho·*goosh de kong·poo·ta·*dor*
cooking	*cozinhar*	koo·zee·*nyaar*
dancing	*dançar*	dang·*saar*
drawing	*desenhar*	de·ze·*nyaar*
films	*ver filmes*	ver *feel·*mesh
gardening	*jardinagem*	zhar·dee·*naa·*zheng
going to the beach	*ir à praia*	eer aa *prai·*a
hiking	*caminhar*	ka·mee·*nyaar*
music	*música*	*moo·*zee·ka
painting	*pintar*	peeng·*taar*
photography	*fazer fotografia*	fa·*zer* foo·too·gra·*fee·*a
reading	*ler*	ler
shopping	*ir às compras*	eer aash *kong·*prash
socialising	*sair com amigos*	sa·*eer* kong a·*mee·*goosh
sport	*fazer desporto*	fa·*zer* desh·*por·*too
surfing the Internet	*navegar na internet*	na·ve·*gaar* na eeng·ter·*net*
travelling	*viajar*	vee·a·*zhaar*

For types of sports, see **sport**, page 135, and the **dictionary**.

music

Do you ...?	Costuma ...?	koosh·too·ma ...
dance	ir dançar	eer dang·saar
go to concerts	ir a concertos	eer a kong·ser·toosh
listen to music	ouvir música	oh·veer moo·zee·ka
play an	tocar algum	too·kaar aal·goong
instrument	instrumento	eeng·shtroo·meng·too
sing	cantar	kang·taar
What ... do	De que ...	de ke ...
you like?	gosta?	gosh·ta
bands	conjuntos	kong·zhoong·toosh
music	tipo de	tee·poo de
	música	moo·zee·ka
artists	artistas	ar·teesh·tash
blues	blues m	blooz
classical music	música	moo·zee·ka
	clássica f	klaa·see·ka
electronic music	música	moo·zee·ka
	electrónica f	ee·le·tro·nee·ka
fado	fado m	faa·doo
folk music	música	moo·zee·ka
	popular f	poo·poo·laar
jazz	jazz m	zhaaz
pop	pop m	pop
rancho	rancho m	raang·shoo
rock	rock m	rrok
traditional	música	moo·zee·ka
Portuguese	tradicional	tra·dee·syoo·naal
music	portuguesa f	poor·too·ge·za
tuna (university	tuna f	too·na
music group)		
world music	música de todo	moo·zee·ka de to·doo
	o mundo f	oo moong·doo

cinema & theatre

I feel like going to a/an ...	Apetece-me ir ao/à ... m/f	a·pe·te·se·me eer ow/aa ...
Did you like the ...?	Gostou ...?	goosh·toh ...
ballet	do ballet	doo ba·le
film	do filme	doo fil·me
opera	da ópera	da o·pe·ra
play	da peça (de teatro)	da pe·sa (de tee·aa·troo)

What's showing at the cinema/theatre tonight?
O que é que está no cinema/teatro hoje à noite?
oo ke e ke shtaa noo see·ne·ma/tee·aa·troo o·zhe aa noy·te

Is it in English?
É em inglês?
e eng eeng·glesh

Does it have English subtitles?
Tem legendas em inglês?
teng le·zheng·dash eng eeng·glesh

Is there a matinee show?
Há alguma matiné?
aa aal·goo·ma ma·tee·ne

Is this seat taken?
Este lugar está ocupado?
esh·te loo·gaar shtaa o·koo·paa·doo

Have you seen (Sorte Nula)?
Já viu a (Sorte Nula)?
zha vee·oo a (sor·te noo·la)

Who's in it?
Com quem é?
kong keng e

It stars (Rui Unas).
É com o . (Rui Unas)
e kong oo (rroo·ee oo·nash)

Do you have tickets for ...?
Tem bilhetes para ...?
teng bee·lye·tesh pa·ra ...

I'd like the best tickets.
Eu queria os melhores bilhetes.
e·oo ke·*ree*·a oosh me·*lyor*·esh bee·*lye*·tesh

I'd like cheap tickets.
Eu queria bilhetes baratos.
e·oo ke·*ree*·a bee·*lye*·tesh ba·*ra*·toosh

I'd like …	Eu queria …	e·oo ke·*ree*·a …
1st/2nd balcony seats	*lugares no primeiro/ segundo balcão*	loo·*gaa*·resh noo pree·*may*·roo/ se·*goong*·doo baal·*kowng*
box seats	*um camarote*	oong ka·ma·*ro*·te
orchestra seats	*lugares na plateia*	loo·*gaa*·resh na pla·*tay*·a
wings seats	*coxias*	koo·*shee*·ash

I thought it was …	Eu achei que era …	e·oo a·*shay* ke e·ra …
boring	*chato/chata* m/f	*shaa*·too/*shaa*·ta
excellent	*excelente*	aysh·se·*leng*·te
OK	*razoável*	rra·zoo·*aa*·vel

action movies	*filmes de acção*	*feel*·mesh de a·*sowng*
animated films	*desenhos animados*	de·*ze*·nyoosh a·nee·*maa*·doosh
comedies	*comédias*	koo·*me*·dyash
documentaries	*documentá-rios*	doo·koo·meng·*taa*·ryoosh
drama	*drama*	*dra*·ma
horror movies	*filmes de terror*	*feel*·mesh de te·*rror*
Portuguese cinema	*cinema português*	see·*ne*·ma poor·too·*gesh*
sci-fi	*ficção científica*	feek·*sowng* see·eng·*tee*·fee·ka
short films	*curtas-metragens*	*koor*·tash·me·*traa*·zhengsh
thrillers	*filmes de suspense*	*feel*·mesh de soosh·*pengs*
war movies	*filmes de guerra*	*feel*·mesh de *ge*·rra

feelings & opinions

feelings

sentimentos

Are you …?	*Está …*	shtaa …
I'm (not) …	*(Não) Estou …*	(nowng) shtoh …
annoyed	*chateado/ chateada* m/f	sha·te·*aa*·doo/ sha·te·*aa*·da
cold	*com frio*	kong *free*·oo
disappointed	*desiludido/ desiludida* m/f	de·zee·loo·*dee*·doo/ de·zee·loo·*dee*·da
embarrassed	*envergonhado/ envergonhada* m/f	eng·ver·goo·*nyaa*·doo/ eng·ver·goo·*nyaa*·da
happy	*feliz*	fe·*leesh*
homesick	*com saudades de casa*	kong sa·oo·*daa*·desh de *kaa*·za
hot	*com calor*	kong ka·*lor*
hungry	*com fome*	kong *fo*·me
in a hurry	*com pressa*	kong *pre*·sa
jealous	*com ciúmes*	kong *syoo*·mesh
sad	*triste*	*treesh*·te
surprised	*surpreendido/ surpreendida* m/f	sur·pre·eng·*dee*·doo/ sur·pre·eng·*dee*·da
thirsty	*com sede*	kong *se*·de
tired	*cansado/ cansada* m/f	kang·*saa*·doo/ kang·*saa*·da
well	*bem*	beng
worried	*preocupado/ preocupada* m/f	pree·o·koo·*paa*·doo/ pree·o·koo·*paa*·da

What's wrong?
Qual é o problema? — kwaal e oo proo·*ble*·ma

What happened?
O que aconteceu? — oo ke aa·kong·te·*se*·oo

If you're not feeling well, see **health**, page 183.

how are you *really*?		
a little	*um bocadinho*	oong boo·ka·*dee*·nyoo
I'm a little sad.	*Estou um bocadinho triste.*	shtoh oong boo·ka·*dee*·nyoo *treesh*·te
very	*muito*	*mweeng*·too
I feel very lucky.	*Sinto-me com muita sorte.*	*seeng*·too·me kong *mweeng*·ta *sor*·te
not at all	*não … nada*	nowng … *naa*·da
I'm not at all tired.	*Não estou nada cansado/ cansada.* m/f	nowng shtoh *naa*·da kang·*saa*·doo/ kang·*saa*·da

opinions

opiniões

Did you like it?
Gostou? gosh·toh

What do you think of it?
O que é que acha disso? oo ke e ke *aa*·sha *dee*·soo

I thought it was … It's …	*Eu achei que …* *É …*	e·oo a·*shay* ke … e …
awful	*horrível* m&f	o·*rree*·vel
beautiful	*lindo/linda* m/f	*leeng*·doo/*leeng*·da
boring	*chato/chata* m/f	*shaa*·too/*shaa*·ta
great	*óptimo/óptima* m/f	*o*·tee·moo/*o*·tee·ma
interesting	*interessante* m&f	eeng·te·re·*sang*·te
OK	*razoável* m&f	rra·zoo·*aa*·vel
strange	*estranho* m *estranha* f	*shtra*·nyoo/ *shtra*·nya
expensive	*caro/cara* m/f	*kaa*·roo/*kaa*·ra

politics & social issues

política & assuntos sociais

Who do you vote for?
Em que partido vota? — eng ke par·*tee*·da *vo*·ta

I support the … party.
Eu apoio o … — e·oo a·*poy*·oo oo …

I'm a member of the … party.
Eu sou membro … — e·oo soh *meng*·broo …

Did you hear about …?
Ouviu falar de …? — oh·*vee*·oo fa·*laar* de …

Do you agree with it?
Concorda? — kong·*kor*·da

I (don't) agree with …
Eu (não) concordo
com … — e·oo (nowng) kong·*kor*·doo
kong …

How do people feel about …?
O que é que as pessoas
pensam sobre …? — oo ke e ke ash pe·*so*·ash
peng·sang *so*·bre …

How can we protest against …?
Como é que podemos
protestar contra …? — ko·moo e ke poo·*de*·moosh
pro·tesh·*taar* kong·tra …

How can we support …?
Como é que podemos
apoiar …? — ko·moo e ke poo·*de*·moosh
a·*poy*·aar …

feelings & opinions

117

abortion	*aborto* m	a·*bor*·too
animal rights	*direitos dos*	dee·*ray*·toosh doosh
	animais m pl	aa·nee·*maish*
bullfighting	*touradas* f pl	toh·*raa*·dash
corruption	*corrupção* f	koo·rroop·*sowng*
crime	*crime* m	*kree*·me
discrimination	*discriminação* f	desh·kree·mee·na·*sowng*
drugs	*drogas* f pl	*dro*·gash
the economy	*a economia* f	a ee·ko·noo·*mee*·a
education	*educação* f	ee·doo·ka·*sowng*
emigration	*emigração* f	e·mee·gra·*sowng*
the environment	*o ambiente* m	oo ang·bee·*eng*·te
equal	*igualdade de*	ee·gwaal·*daa*·de de
opportunity	*oportunidades* f	o·poor·too·nee·*daa*·desh
the European	*a União*	a oo·*nyowng*
Union	*Europeia* f	e·oo·roo·*pay*·a
euthanasia	*eutanásia* f	e·oo·ta·*naa*·zya
globalisation	*globalização* f	glo·ba·lee·za·*sowng*
human rights	*direitos*	dee·*ray*·toosh
	humanos m pl	oo·*ma*·noosh
immigration	*imigração* f	ee·mee·gra·*sowng*
inequality	*desigualdade* f	de·zee·gwaal·*daa*·de
military service	*serviço militar* m	ser·*vee*·soo mee·lee·*taar*
party politics	*política*	poo·*lee*·tee·ka
	partidária f	par·tee·*daa*·rya
poverty	*pobreza* f	poo·*bre*·za
privatisation	*privatização* f	pree·va·tee·za·*sowng*
public health care	*saúde pública* f	sa·*oo*·de poo·blee·ka
racism	*racismo* m	rraa·*seezh*·moo
sexism	*sexismo* m	se·*seezh*·moo
social welfare	*segurança*	se·goo·*rang*·sa
	social f	soo·*syaal*
terrorism	*terrorismo* m	te·rroo·*reesh*·moo
unemployment	*desemprego* m	de·zeng·*pre*·goo
US foreign policy	*política*	poo·*lee*·tee·ka
	externa	aysh·*ter*·na
	americana f	a·me·ree·*kaa*·na
the war in …	*a guerra em* …f	a ge·rra eng …

the environment

Is there a … problem here?
Há algum problema   aa aal·*goong* pro·*ble*·ma
de … aqui?   de … a·*kee*

What should be done about …?
O que é que deve ser   oo ke e ke *de*·ve ser
feito em relação …?   fay·too eng rre·la·*sowng* …

conservation	*à conservação* f	aa kong·ser·va·*sowng*
deforestation	*à desflorestação* f	aa desh·floo·resh·ta·*sowng*
drought	*à seca* f	aa *se*·ka
ecosystem	*ao ecosistema* f	ow e·ko·seesh·*te*·ma
endangered	*às espécies em*	aash *shpe*·syesh eng
species	*via de extinção* f pl	*vee*·a de aysh·teeng·*sowng*
forest fires	*aos fogos*	owsh *fo*·goosh
	florestais m pl	floo·resh·*taish*
genetically	*à comida*	aa koo·*mee*·da
modified food	*geneticamente*	zhe·ne·tee·ka·*meng*·te
	modificada f	mo·dee·fee·*kaa*·da
hunting	*à caça* f	aa *kaa*·sa
hydroelectricity	*à*	aa
	hidroelectricidade f	ee·dro·ee·le·tree·see·*daa*·de
irrigation	*à irrigação* f	aa ee·rree·ga·*sowng*
nuclear energy	*à energia*	aa ee·ner·*zhee*·a
	nuclear f	noo·klee·*aar*
nuclear testing	*aos testes*	owsh *tesh*·tesh
	nucleares m pl	noo·klee·*aa*·resh
ozone layer	*à camada de*	aa ka·*maa*·da de
	ozono f	o·*zo*·noo
pesticides	*aos pesticidas* m pl	owsh pesh·tee·*see*·dash
pollution	*à poluição* f	aa poo·loo·ee·*sowng*
recycling	*aos programas*	owsh proo·*gra*·mash
programme	*de reciclagem* m pl	de rre·see·*klaa*·zheng
toxic waste	*ao lixo tóxico* m	ow *lee*·shoo tok·*see*·koo
water supply	*ao abastecimento*	ow a·bash·te·see·*meng*·too
	de água m	de *aa*·gwa

Is this a protected ...?	... está protegido/ protegida? m/f	... shtaa proo·te·_zhee_·doo/ proo·te·_zhee_·da
forest	Esta floresta f	esh·ta flo·_resh_·ta
park	Este parque m	esh·te _par_·ke
species	Esta espécie f	esh·ta _shpe_·sye

r.e.s.p.e.c.t

You might have noticed that Portuguese makes a distinction between 'polite' (marked with pol) and 'informal' (inf) pronouns. In the phrases throughout this book, we've used the form that best suits the situation. As a general rule, if you're talking to people who are older than you or that you don't know very well, it's polite to use _você_ vo·_se_ (you pol) and the third person singular verb form (rather than using _tu_ too and the second person verb form). 'Can you show me the way?', for example, would be _Você pode indicar-me o caminho?_ vo·_se po_·de eeng·dee·_kaar_·me oo ka·_mee_·nyoo. In practice, however, the word _você_ is almost always dropped, so it would usually be _Pode indicar-me o caminho?_ _po_·de eeng·dee·_kaar_·me oo ka·_mee_·nyoo. Another option is to use the person's name or title – you might say, for example, _A senhora pode indicar-me o caminho?_ a se·_nyo_·ra _po_·de eeng·dee·_kaar_·me oo ka·_mee_·nyoo (Can the lady show me the way?). See the **phrasebuilder** for more on personal pronouns.

where to go

What's there to do in the evenings?
O que é que se pode   oo ke e ke se *po*·de
fazer à noite?   fa·*zer* aa *noy*·te

What's on …?	*O que é que há …?*	oo ke e ke aa …
this weekend	*este*	*esh*·te
	fim-de-semana	feeng·de·se·*ma*·na
today	*hoje*	*o*·zhe
tonight	*hoje à noite*	*o*·zhe aa *noy*·te

I feel like	*Está-me a*	*shtaa*·me a
going to a …	*apetecer ir a …*	a·pe·te·*ser* eer a …
bar	*um bar*	oong bar
bullfight	*uma tourada*	*oo*·ma toh·*raa*·da
café	*um café*	oong ka·*fe*
concert	*um concerto*	oong kong·*ser*·too
fado house	*uma casa*	*oo*·ma *kaa*·za
	de fados	de *faa*·doosh
film	*um filme*	oong *feel*·me
nightclub	*uma discoteca*	*oo*·ma deesh·koo·*te*·ka
party	*uma festa*	*oo*·ma *fesh*·ta
play	*uma peça*	*oo*·ma *pe*·sa
	de teatro	de tee·*aa*·troo
restaurant	*um restaurante*	oong rresh·tow·*rang*·te
street party	*uma festa*	*oo*·ma *fesh*·ta
	de rua	de *rroo*·a

Is there a	*Há um guia*	aa oong *gee*·a
local … guide?	*local de …?*	loo·*kaal* de …
entertainment	*entertenimento*	eng·ter·te·nee·*meng*·too
film	*filmes*	*feel*·mesh
music	*música*	moo·*zee*·ka

Where can I find …?	Onde é que há …?	ong·de e ke aa …
bars	bares	ba·resh
clubs	discotecas	deesh·koo·te·kash
gay/lesbian venues	lugares de gays/ lésbicas	loo·gaa·resh de gaysh/ lezh·bee·kash
places to eat	sítios para comer	see·tyoosh pa·ra koo·mer

invitations

What are you doing …?	O que é que …?	oo ke e ke …
now	está a fazer agora	shtaa a fa·zer a·go·ra
this weekend	vai fazer este fim-de-semana	vai fa·zer esh·te feeng·de·se·ma·na
tonight	vai fazer hoje à noite	vai fa·zer o·zhe aa noy·te

Would you like to go (for a) …?	Gostava de ir …?	goosh·taa·va de eer …
I feel like going (for a) …	Apetece-me ir …	a·pe·te·se·me eer …
coffee	a um café	a oong ka·fe
dancing	dançar	dang·saar
drink	beber alguma coisa	be·ber aal·goo·ma koy·za
meal	comer	koo·mer
out	sair	sa·eer
walk	andar a pé	ang·daar a pe

Do you know a good restaurant?
Conhece um bom restaurante? — kong·nye·se oong bong rresh·tow·rang·te

Do you want to come to the concert with me?
Quer vir ao concerto comigo? — ker veer ow kong·ser·too koo·mee·goo

We're having a party.
Vamos dar uma festa.   vaa·moosh daar oo·ma fesh·ta

You should come.
Devia vir.   de·vee·a veer

responding to invitations

Yes, I'd love to.
Sim, adorava.   seeng a·doo·raa·va

That's very kind of you.
É muito simpático   e mweeng·too seeng·paa·tee·koo
da sua parte.   da soo·a par·te

Where shall we go?
Onde é que podemos ir?   ong·de e ke poo·de·moosh eer

No, I'm afraid I can't.
Tenho muita pena,   ta·nyoo mweeng·ta pe·na
mas não posso.   mash nowng po·soo

What about tomorrow?
E que tal amanhã?   ee ke taal aa·ma·nyang

Sorry, I can't sing/dance.
Tenho muita pena, mas   ta·nyoo mweeng·ta pe·na mas
não sei cantar/dançar.   nowng say kang·taar/dang·saar

arranging to meet

Where will we meet?
Onde é que nos   ong·de e ke noosh
encontramos?   eng·kong·traa·moosh

What time do you want to meet?
A que horas é que   a ke o·rash e ke
nos encontramos?   noosh eng·kong·traa·moosh

Let's meet (at the entrance).
Encontramo-nos   eng·kong·*traa*·moo·noosh
(à entrada).   (aa eng·*traa*·da)

I'll pick you up.
Eu vou buscá-lo/-la. m/f   e·oo voh boosh·*kaa*·loo/la

Are you ready?
Está pronto/pronta? m/f   shtaa *prong*·too/*prong*·ta

I'm ready.
Estou pronto/pronta. m/f   shtoh *prong*·too/*prong*·ta

I'll be coming later.
Eu vou mais tarde.   e·oo voh maish *taar*·de

Where will you be?
Onde é que vais estar?   *ong*·de e ke vaish shtaar

I'll see you then.
Até já.   a·*te* zhaa

I'm looking forward to it.
Vai ser um prazer.   vai ser oong pra·*zer*

Sorry I'm late.
Desculpe o atraso.   desh·*kool*·pe oo a·*traa*·zoo

drugs

drogas

Do you want to have a smoke?
Quer um cigarro?   ker oong see·*gaa*·rroo

Do you have a light?
Tem lume?   teng *loo*·me

I take ... occasionally.
Eu tomo ... de vez   e·oo to·moo ... de vezh
em quando.   eng *kwang*·doo

I don't take drugs.
Eu não tomo drogas.   e·oo nowng to·moo *dro*·gash

If the police are talking to you about drugs, see **police**, page 180, for useful phrases.

The phrases in this chapter are generally in the informal form, as you use them to talk to people you know fairly well. See the box on page 120 for more details on polite and informal.

asking someone out

convidar alguém para sair

Where would you like to go (tonight)?
Onde é que queres ir — ong·de e ke ke·resh eer
(hoje à noite)? — (o·zhe aa noy·te)

Would you like to do something (tomorrow)?
Queres fazer alguma — ke·resh fa·zer aal·goo·ma
coisa (amanhã)? — koy·za (aa·ma·nyang)

Yes, I'd love to.
Sim, adorava. — seeng a·doo·raa·va

Sorry, I can't.
Desculpa, mas não posso. — desh·kool·pa mash nowng po·soo

---

local talk

He is a babe.
Ele é muito giro. — e·le e mweeng·too zhee·roo

She is a babe.
Ela é muito gira. — e·la e mweeng·too zhee·ra

He/She is hot.
Ele/Ela é bom/boa. — e·le/e·la e bong/bo·a

He's a bastard.
É um cabrão. — e oong ka·browng

She's a bitch.
É uma cabra. — e oo·ma kaa·bra

---

pick-up lines

Would you like a drink?
Queres uma bebida? ke·resh oo·ma be·bee·da

You look like someone I know.
Pareces-te mesmo pa·re·sesh·te mezh·moo
com uma pessoa que kong oo·ma pe·so·a ke
eu conheço. e·oo koo·nye·soo

You're a fantastic dancer.
Danças muito bem. daang·sash mweeng·too beng

Can I …?	*Posso …?*	po·soo …
dance with you	*dançar*	dang·saar
	contigo	kong·tee·goo
sit here	*sentar-me aqui*	seng·taar·me a·kee

rejections

No, thank you.
Não, obrigado/ nowng o·bree·gaa·doo/
obrigada. m/f o·bree·gaa·da

I'd rather not.
É melhor não. e me·lyor nowng

I'm here with my girlfriend.
Estou aqui com a minha shtoh a·kee kong a mee·nya
namorada. na·moo·raa·da

I'm here with my boyfriend.
Estou aqui com o meu shtoh a·kee kong oo me·oo
namorado na·moo·raa·doo

Excuse me, I have to go now.
Desculpa, tenho de desh·kool·pa ta·nyoo de
me ir embora. me eer eng·bo·ra

Leave me alone!	*Deixa-me!*	*day*·sha·me
Piss off!	*Desaparece!*	de·za·pa·*re*·se

getting closer

aproximar-se de alguém

I really like you.
Eu gosto mesmo de ti.   e·oo *gosh*·too *mezh*·moo de tee

You're great.
És fantástico/   esh fang·*taash*·tee·koo/
fantástica. m/f   fang·*taash*·tee·ka

Can I kiss you?
Posso dar-te um beijo?   po·soo *dar*·te oong *bay*·zhoo

Do you want to come inside for a while?
Queres entrar?   ke·resh eng·*traar*

Do you want a massage?
Queres uma massagem?   ke·resh oo·ma ma·*saa*·zheng

Would you like to stay over?
Queres passar a noite aqui? ke·resh pa·*saar* a *noy*·te a·*kee*

Can I stay over?
Posso passar a noite aqui? po·soo pa·*saar* a *noy*·te a·*kee*

Can I make you breakfast?
Posso fazer-te o   po·soo fa·*zer*·te oo
pequeno-almoço?   pe·*ke*·noo·aal·*mo*·soo

is it a date?

There's no specific word for 'date' in Portuguese – the Portuguese use the word *encontro* eng·*kong*·troo, which is just a general word for 'meeting'. Be sure you know what kind of meeting you're going to before you turn up with chocolates or flowers!

sex

Kiss me.
Dá-me um beijo.   daa·me oong *bay*·zhoo

I want you.
Quero-te.   ke·roo·te

Touch me here.
Toca-me aqui.   to·ka·me a·*kee*

Do you like this?
Gostas disto?   gosh·tash *deesh*·too

I (don't) like that.
Eu (não) gosto disso.   e·oo (nowng) gosh·too dee·soo

I think we should stop now.
Acho que é melhor   aa·shoo ke e me·*lyor*
pararmos.   pa·*raar*·moosh

Let's go to bed.
Vamos para a cama.   vaa·moosh pa·ra a *kaa*·ma

Do you have a (condom)?
Tens (um   tengsh (oong
preservativo)?   pre·zer·va·*tee*·voo)

Let's use a (condom).
Vamos usar (um   vaa·moosh oo·*zaar* (oong
preservativo).   pre·zer·va·*tee*·voo)

I won't do it without protection.
Eu não faço isso   e·oo nowng faa·soo ee·soo
sem protecção.   seng proo·te·*sowng*

It's my first time.
É a minha primeira vez.   e a *mee*·nya pree·*may*·ra vezh

Don't worry, I'll do it myself.
Não te preocupes,   nowng te pree·o·*koo*·pesh
eu faço isso   e·oo faa·soo ee·soo
sozinho/sozinha. m/f   so·*zeeng*·nyoo/so·*zeeng*·nya

It helps to have a sense of humour.
Ajuda ter sentido   a·*zhoo*·da ter seng·*tee*·doo
de humor.   de oo·*mor*

sweet nothings		
dear	*querido* m	ke·*ree*·doo
	querida f	ke·*ree*·da
my love	*meu amor*	me·oo a·*mor*
sweetie	*fofa*	*fo*·fa

Oh my god!	*Meu Deus!*	me·oo de·oosh
That's great.	*Fantástico!*	fang·*taash*·tee·koo
Easy tiger!	*Calma!*	*kaal*·ma

faster	*mais rápido*	maish *rraa*·pee·doo
harder	*com mais força*	kong maish *for*·sa
slower	*mais devagar*	maish de·va·*gaar*
softer	*mais suave*	maish *swaa*·ve

That was …	*Foi …*	foy …
amazing	*extraordinário*	shtra·or·dee·*naa*·ree·oo
romantic	*romântico*	rroo·*mang*·tee·koo
wild	*selvagem*	sel·*vaa*·zheng

love

amor

I think we're good together.
Eu acho que nós   e·oo *aa*·shoo ke nosh
estamos bem   *shta*·moosh beng
juntos.   *zhoong*·toosh

I love you.
Amo-te.   a·*moo*·te

Will you …?	*Queres …?*	ke·resh …
go out with me	*sair comigo*	sa·*eer* koo·*mee*·goo
marry me	*casar*	ka·*zaar* koo·*mee*·goo
meet my parents	*conhecer os meus pais*	koo·nye·*ser* oosh me·oosh paish

problems

Are you seeing someone else?
Estás a andar com   shtaash a ang·*daar* kong
outra pessoa?   *oh*·tra pe·*so*·a

He/She is just a friend.
Ele/Ela é só um   e·le/e·la e so oong
amigo/uma amiga. m/f   a·*mee*·goo/*oo*·ma a·*mee*·ga

You're just using me for sex.
Tu só me estás a   too so me shtaash a
usar para sexo.   oo·*zaar* pa·ra *sek*·soo

I never want to see you again.
Nunca mais te quero ver.   *noong*·ka maish te *ke*·roo ver

I don't think it's working out.
Eu acho que estamos   e·oo *aa*·shoo ke *shta*·moosh
com problemas.   kong proo·*ble*·mash

We'll work it out.
Nós vamos resolver   nosh *va*·moosh rre·zol·*ver*
os problemas.   oosh proo·*ble*·mash

leaving

I have to leave (tomorrow).
Vou ter que me ir   voh ter ke me eer
embora (amanhã).   eng·*bo*·ra (aa·ma·*nyang*)

I'll …	Eu vou …	e·oo voh …
keep	*manter-me*	mang·*ter*·me
in touch	*em contacto*	eng kong·*taak*·too
miss you	*ter saudades*	ter sow·*daa*·desh
	tuas	*too*·ash
visit you	*visitar-te*	vee·zee·*taar*·te

beliefs & cultural differences
crenças & diferenças culturais

religion

What's your religion?
Qual é a sua religião?   kwaal e a soo·a rre·lee·zhee·owng

I'm not religious.
Não sou religioso/   nowng soh rre·lee·zhee·o·zoo/
religiosa. m/f   rre·lee·zhee·o·za

I'm ...	Eu sou ...	e·oo soh ...
Buddhist	*budista*	boo·deesh·ta
Catholic	*católico/*	ka·to·lee·koo/
	católica m/f	ka·to·lee·ka
Christian	*cristão/*	kreesh·towng/
	cristã m/f	kreesh·tang
Hindu	*hindu*	eeng·doo
Jewish	*judeu/judia* m/f	zhoo·de·oo/zhoo·dee·a
Muslim	*muçulmano/*	moo·sool·maa·noo/
	muçulmana m/f	moo·sool·maa·na

I (don't)	Eu (não)	e·oo (nowng)
believe in ...	*acredito em ...*	a·kre·dee·too eng ...
astrology	*astrologia*	ash·troo·loo·zhee·a
fate	*destino*	desh·tee·noo
God	*Deus*	de·oosh

Can I ... here?	Posso ... aqui?	po·soo ... a·kee
Where can I ...?	*Onde posso ...?*	ong·de po·soo ...
attend a	*assistir a*	a·seesh·teer a
service	*oong serviço*	oong ser·vee·soo
	religioso	rre·lee·zhee·o·zoo
attend mass	*assistir a*	a·seesh·teer a
	uma missa	oo·ma mee·sa
pray	*rezar*	rre·zaar

cultural differences

Is this a local or national custom?
Este é um costume esh·te e oong koosh·*too*·me
local ou nacional? loo·*kaal* oh na·syoo·*naal*

I don't want to offend you.
Não quero ofendê-lo/ nowng *ke*·roo oo·feng·*de*·lo/
ofendê-la. m/f oo·feng·*de*·la

I'm not used to this.
Não estou nowng shtoh
acostumado/ a·koosh·too·*maa*·doo/
acostumada a isso. m/f a·koosh·too·*maa*·da a ee·soo

I'll try it.
Vou experimentar. voh shpree·meng·*taar*

I'd rather not join in.
Prefiro não pre·*fee*·roo nowng
tomar parte. too·*maar paar*·te

I didn't mean to do/say anything wrong.
Não tive intenção de nowng *tee*·ve eeng·teng·*sowng* de
fazer/dizer nada de mal. fa·*zer*/dee·*zeer naa*·da de maal

I'm sorry, it's *Desculpe, mas é* desh·*kool*·pe mash e
against my ... *contra a minha ...* *kong*·tra a *mee*·nya ...
   beliefs   *crença*   *kreng*·sa
   religion   *religião*   rre·lee·zhee·*owng*

This is ... *Isto é ...* *eesh*·too e ...
   different   *diferente*   dee·fe·*reng*·te
   fun   *divertido*   dee·ver·*tee*·doo
   interesting   *interessante*   eeng·te·re·*sang*·te

When's the gallery/museum open?
*Quando é que o museu
está aberto?*
kwaang·doo e ke oo moo·ze·oo
shtaa a·ber·too

What kind of art are you interested in?
*Qual é o tipo de arte que
mais lhe interessa?*
kwaal e oo tee·poo de aar·te ke
maish lye eeng·te·re·sa

What's in the collection?
Que obras há no museu?
ke o·brash aa noo moo·ze·oo

What do you think of …?
O que acha de …?
oo ke aa·sha de …

It's an exhibition of …
É uma exposição de …
e oo·ma shpoo·zee·sowng de …

I'm interested in …
*Eu estou interessado/
interessada em …* m/f
e·oo shtoh eeng·te·re·saa·doo/
eeng·te·re·saa·da eng …

… art	arte …	aar·te …
baroque	barroca	ba·rro·ka
classical	clássica	klaa·see·ka
Gothic	gótica	go·tee·ka
graphic	gráfica	graa·fee·ka
impressionist	impressionista	eeng·pre·syoo·neesh·ta
Manueline	manuelina	man·wel·ee·na
modern	moderna	moo·der·na
Moorish	mourisca	moh·reesh·ka
prehistoric	pré-histórica	pre·shto·ree·ka
Renaissance	renascentista	rre·nash·seng·teesh·ta
Roman	românica	rroo·maa·nee·ka
Romanesque	romanesca	roo·ma·nesh·ka

architecture	*arquitectura* f	aar·kee·te·*too*·ra
art	*arte* f	*aar*·te
artwork	*obra de arte* f	o·bra de *aar*·te
curator	*conservador/*	kong·ser·va·*dor/*
	conservadora m/f	kong·ser·va·*do*·ra
design	*design* m	de·*zain*
etching	*água-forte* f	aa·gwa·*for*·te
exhibit	*exposição* f	esh·poo·zee·*sowng*
exhibition hall	*galeria* f	ga·le·*ree*·a
installation	*instalação* f	eengsh·ta·la·*sowng*
opening	*inauguração* f	ee·now·goo·ra·*sowng*
painted tiles	*azulejos* m pl	a·zoo·le·zhoos
painter	*pintor/*	*peeng*·tor/
	pintora m/f	peeng·*to*·ra
painting	*pintura* f	peeng·*too*·ra
period	*período* m	pe·*ree*·oo·doo
permanent	*colecção*	koo·le·*sowng*
collection	*permanente* f	per·ma·*neng*·te
pillories	*pilares* m pl	pee·*laa*·resh
(stone columns)		
print	*gravura* f	gra·*voo*·ra
sculptor	*escultor/*	shkool·*tor/*
	escultora m/f	shkool·*to*·ra
sculpture	*escultura* f	shkool·*too*·ra
statue	*estátua* f	*shtaa*·too·a
studio	*estúdio* m	*shtoo*·dyoo
style	*estilo* m	*shtee*·loo
technique	*técnica* f	*tek*·nee·ka

arts and crafts

A number of regions in Portugal are well-known for specific arts and crafts. Types of ceramics include *porcelana da vista Alegre* (poor·se·*la*·na da *veesh*·ta a·*le*·gre) from Ílhavo, Barcelos roosters (*galo de Barcelos* gaa·loo de bar·*se*·loosh) and black ceramics from Bisalhães. Basketry (*cestaria* ses·ta·*ree*·a), bobbin lace from the Peniche harbour region (*renda de bilros* *rreng*·da de *beel*·rroosh) and embroidery from northern Portugal (*bordados* boor·*daa*·doosh) are also highly regarded.

Some of the phrases in the 'playing sport' section of this chapter are in the informal form, as people tend to be casual in the middle of a game. See the box on page 120 for more details on polite and informal.

sporting interests

interesses desportivos

What sport do you follow?
Que desporto é que segue? ke desh·*por*·too e ke *se*·ge

What sport do you play?
Que desporto é que pratica? ke desh·*por*·too e ke pra·*tee*·ka

I play/do …	*Eu faço/ pratico …*	e·oo *faa*·soo/ pra·*tee*·koo …
I follow …	*Eu sigo …*	e·oo *see*·goo …
athletics	*atletismo*	at·le·*teezh*·moo
basketball	*basquetebol*	bash·ke·te·*bol*
football (soccer)	*futebol*	foo·te·*bol*
karate	*karaté*	ka·ra·*te*
roller-blading	*hóquei em*	o·kay eng
hockey	*patins*	pa·*teengsh*
scuba diving	*mergulho*	mer·*goo*·lyoo
tennis	*ténis*	*te*·neesh
volleyball	*voleibol*	*vo*·lay·bol
Who's your favourite …?	*Qual é …?*	kwaal e …
sportsperson	*o seu atleta favorito*	oo se·oo at·*le*·ta fa·voo·*ree*·too
team	*a sua equipa favorita*	a soo·a e·*kee*·pa fa·voo·*ree*·ta

I …	Eu …	e·oo …
cycle	faço ciclismo	faa·soo see·kleesh·moo
run	corro	ko·rroo
walk	ando a pé	ang·doo a pe

Do you like (football)?
Gosta de (futebol)?   gosh·ta de (foo·te·bol)

Yes, very much.
Sim, gosto muito.   seeng gosh·too mweeng·too

Not really.
Nem por isso.   neng poor ee·soo

I like watching it.
Eu gosto de ver.   e·oo gosh·too de ver

going to a game

ir a um jogo

Would you like to go to a game?
Quer ir a um jogo?   ker eer a oong zho·goo

Who are you supporting?
Por quem está?   poor keng shtaa

Who's playing?
Quem está a jogar?   keng shtaa a zhoo·gaar

Who's winning?
Quem está a ganhar?   keng shtaa a ga·nyaar

scoring

What's the score?
Qual é o resultado?   kwaal e oo rre·zool·taa·doo

draw/even	empate	eng·paa·te
love (zero)	nada	naa·da
match-point	bola de partida	bo·la de par·tee·da
nil (zero)	zero	ze·roo

That was a ... game!	Foi um ...!	foy oong ...
bad	mau jogo	mow zho·goo
boring	jogo chato	zho·goo shaa·too
great	jogo óptimo	zho·goo o·tee·moo

playing sport

praticar desporto

Do you want to play?
Quer jogar?
ker zhoo·gaar

Can I join in?
Posso entrar?
po·soo eng·traar

That would be great.
Isso era óptimo.
ee·soo e·ra o·tee·moo

I can't.
Não posso.
nowng po·soo

I have an injury.
Estou lesado/lesada. m/f
shtoh le·zaa·doo/le·zaa·da

Your/My point.
O ponto é teu/meu.
oo pong·too e te·oo/me·oo

Kick/Pass it to me!
Passa!
paa·sa

You're a good player.
És um bom jogador. m
esh oong bong zhoo·ga·dor
És uma boa jogadora. f
esh oo·ma bo·a zhoo·ga·do·ra

Thanks for the game.
Obrigado/Obrigada
o·bree·gaa·doo/o·bree·gaa·da
pelo jogo. m/f
pe·loo zho·goo

Where's the nearest ...?	Onde é que é o ... mais próximo?	ong·de e ke e oo ... maish pro·see·moo
golf course	campo de golfe	kang·poo de gol·fe
gym	ginásio	zhee·naa·zyoo
tennis court	campo de ténis	kang·poo de te·neesh

What's the charge per ...?	Quanto se paga por ...?	kwang·too se paa·ga poor ...
day	dia	dee·a
game	jogo	zho·goo
hour	hora	o·ra
visit	visita	vee·zee·ta

Can I hire a ...?	Pode-se alugar ...?	po·de·se a·loo·gaar ...
ball	uma bola	oo·ma bo·la
bicycle	uma bicicleta	oo·ma bee·see·kle·ta
court	um campo	oong kang·poo
racquet	uma raquete	oo·ma rra·ke·te

Where's a good place to ...?	Onde é que há um bom lugar para ...?	ong·de e ke aa oong bong loo·gaar pa·ra ...
fish	pescar	pesh·kaar
go	andar a	ang·daar a
horseriding	cavalo	ka·vaa·loo
run	correr	koo·rrer
ski	esquiar	shkee·aar
snorkel	fazer snorkel	fa·zer snor·kel
surf	fazer surf	fa·zer sarf

Where's the nearest swimming pool?
Onde é que é a piscina mais próxima?
ong·de e ke e a pesh·see·na maish pro·see·ma

Do I have to be a member to attend?
Tenho de ser membro para entrar?
ta·nyoo de ser meng·broo pa·ra eng·traar

Is there a women-only session?
Há alguma sessão só para mulheres?
aa aal·goo·ma se·sowng so pa·ra moo·lye·resh

Where are the changing rooms?
Onde são os balneários?
ong·de sowng oosh bal·nee·aa·ree·oosh

football/soccer

Who plays for (Porto)?
Quem joga no (Porto)?   keng *zho*·ga noo (*por*·too)

He's a great (player).
Ele é um grande   *e*·le e oong *grang*·de
(jogador).   (zhoo·ga·*dor*)

He played brilliantly in the match against (Italy).
Ele jogou muito bem   *e*·le zho·*goh* mweeng·too beng
contra (a Itália).   *kong*·tra (a ee·*taa*·lya)

Which team is at the top of the league?
Qual é a equipa que   kwaal e a e·*kee*·pa ke
vai à frente no   vai aa *freng*·te noo
campeonato?   kang·pee·oo·*naa*·too

What a great/terrible team!
Que equipa   ke e·*kee*·pa
fantástica/horrível!   fang·*taash*·tee·ka/o·*rree*·vel

ball	*bola* f	*bo*·la
coach	*treinador* m	tray·na·*dor*
corner (kick)	*canto* m	*kang*·too
foul	*falta* f	*faal*·ta
free kick	*livre* m	*lee*·vre
goal (structure)	*baliza* f	ba·*lee*·za
goalkeeper	*guarda-redes* m	*gwaar*·da·*rre*·desh
offside	*fora-de-jogo*	*fo*·ra·de·*zho*·goo
penalty	*grande penalidade* f	*grang*·de pe·na·lee·*daa*·de
player	*jogador* m	zhoo·ga·*dor*
red card	*cartão vermelho* m	kar·*towng* ver·*me*·lyoo
referee	*árbitro* m	*ar*·bee·troo
striker	*atacante* m	a·ta·*kang*·te
throw-in	*lançamento*	lang·sa·*meng*·too
	lateral m	la·te·*raal*
yellow card	*cartão amarelo* m	kar·*towng* a·ma·*re*·loo

water sports

Can I book a lesson?
Posso marcar uma aula?   po·soo mar·kaar oo·ma ow·la

Can I hire (a) …?	*Posso alugar …?*	po·soo a·loo·gaar …
boat	*um barco*	oong baar·koo
canoe	*uma canoa*	oo·ma ka·no·a
kayak	*um kayak*	oong kai·ak
life jacket	*um colete salva-vidas*	oong koo·le·te saal·va·vee·dash
snorkelling gear	*equipamento de snorkelling*	e·kee·pa·meng·too de snor·ke·leeng
water-skis	*esquis aquáticos*	shkeesh a·kwaa·tee·koosh
wetsuit	*fato de mergulho*	faa·too de mer·goo·lyoo

Are there any …?	Há …?	aa …
reefs	alguns	aal·*goongsh*
	recifes	rre·*see*·fesh
rips	correntes	koo·*rreng*·tesh
	perigosas	pree·*go*·zash
water hazards	zonas	*zo*·nash
	perigosas	pree·*go*·zash

I'd like to (go) …	Eu gostava de …	e·oo goosh·*taa*·va de …
scuba diving	mergulhar	mer·goo·*lyaar*
	com botija	kong boo·*tee*·zha
snorkelling	fazer snorkelling	fa·*zer snor*·ke·leeng
learn to dive	aprender a fazer	a·preng·*der* a fa·*zer*
	mergulho	mer·*goo*·lyoo

guide	guia f	*gee*·a
motorboat	barco a motor m	*baar*·koo a moo·*tor*
oars	remos m pl	*rre*·moosh
sailboarding	windsurf f	*weend*·sarf
sailing boat	barco à vela m	*baar*·koo aa *ve*·la
surfboard	prancha de surf f	*prang*·sha de sarf
surfing	surf m	sarf
wave	onda f	*ong*·da

bullfighting

The ancient rite of bullfighting (*tourada* toh·*raa*·da) remains one of Portugal's most popular spectator sports. If you decide to go, prepare yourself for something a bit different from the Spanish version. The bull (*touro* toh·*roo*) first faces a horseman (*cavaleiro* ka·va·*lay*·roo) who must plant a number of barbs into the bull's neck muscle. Then a crew of foot soldiers (*forcados* foor·*kaa*·doosh) enters the ring, taunts the bull into charging forcefully, and eventually wrestles him to a standstill.

In case you were thinking it's a fair fight, bear in mind that the bull's horns are cut so as not to have sharp points and padded with leather. The sport is called 'bloodless' because the bull doesn't die in the ring, but he's almost always killed just afterwards by a butcher.

extreme sports

I'd like to go …	Eu gostava de fazer …	e·oo goosh·taa·va de fa·zer …
canyoning	canyoning	ka·nyo·neeng
caving	espeleologia	shpe·lee·oo·loo·zhee·a
game fishing	caça submarina	kaa·sa soob·ma·ree·na
hang-gliding	asa-delta	aa·za·del·ta
mountain biking	ciclismo de montanha	see·kleesh·moo de mong·tang·nya
parasailing	parapente	paa·ra·peng·te
rock climbing	escalada	shka·laa·da
scuba-diving	mergulhar com botija	mer·goo·lyaar kong boo·tee·zha
skydiving	paraquedismo	paa·ra·ke·deesh·moo
white-water rafting	rafting	rraaf·teeng

sports talk

What a …!	Que …!	ke …
goal	golo	go·loo
hit	pancada	pang·kaa·da
kick	pontapé	pong·ta·pe
pass	passe	paa·se
performance	actuação	a·too·a·sowng

hiking

caminhada

English	Portuguese	Pronunciation
Where can I ...?	*Onde é que posso ...?*	ong·de e ke po·soo ...
buy supplies	*comprar*	kong·*praar*
	mantimentos	mang·tee·*meng*·toosh
find someone	*encontrar*	eng·kong·*traar*
who knows	*alguém que*	aal·*geng* ke
this area	*conheça esta*	koo·*nye*·sa *esh*·ta
	área	*aa*·re·a
get a map	*arranjar*	a·rrang·*zhaar*
	um mapa	oong *maa*·pa
hire hiking	*alugar*	a·loo·*gaar*
gear	*equipamento*	e·kee·pa·*meng*·too
	de caminhada	de ka·mee·*nyaa*·da

How high is the climb?
Qual é a altura   kwaal e a aal·*too*·ra
da escalada?   da shka·*laa*·da

How long is the trail?
Qual é o comprimento   kwaal e oo kong·pree·*meng*·too
do atalho?   doo a·*taa*·lyoo

Is it safe?
É seguro?   e se·*goo*·roo

Do we need a guide?
Precisamos de um guia?   pre·see·*za*·moosh de oong *gee*·a

Are there guided treks?
Há caminhadas com guia?   aa ka·mee·*nyaa*·dash kong *gee*·a

Do we need to take (a) …?	Precisamos de levar …?	pre·see·za·moosh de le·vaar …
food	comida	koo·mee·da
sleeping bag	saco-cama	saa·koo·kaa·ma
water	água	aa·gwa

Is the track …?	O trilho …?	oo tree·lyoo …
(well-)marked	está (bem) sinalizado	shtaa (beng) see·na·lee·zaa·doo
open	está aberto	shtaa a·ber·too
scenic	tem vistas bonitas	teng veesh·tash boo·nee·tash

Which is the … route?	Qual é a rota mais …?	kwaal e a rro·ta maish …
easiest	fácil	faa·seel
most interesting	interessante	eeng·te·re·sang·te
shortest	curta	koor·ta

Where can I find the …?	Onde …?	ong·de …
camping ground	é o parque de campismo	e oo par·ke de kang·peesh·moo
nearest village	é a aldeia mais próxima	e a aal·day·a maish pro·see·ma
showers	são os chuveiros	sowng oosh shoo·vay·roosh
toilets	são as casas de banho	sowng ash kaa·zash de ba·nyoo

Is there a hut?
Há alguma cabana?   aa aal·goo·ma ka·ba·na

When does it get dark?
A que horas fica escuro?   a ke o·rash fee·ka shkoo·roo

Where have you come from?
Donde é que vocês vieram?   dong·de e ke vo·sesh vee·e·rowng

How long did it take?
Quanto tempo demorou?   kwaang·too teng·poo de·moo·roh

Does this path go to (Alcoutim)?
Este caminho leva   esh·te ka·mee·nyoo le·va
a (Alcoutim)?   a (aal·koh·teeng)

Can I go through here?
Posso ir por aqui?   po·soo eer poor a·kee

Is the water OK to drink?
Pode-se beber esta água?   po·de·se be·ber esh·ta aa·gwa

I'm lost.
Estou perdido/perdida. **m/f**   shtoh per·dee·doo/per·dee·da

beach

praia

In Portugal, a plain red flag on the beach warns you that swimming is forbidden. A yellow flag signals that conditions are dangerous and you should stay near the shore. A green flag indicates the sea is calm and you can swim.

Where's the ...	*Onde é que*	*ong·*de e ke
beach?	*é a ...?*	e a ...
best	*melhor praia*	me·lyor prai·a
nearest	*praia mais*	prai·a maish
	próxima	pro·see·ma
nudist	*praia de*	prai·a de
	nudismo	noo·deesh·moo
public	*praia pública*	prai·a poo·blee·ka

listen for ...

Cuidado com a corrente!
kwee·*daa*·doo kong a
koo·*rreng*·te

**Be careful of
the undertow!**

É perigoso!
e pree·*go*·zoo

It's dangerous!

Não Mergulhar	nowng mer·goo·*lyaar*	**No Diving**
Não Nadar	nowng na·*daar*	**No Swimming**

Is it safe to dive/swim here?
É seguro mergulhar/   e se·*goo*·roo mer·goo·*lyaar*/
nadar aqui?   na·*daar* a·*kee*

What time is high/low tide?
A que horas é a maré   a ke *o*·rash e a ma·*re*
alta/baixa?   *aal*·ta/*bai*·sha

Do we have to pay?
Temos que pagar?   te·moosh ke pa·*gaar*

How much to rent a/an ...?	*Quanto custa para alugar ...?*	*kwang*·too *koosh*·ta *pa*·ra a·loo·*gaar* ...
chair	*uma cadeira*	*oo*·ma ka·*day*·ra
hut	*uma cabana*	*oo*·ma ka·*ba*·na
umbrella	*um guarda-sol*	oong gwaar·da·*sol*
wind stopper	*um pára-vento*	oong *paa*·ra·*veng*·too

weather

tempo

What's the weather like?
Como está o   *ko*·moo shtaa oo
tempo?   *teng*·poo

What will the weather be like tomorrow?
Como vai estar o   *ko*·moo vai shtaar oo
tempo amanhã?   *teng*·poo aa·ma·*nyang*

Where can I buy a/an ...?	*Onde é que posso comprar ...?*	*ong*·de e ke *po*·soo kong·*praar* ...
rain jacket	*uma gabardina*	*oo*·ma ga·baar·*dee*·na
umbrella	*um guarda-chuva*	oong gwaar·da·*shoo*·va

It's …	Está …	shtaa …
cloudy	enublado	e·noo·blaa·doo
(very) cold	(muito) frio	(mweeng·too) free·oo
fine	bom	bong
hot	muito quente	mweeng·too keng·te
raining	a chover	a shoo·ver
snowing	a nevar	a ne·vaar
sunny	sol	sol
warm	quente	keng·te
windy	ventoso	veng·to·zoo

flora & fauna

What … is that?	Que …?	ke …
animal	animal é aquele	aa·nee·maal e a·ke·le
flower	flor é aquela	flor e a·ke·la
plant	planta é aquela	plang·ta e a·ke·la
tree	árvore é aquela	aar·vo·re e a·ke·la

Is it …?	É …?	e …
dangerous	perigoso/	pree·go·zoo/
	perigosa m/f	pree·go·za
poisonous	venenoso/	ve·ne·no·zoo/
	venenosa m/f	ve·ne·no·za
protected	protegido/	proo·te·zhee·doo/
	protegida m/f	proo·te·zhee·da

local animals & plants

Iberian wolf	lobo ibérico m	lo·boo ee·be·ree·koo
lynx	lince da malcata m	leeng·se da maal·kaa·ta
carob tree	alfarrobeira f	aal·fa·rroo·bay·ra
cork tree	sobreiro m	soo·bray·roo
oak tree	carvalho m	kar·vaa·lyoo
olive tree	oliveira f	o·lee·vay·ra
pine tree	pinheiro m	pee·nyay·roo

outdoors

Can you eat the fruit?
Pode-se comer esta fruta?   po·de·se koo·*mer esh*·ta *froo*·ta

What's it used for?
Para que é que é   *pa*·ra ke e ke e
usado/usada? m/f   oo·*zaa*·doo/oo·*zaa*·da

Is it endangered?
Está em vias de   shtaa eng *vee*·ash de
extinção?   aysh·teeng·*sowng*

signs

Aberto	a·*ber*·too	**Open**
Casa de Banho	*kaa*·za de *ba*·nyoo	**Toilets/WC**
Entrada	eng·*traa*·da	**Entrance**
Fechado	fe·*shaa*·doo	**Closed**
Homens	o·mengsh	**Men**
Informação	eeng·for·ma·*sowng*	**Information**
Mulheres	moo·*lye*·resh	**Women**
Não Fotografar	nowng foo·too·gra·*faar*	**No Photography**
Não Fumar	nowng foo·*maar*	**No Smoking**
Proibido	pro·ee·*bee*·doo	**Prohibited**
Saída	sa·*ee*·da	**Exit**

basics

básicos

Breakfast is a quick affair in Portugal, usually consisting of a coffee with toast or a pastry. Lunch (usually taken around 1pm) is the main meal of the day, and generally includes meat or fish, vegetables, and rice or potatoes – plus wine, cheese, olives and bread. Dinner is generally lighter and is eaten around 8 or 9pm – even later on weekends.

breakfast	*pequeno almoço* m	pe·ke·noo aal·mo·soo
lunch	*almoço* m	aal·mo·soo
dinner	*jantar* m	zhang·taar
snack	*lanche* m	lang·she
eat v	*comer*	koo·mer
drink v	*beber*	be·ber
I'd like ...	*Eu queria ...*	e·oo ke·ree·a ...
I'm starving!	*Estou*	shtoh
	esfomeado/	shfo·mee·aa·doo/
	esfomeada! m/f	shfo·mee·aa·da

finding a place to eat

Where would you go for (a) ...?	Onde é que iria para ...?	ong·de e ke ee·ree·a pa·ra ...
celebration	festejar	fesh·te·zhaar
cheap meal	uma refeição barata	oo·ma rre·fay·sowng ba·raa·ta
local specialities	especiali- dades locais	shpe·see·a·lee· daa·desh lo·kaish

Can you recommend a ...?	Pode-me recomendar ...?	po·de·me rre·koo·meng·daar ...
bar	um bar	oong bar
beer house	uma cervejaria	oo·ma ser·ve·zha·ree·a
café	um café	oong ka·fe
grill restaurant	uma churrasqueira	oo·ma shoo·rraash·kay·ra
neighbourhood restaurant	uma tasca	oo·ma taash·ka
pastry shop	uma pastelaria	oo·ma pash·te·la·ree·a
restaurant	um restaurante	oong rresh·tow·rang·te
tavern	uma taberna	oo·ma ta·ber·na
tea house	uma casa de chá	oo·ma kaa·za de shaa

I'd like to reserve a table for ...	Eu queria reservar uma mesa para ...	e·oo ke·ree·a rre·zer·vaar oo·ma me·za pa·ra ...
(two) people	(duas) pessoas	(doo·ash) pe·so·ash
(eight) o'clock	as (oito da noite)	ash (oy·too da noy·te)

Are you still serving food?
Ainda servem comida?   a·eeng·da ser·veng koo·mee·da

How long is the wait?
Quanto tempo é que se tem de estar à espera?   kwang·too teng·poo e ke se teng de shtaar aa shpe·ra

Onde é que se quer/querem sentar? sg/pl	ong·de e ke ke ker/ke·reng seng·taar	Where would you like to sit?
Já decidiram?	zha de·see·dee·rowng	What can I get for you?
Gosta/gostam de ...? sg/pl	goosh·ta/goosh·towng de ...	Do you like ...?
Eu aconselho ...	e·oo a·kong·sa·lyoo ...	I suggest the ...
Bem passado ou mal passado?	beng pa·saa·doo oh mal pa·saa·doo	How would you like that cooked?
Aqui está! a·kee shtaa		Here you go!
Bom apetite. bong a·pe·tee·te		Enjoy your meal.

at the restaurant

no restaurante

What would you recommend?
O que é que recomenda? oo ke e ke rre·koo·meng·da

What's in that dish?
Quais são os ingredientes daquele prato? kwaish sowng oosh eeng·gre·dee·eng·tesh da·ke·le praa·too

What's that called?
Como é que se chama aquilo? ko·moo e ke se shaa·ma a·kee·loo

I'll have that.
Eu quero aquilo. eu ke·roo a·kee·loo

Does it take long to prepare?
Demora muito tempo a preparar? de·mo·ra mweeng·too teng·poo a pre·pa·raar

eating out

151

Is it self-serve?
É self-service?   e self·*ser*·vees

Are these complimentary?
Isto é gratuito?   eesh·too e gra·*twee*·too

Can you recommend a good local wine?
Pode-me recomendar   po·de·me rre·koo·meng·*daar*
um bom vinho daqui   oong bong *vee*·nyoo da·*kee*
da zona?   daa *zo*·na

I'd like (a/the)	*Queria ...,*	ke·*ree*·a ...
..., please.	*por favor.*	poor fa·*vor*
children's	*o menu das*	oo me·*noo* dash
menu	*crianças*	kree·*ang*·sash
drink list	*a lista das*	a *leesh*·ta dash
	bebidas	be·*bee*·dash
local speciality	*uma*	*oo*·ma
	especialidade	shpe·see·a·lee·*daa*·de
	local	loo·*kaal*
meal fit for a king	*um banquete*	oong bang·*ke*·te
menu	*um menu*	oong me·*noo*
(in English)	*(em inglês)*	(eng eeng·*lesh*)
(non)smoking	*uma mesa de*	*oo*·ma *me*·za de
table	*(não) fumador*	(nowng) foo·ma·*dor*
table for (five)	*uma mesa*	*oo*·ma *me*·za
	para (cinco)	*pa*·ra (*seeng*·koo)
wine list	*uma lista dos*	*oo*·ma *leesh*·ta doosh
	vinhos	*vee*·nyoosh

I'd like it	*Eu queria*	e·oo ke·*ree*·a
with/without ...	*com/sem ...*	kong/seng ...
cheese	*queijo*	*kay*·zhoo
chilli	*píri-píri*	pee·ree·*pee*·ree
garlic	*alho*	*aa*·lyoo
nuts	*oleaginosas*	o·lee·a·zhee·*no*·zash
pepper	*pimenta*	pee·*meng*·ta
salt	*sal*	saal
tomato sauce	*molho de*	*mo*·lyoo de
	tomate	too·*maa*·te

For other specific meal requests, see **vegetarian & special meals**, page 165.

In Portugal restaurants usually have what is called *couvert* koo·*ver* – bread, butter, paté, olives and sometimes prosciutto at the tables. If you eat them you'll be charged a (normally small) fee.

Aperitivos	a·per·ee·*tee*·voosh	Appetisers
Sopas	*so*·pash	Soups
Entradas	eng·*traa*·dash	Entrées
Saladas	sa·*laa*·dash	Salads
Pratos Principais	*praa*·toosh preeng·see·*paish*	Main Courses
Extras	*aysh*·trash	Side Dishes
Sobremesa	soo·bre·*me*·za	Desserts
Bebidas	be·*bee*·dash	Drinks
Aperitivos	a·pe·ree·*tee*·voosh	Apéritifs
Espirituosos	shpee·ree·too·o·*zoosh*	Spirits
Cerveja	ser·*ve*·zha	Beers
Refrigerantes	rre·free·zhe·*rang*·tesh	Soft Drinks
Vinhos ...	vee·*nyoosh*	... Wines
Espumantes	shpoo·*mang*·tesh	Sparkling
Brancos	*brang*·koosh	White
Tintos	*teeng*·toosh	Red
de Sobremesa	de soo·bre·*me*·za	Dessert
Digestivos	dee·zhesh·*tee*·voosh	Digestifs

See also the **culinary reader**, page 167.

talking food

falar de comida

I love this dish.
Eu adoro este prato.   e·oo a·*do*·roo *esh*·te *praa*·too

I love the local cuisine.
Eu adoro a comida local.   e·oo a·*do*·roo a koo·*mee*·da loo·*kaal*

That was delicious!
Isto estava delicioso!   eesh·too shtaa·va de·lee·see·o·zoo

My compliments to the chef.
Os meus parabéns   oosh me·oosh pa·ra·bengzh
ao cozinheiro chefe.   ow koo·zee·nyay·roo she·fe

I'm full.
Estou cheio/cheia. m/f   shtoh shay·oo/shay·a

methods of preparation

métodos de preparação

I'd like it …	*Eu queria …*	e·oo ke·ree·a …
I don't want it …	*Eu não quero …*	e·oo nowng ke·roo …
boiled	*cozido* m	koo·zee·doo
	cozida f	koo·zee·da
broiled/	*grelhado* m	gre·lyaa·doo
grilled	*grelhada* f	gre·lyaa·da
(deep-)fried	*frito* m	free·too
	frita f	free·ta
mashed	*esmagado* m	shma·gaa·doo
	esmagada f	shma·gaa·da
medium	*nem bem nem*	neng beng neng
	mal-passado/	maal·pa·saa·doo/
	mal-passada m/f	maal·pa·saa·da
rare	*mal-passado* m	maal·pa·saa·doo
	mal-passada f	maal·pa·saa·da
reheated	*reaquecido* m	rre·a·ke·see·doo
	reaquecida f	rre·a·ke·see·da
steamed	*cozido/*	koo·zee·doo/
	cozida	koo·zee·da
	a vapor m/f	a va·por
well-done	*bem-passado* m	beng·pa·saa·doo
	bem-passada f	beng·pa·saa·da
with the	*o molho da*	oo mo·lyoo da
dressing on	*salada à parte*	sa·laa·da aa paar·te
the side		
without …	*sem …*	seng …

at the table

Please bring (a/the) ...	Pode-me trazer ...	po·de·me tra·zer ...
bill	a conta	a kong·ta
cutlery	os talheres	oosh ta·lye·resh
(wine)glass	um copo (de vinho)	oong ko·poo (de vee·nyoo)
napkin	o guardanapo	oo gwar·da·naa·poo
tablecloth	a toalha de mesa	a twaa·lya de me·za
This is ...	Isto está ...	eesh·too shtaa ...
burnt	queimado	kay·maa·doo
(too) cold	(demasiado) frio	(de·ma·zee·aa·doo) free·oo
(too) spicy	(demasiado) picante	(de·ma·zee·aa·doo) pee·kang·te
stale	duro	doo·roo
superb	magnífico	maag·nee·fee·koo

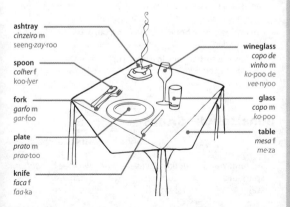

ashtray
cinzeiro m
seeng·zay·roo

spoon
colher f
koo·lyer

fork
garfo m
gar·foo

plate
prato m
praa·too

knife
faca f
faa·ka

wineglass
copo de vinho m
ko·poo de vee·nyoo

glass
copo m
ko·poo

table
mesa f
me·za

I need a coffee

For a nation whose preferred drink at lunch, dinner and sometimes even breakfast, tends to be wine, the Portuguese make pretty decent coffee. As in Italy, if you just order a *café* (ka·*fe*) what you'll get is an espresso or short black – strong black coffee in a demitasse (small cup). The variations on the basic espresso run to over twenty, but the main terms are listed below. Choose your preferred brew and enjoy – just beware, if you ask for decaffeinated coffee (*café sem cafeína* ka·fe seng ka·fe·*ee*·na), a sachet of instant coffee will usually arrive with a pot of hot water for you to make yourself.

an espresso
uma bica	oo·ma *bee*·ka
um café	oong ka·*fe*
um cimbalino	oong seeng·ba·*lee*·noo
um expresso	oong *shpre*·soo

a double espresso
uma bica dupla	oo·ma *bee*·ka *doo*·pla
um café duplo	oong ka·fe *doo*·ploo

a weak espresso
um carioca	oong ka·ree·*o*·ka

an espresso with a dash of milk
um garoto	oong ga·*ro*·too

an espresso with hot milk served in a tall glass
um galão	oong ga·*lowng*

half espresso, half milk in a large cup (caffe latte)
um café com leite	oong ka·*fe* kong *lay*·te

nonalcoholic drinks

bebidas sem ser alcoólicas

... mineral water	*água mineral ...*	*aa*·gwa mee·ne·*raal* ...
sparkling	*com gás*	kong gaash
still	*sem gás*	seng gaash

orange juice	sumo de laranja natural m	soo·moo de la·rang·zha na·too·raal
soft drink	refrigerante m	rre·free·zhe·rang·te
(hot) water	água (quente) f	aa·gwa (keng·te)
(cup of) tea …	(chávena de) chá …	(shaa·ve·na de) shaa …
(cup of) coffee …	(chávena de) café …	(shaa·ve·na de) ka·fe …
with (milk)	com (leite)	kong (lay·te)
without (sugar)	sem (açúcar)	seng (a·soo·kar)

alcoholic drinks

bebidas alcoólicas

beer	cerveja f	ser·ve·zha
brandy	brandy f	brang·dee
champagne	champanhe m	shang·pa·nye
cocktail	cocktail m	kok·tayl
firewater	água-ardente m	aa·gwaar·deng·te
a shot of …	um copinho de …	oong koo·pee·nyoo de …
gin	gin	zheeng
rum	rum	rroong
tequila	tequila	te·kee·la
vodka	vodka	vo·de·ka
whisky	uísque	oo·eesh·kee
a bottle	uma garrafa	oo·ma ga·rraa·fa
of … wine	de vinho …	de vee·nyoo …
a glass	um copo de	oong ko·poo de
of … wine	vinho …	vee·nyoo …
dessert	de sobremesa	de soo·bre·me·za
red	tinto	teeng·too
rosé	rosé	rro·ze
sparkling	espumante	shpoo·mang·te
white	branco	brang·koo
young (green)	verde	ver·de

For additional items, see the **culinary reader**, page 167, and the **dictionary**.

know your beer

à pressão	aa pre·*sowng*	draft
uma caneca	*oo*·ma ka·*ne*·ka	larger (33cl) draft beer
uma garrafa de cerveja	*oo*·ma ga·*rraa*·fa de ser·*ve*·zha	large bottle of beer
uma mini	*oo*·ma *mee*·nee	small bottle of beer
um jarro	oong *zhaa*·roo	a jug of beer
um quartilho	oong kwar·*tee*·lyoo	a pint of beer
uma imperial	*oo*·ma eeng·pree·*aal*	small (20cl) draft beer in the south, including Lisbon
um fino	oong *fee*·noo	small (20cl) draft beer in the center and north of Portugal

in the bar

Excuse me!
Desculpe!　　　desh·*kool*·pe

I'm next.
Eu sou a seguir.　　　e·oo soh a se·*geer*

I'll have (a moscatel).
Eu queria (um moscatel).　　　e·oo ke·*ree*·a (oong moosh·ka·*tel*)

Same again, please.
O mesmo, por favor.　　　oo *mezh*·moo poor fa·*vor*

No ice, thanks.
Sem gelo, por favor.　　　seng *zhe*·loo poor fa·*vor*

I'll buy you a drink.
Eu pago-lhe uma bebida.　　　e·oo *paa*·goo·lye *oo*·ma be·*bee*·da

What would you like?
O que é que quer? oo ke e ke ker

I don't drink alcohol.
Eu não bebo álcool. e·oo nowng be·boo aal·koo·ol

It's my round.
É a minha rodada. e a mee·nya rroo·daa·da

Do you serve meals here?
Vocês servem vo·sesh ser·veng
refeições aqui? rre·fay·soyngsh a·kee

---

listen for ...

O que é que vão comer/tomar?
oo ke e ke vowng **What are you having**
koo·mer/too·maar **to eat/drink?**

Eu acho que já bebeu demais.
e·oo aa·shoo ke zhaa **I think you've had**
be·be·oo de·maish **enough.**

Últimos pedidos.
ool·tee·moosh pe·dee·doosh **Last orders.**

---

drinking up

beber

Cheers!
À nossa! aa no·sa

This is hitting the spot.
Está a saber-me shtaa a sa·ber·me
mesmo bem. mesh·moo beng

I feel fantastic!
Estou a sentir-me shtoh a seng·teer·me
mesmo bem. mesh·moo beng

I think I've had one too many.
Acho que bebi demais. aa·shoo ke be·bee de·maish

I'm feeling drunk.
   Estou a sentir-me   shtoh a seng·*teer*·me
   bêbado/bêbada. **m/f**   be·ba·doo/*be*·ba·da

I'm pissed.
   Estou completamente   shtoh kong·ple·ta·*meng*·te
   bêbado/bêbada. **m/f**   be·ba·doo/*be*·ba·da

I feel ill.
   Sinto-me mal.   *seeng*·too·me maal

Where's the toilet?
   Onde é a casa de banho.   *ong*·de e a *kaa*·za de *ba*·nyoo

I'm tired, I'd better go home.
   Estou cansado/   shtoh kang·*saa*·doo/
   cansada, é melhor   kang·*saa*·da e me·*lyoor*
   ir para casa. **m/f**   eer *pa*·ra *kaa*·za

Can you call a taxi for me?
   Pode chamar-me um   *po*·de sha·*maar*·me oong
   táxi?   *taak*·see

I don't think you should drive.
   Eu acho que não   *e*·oo *aa*·shoo ke nowng
   devia conduzir.   de·*vee*·a kong·doo·*zeer*

---

the beef of the sea

It's famed as being in so many recipes that you could eat it a different way every day for a year, it's white and hard as a rock and it smells decidedly fishy … Yes, it's *bacalhau* ba·ka·*lyow*, what many consider the Portuguese national food. The word is often translated as simply 'cod', but if that conjures up images involving five minutes with a frypan and a slice of lemon (or chips and newspaper, Britons!), forget them – this is salted and dried fish, and needs serious soaking.

buying food

comprar comida

What's the local speciality?
Qual é a especialidade local?
kwaal e a shpe·see·a·lee·*daa*·de loo·*kaal*

What's that?
O que é aquilo?
oo ke e a·*kee*·loo

Can I taste it?
Posso provar?
po·soo proo·*vaar*

Can I have a bag, please?
Pode-me dar um saco, por favor?
po·de·me daar oong saa·koo poor fa·*vor*

I don't need a bag, thanks.
Não preciso de um saco, obrigado/obrigada. m/f
nowng pre·*see*·zoo de oong saa·koo o·bree·*gaa*·doo/o·bree·*gaa*·da

How much is (a kilo of cheese)?
Quanto é (um quilo de queijo)?
kwang·too e (oong kee·loo de kay·zhoo)

listen for ...

Em que é que posso ajudar?
eng ke e ke po·soo aa·zhoo·*daar* **Can I help you?**

O que deseja?
oo ke de·ze·zha **What would you like?**

Mais alguma coisa?
maish aal·*goo*·ma *koy*·za **Anything else?**

Não temos.
nowng *te*·moosh **There isn't any.**

how would you like that?

cooked	cozinhado/	koo·zee·*nyaa*·doo/
	cozinhada m/f	koo·zee·*nyaa*·da
cured	curado/curada m/f	koo·*raa*·doo/koo·*raa*·da
dried	seco/seca m/f	se·koo/se·ka
fresh	fresco/fresca m/f	fresh·koo/fresh·kaa
frozen	congelado/	kong·zhe·*laa*·doo/
	congelada m/f	kong·zhe·*laa*·da
smoked	fumado/	foo·*maa*·doo/
	fumada m/f	foo·*maa*·da
raw	cru/crua m/f	kroo/*kroo*·a

I'd like …	Eu queria …	e·oo ke·*ree*·a …
(200) grams	(duzentos) gramas	(doo·*zeng*·toosh) *graa*·mash
half a dozen	meia dúzia	*may*·a doo·zya
a dozen	uma dúzia	oo·ma doo·zya
half a kilo	meio quilo	*may*·oo *kee*·loo
a kilo	um quilo	oong *kee*·loo
(two) kilos	(dois) quilos	(doysh) *kee*·loosh
a bottle	uma garrafa	oo·ma ga·*rraa*·fa
a jar	um frasco	oong *fraash*·koo
a packet	um pacote	oong pa·*ko*·te
a piece	uma peça	oo·ma *pe*·sa
(three) pieces	(três) peças	(tresh) *pe*·sash
a slice	uma fatia	oo·ma fa·*tee*·a
(six) slices	(seis) fatias	(saysh) fa·*tee*·ash
a tin (can)	uma lata	oo·ma *laa*·ta
(just) a little	(só) um bocadinho	(so) oong boo·ka·*dee*·nyoo
more	mais	maish
some	uns/	oongsh/
	umas m/f	oo·mash
that one	aquele/aquela m/f	a·*ke*·le/a·*ke*·la
this one	este/esta m/f	esh·te/*esh*·ta

Less.	Menos.	me·noosh
A bit more.	Um pouco mais.	oong *poh*·koo maish
Enough.	Chega.	she·ga

Do you have …?	Há …?	aa …
anything	alguma coisa	aal·*goo*·ma *koy*·za
cheaper	mais barata	maish ba·*raa*·ta
other kinds	de outros	de *oh*·troosh
	tipos	tee·poosh
Where can I find	Onde é	ong·de e
the … section?	que é …?	ke e …
dairy	a secção de	a sek·*sowng* de
	produtos	proo·*doo*·toosh
	lácteos	laak·tee·oosh
fish	a peixaria	a pay·sha·*ree*·a
frozen goods	os	oosh
	congelados	kong·zhe·*laa*·doosh
fruit and	a fruta e	a *froo*·ta e
vegetable	vegetais	ve·zhe·*taish*
meat	a carne	a *kaar*·ne
poultry	a secção	a sek·*sowng*
	de aves	de *aa*·vesh

cooking utensils

Could I please borrow a ...?	Podia-me emprestar ...?	poo·*dee*·a·me eng·presh·*taar* ...
I need a ...	Preciso de uma ...	pre·*see*·zoo de oo·ma ...
chopping board	tábua para cortar	*taa*·boo·a *pa*·ra kor·*taar*
frying pan	frigideira	free·gee·*day*·ra
knife	faca	*faa*·ka
saucepan	caçarola	ka·sa·*ro*·la

false friends

You can often guess the meanings of Portuguese words, as many are similar to English words which were originally borrowed from a Romance language (usually French). But beware! Things aren't always what they seem, and you could cause general hilarity by asking for a briefcase (pasta *pash*·ta) in a restaurant. Here are a few examples:

cola   *ko*·la
   means 'glue', not a caffeinated soft drink

depressa   de·*pre*·sa
   means 'fast' rather than 'depressed'

massa   *maa*·sa
   means 'noodles' rather than 'Catholic Mass'

salsa   *saal*·sa
   means 'parsley' rather than 'sauce' or 'dip'

sumo   *soo*·mo
   means 'juice', not Japanese wrestling

And the classic:

uma constipação   oo·ma kong·shtee·pa·*sowng*
   is a headcold, not constipation

The Portuguese by and large don't understand vegetarianism – like many European countries, Portugal has ridden on the pig's back since medieval times, and even the pastries can be made with lard. The big cities and the trendy Algarve region tend to be more vegetarian-friendly, but anywhere else you may have difficulty. Of course, if you're a 'pescatarian' (ie you eat fish but no other meat) you won't have too many problems, as Portugal's other staple protein is salt cod (*bacalhau* ba·ka·*lyow* – see the box on page 160 for more).

ordering food

pedir comida

Is there a ... restaurant near here?

Há algum restaurante ...	aa aal·*goong* rresh·tow·*rang*·te ...	
perto daqui?	*per*·too da·*kee*	

Do you	*Tem*	teng
have ... food?	*comida ...?*	koo·*mee*·da ...
halal	*halal*	a·*laal*
kosher	*kosher*	*ko*·sher
vegetarian	*vegetariana*	ve·zhe·ta·ree·*aa*·na

butter	*manteiga* f	mang·*tay*·ga
eggs	*ovos* m pl	*o*·voosh
fish	*peixe* m	*pay*·she
fish stock	*caldo de peixe* m	*kaal*·doo de *pay*·she
(red) meat	*carne (vermelha)* f	*kaar*·ne (ver·*me*·lya)
meat stock	*caldo de carne* m	*kaal*·doo de *kaar*·ne
oil	*óleo* m	*o*·lee·oo
pork	*carne de porco* f	*kaar*·ne de *por*·koo
poultry	*aves* f pl	*aa*·vesh

I don't eat …
Eu não como …   e·oo nowng *ko*·moo …

Is it cooked with …?
Leva …?   *le*·va …

Could you prepare a meal without …?
Pode preparar sem …?   po·de pre·pa·*raar* seng …

special diets & allergies

I'm on a special diet.	*Eu tenho uma dieta especial.*	e·oo *ta*·nyoo oo·ma dee·*e*·ta shpe·see·*aal*
I'm (a) …	*Eu sou …*	e·oo soh …
Buddhist	*budista*	boo·*deesh*·ta
Hindu	*hindu*	*eeng*·doo
Jewish	*judeu* m	zhoo·*de*·oo
	judia f	zhoo·*dee*·a
Muslim	*muçulmano* m	moo·sool·*ma*·noo
	muçulmana f	moo·sool·*ma*·na
vegan	*vegan*	*vee*·gang
vegetarian	*vegetariano* m	ve·zhe·ta·ree·*a*·noo
	vegetariana f	ve·zhe·ta·ree·*a*·na
I'm allergic to …	*Eu sou alérgico/ alérgica a …* m/f	e·oo soh a·*ler*·zhee·koo/ a·*ler*·zhee·ka a …
dairy produce	*produtos lácteos*	pro·*doo*·toosh *laak*·tee·oosh
eggs	*ovos*	o·voosh
gelatine	*gelatina*	zhe·la·*tee*·na
gluten	*glúten*	*gloo*·teng
honey	*mel*	mel
MSG	*MSG*	e·me·e·se·*zhe*
nuts	*oleaginosas*	o·lee·a·zhe·*no*·zash
peanuts	*amendoins*	a·meng·doo·*eengsh*
seafood	*marisco*	ma·*reesh*·koo
shellfish	*crustáceos*	kroosh·*taa*·se·oosh

This miniguide to Portuguese cuisine is designed to help you navigate menus and get the most out of your gastronomic experience in Portugal. *Bom apetite!*

A

abacate ⓜ a-ba-*kaa*-te *avocado*
abóbora ① a-*bo*-boo-ra *pumpkin*
abobrinha ① a-boo-*bree*-nya *zucchini*
açafrão ⓜ a-sa-*frowng* *saffron*
acepipes ⓜ pl a-se-*pee*-pesh
  delicacies • hors d'oeuvres • titbits
achigã ⓜ a-shee-*gang* *black bass (fish)*
ácido/ácida ⓜ/①
  *aa-*see-doo/*aa*-see-da *sour*
açorda ① a-*sor*-da
  *bread-based thick soup, often flavoured
  with garlic, coriander & olive oil*
  — de bacalhau de ba-ka-*lyow* **açorda**
    with shredded salt cod
  — de gambas de *gang*-bash **açorda**
    containing prawns
  — de marisco de ma-*reesh*-koo **açorda**
    with prawns, mussels & cockles
  — de sável de *saa*-vel *spicy* **açorda**
    flavoured with shad (fish) broth
açúcar ⓜ a-*soo*-kar *sugar*
  — amarelo a-ma-*re*-loo *brown sugar*
  — granulado gra-noo-*laa*-doo
    granulated or refined sugar
agriões ⓜ pl a-gree-*oyngsh* *watercress*
água ① *aa*-gwa *water*
  — da nascente da nash-*seng*-te
    spring water
  — da torneira da toor-*nay*-ra *tap water*
  — mineral (com/sem gás)
    mee-ne-*raal* (kong/seng gaash) *mineral
    water (with/without carbonation)*
água-ardente ① *aa*-gwaar-*deng*-te
  brandy-like spirit
  — de cana de *ka*-na *sugar cane spirit*
  — de figo de *fee*-goo *fig brandy*
  — de medronho de me-*dro*-nyoo
    brandy made from arbutus berry
  — velha *ve*-lya *fine brandy*

aipo ⓜ *ai*-poo *celery*
alcachofra ① aal-ka-*sho*-fra *artichoke*
alecrim ⓜ a-le-*kreeng* *rosemary*
Alentejana, à a-leng-te-*zha*-na, aa *'Alentejo
  style' – dish made with garlic, olive oil,
  paprika, usually pork & small cockles*
alface ① aal-*faa*-se *lettuce*
alheiras ① pl a-*lyay*-rash *sausage of bread,
  garlic, chilli & meats*
alho ⓜ *aa*-lyoo *garlic*
  — francês frang-*sesh* *leek*
  — porro po-*rroo* *leek*
almoço ⓜ aal-*mo*-soo *lunch*
almôndegas ① pl aal-*mong*-de-gash
  beef or pork meatballs
alperce ⓜ aal-*per*-se *apricot*
amanteigado ⓜ a-mang-tay-*gaa*-doo
  'buttery' – term describing creamy cheeses
amarguinha ① a-mar-*gee*-nya
  almond-flavoured liqueur
amêijoas ① pl a-may-*zhoo*-ash *cockles*
  — à Bulhão Pato aa boo-*lyowng
    paa*-too *broth of small cockles in
    coriander, white wine & garlic sauce*
  — ao natural ow na-too-*raal*
    steamed cockles
  — na cataplana na ka-ta-*pla*-na
    *small cockles cooked with onion, chopped
    chouriço, ham and red & green capsicum*
ameixa ① a-*may*-sha *plum*
ameixas de Elvas ① pl
  a-*may*-shash de el-vash *'plums of Elvas' –
  sweet dessert plums preserved in sugar*
ameixa seca ① a-*may*-sha se-ka *prune*
amêndoa ① a-*meng*-doo-a *almond*
amendoim ⓜ a-meng-doo-*eeng* *peanut*
amora ① a-*mo*-ra *blackberry*
ananás ⓜ a-na-*naash* *pineapple*
anho ⓜ *a*-nyoo *lamb (see also **borrego**)*
anis ⓜ a-*neesh* *aniseed*

anona ⓕ a-*no*-na custard apple

aperitivo ⓜ a-pe-ree-*tee*-voo apéritif

areias ⓕ pl a-*ray*-ash
sweet biscuit flavoured with lemon

arenque ⓜ a-*reng*-ke herring

arjamolho ⓜ ar-zha-*mo*-lyoo Algarve name
for gaspacho

arrepiadas ⓕ pl a-rre-pee-*aa*-dash sliced
almonds, held together with meringue

arroz ⓜ a-*rrosh* rice
— **árabe** *aa*-ra-be rice with raisins, nuts &
sometimes chopped dried fruit
— **à valenciana** aa va-leng-see-*a*-na a
saffron-flavoured rice dish similar to paella
— **cozido** koo-*zee*-doo boiled rice
— **de bacalhau** de ba-ka-*lyow* tomato-
flavoured rice with shredded salt cod
— **de berbigão** de ber-bee-*gowng* rice
with cockles, seasoned with coriander
— **de bucho** de *boo*-shoo creamy rice
cooked in pork broth
— **de cabidela** de ka-bee-*de*-la chicken &
rice casserole with fresh chicken blood
— **de ervilhas** de er-*vee*-lyash
rice with peas
— **de espigos** de *shpee*-goosh
rice with cabbage
— **de feijão** de fay-*zhowng*
rice with red beans
— **de forno** de *for*-noo baked rice with
onion & prosciutto or **salpicão**
— **de grelos** de gre-*loosh*
rice with cabbage
— **de lampreia** de lang-*pray*-a
lamprey & rice stew with onion, parsley,
white wine, **chouriço** & lamprey blood
— **de langueirão** de lang-gay-*rowng*
rice with razor clams & onion, seasoned
with garlic & parsley
— **de lapas** de *laa*-pash rice with limpets
— **de marisco** de ma-*reesh*-koo
casserole of seafood & rice in tomato sauce
— **de pato** de *paa*-too
baked or braised casserole of rice with
shredded duck & sausage slices
— **de polvo** de *pol*-voo chunks of octopus & onion in a tomato-rice stew
— **de sarrabulho** de sa-rra-*boo*-lyoo stew
with rice, pork, beef, chicken & sauce made
of onion & pig's blood

— **de tamboril** de tang-boo-*reel*
tomato-rice stew with chunks of frog-fish
— **de tomate** de too-*maa*-te
rice cooked in a tomato broth, often served
with fried fish
— **doce** *do*-se creamy rice sprinkled
with cinnamon
— **integral** eeng-te-*graal* brown rice

arrufadas de Coimbra ⓕ pl
a-rroo-*faa*-dash de *koyng*-bra dome-
shaped, cinnamon-flavoured bread

asa ⓕ *aa*-za wing
— **de frango** de *frang*-goo chicken wing
— **de perú** de pe-*roo* turkey wing

assado/assada ⓜ/ⓕ a-*saa*-doo/a-*saa*-da
roast

assado de peixe ⓜ a-*saa*-doo de *pay*-she
mixture of different roasted or baked fish

atum ⓜ a-*toong* tuna
— **de escabeche** de shka-*be*-she raw
tuna 'pickled' or 'cooked' in vinegar

avelã ⓕ a-ve-*lang* hazelnut

aves ⓕ pl *aa*-vesh poultry

avestruz ⓜ&ⓕ a-*vesh*-troosh ostrich

azeite ⓜ a-*zay*-te olive oil

azeitonas ⓕ pl a-zay-*to*-nash olives
— **pretas** *pre*-tash black olives
— **recheadas** rre-shee-*aa*-dash
stuffed olives
— **sem caroço** seng ka-ro-*soo*
pitted olives
— **verdes** *ver*-desh green olives

azevias ⓕ pl a-ze-*vee*-ash fried puff pastry
with a sweet chickpea filling

B

baba de camelo ⓕ *baa*-ba de ka-*me*-loo
'camel drool' – caramel mousse made with
condensed milk

bacalhau ⓜ ba-ka-*lyow* dried salt cod
— **à Assis** aa a-*sees* crumbled salt cod
cooked in olive oil with vegetables, mixed
with eggs & parsley, then baked
— **à Brás** aa braas flaked cod scramble-
fried with egg, potato & olives
— **à cozinha velha** aa koo-*zee*-nya *ve*-lya
chopped salt cod, onions & carrots fried in
olive oil & cooked in a white sauce, covered
with breadcrumbs, then baked

— à Gomes de Sá aa *go*-mes de saa
flaked salt cod soaked in milk & browned
in the oven with vegetables & eggs

— albardado aal-bar-*daa*-doo salt cod
fried in a doughy batter

— assado com batatas a murro
a-*saa*-doo kong ba-*taa*-tash a *moo*-rroo
baked or roasted salt cod with smashed
baked potatoes, garlic & olive oil

— assado com pão de centeio
a-*saa*-doo kong powng de seng-*tay*-oo
baked salt cod steak sprinkled with garlic,
olive oil & crumbled rye bread

— com todos kong *to*-doosh boiled salt
cod served with boiled egg & vegetables

— cozido koo-*zee*-doo boiled salt cod

— cru desfiado kroo desh-fee-*aa*-doo
shredded raw salt cod in an olive oil &
vinegar dressing

— desfiado desh-fee-*aa*-doo
fine strips of raw salt cod served with
chopped onion & garlic

— guisado gee-*zaa*-doo stewed salt cod
steaks with olive oil, tomatoes, onion,
potatoes, butter, herbs & spices

— no borralho noo boo-*rraa*-lyoo
salt cod steak wrapped in cabbage leaves
& bacon & cooked in burning embers

— no forno noo *for*-noo
baked salt cod, often smothered in an
onion & olive oil sauce

— roupa-velha rroh-pa-*ve*-lya
'old clothes' – mixture of cabbage, salt cod
& potatoes, sautéed in olive oil & garlic

bagaço ⓜ ba-*gaa*-soo **água-ardente**,
often drunk with an espresso coffee

banha ⓕ *baa*-nya lard

barriga-de-freira ⓕ ba-*rree*-ga-de-*fray*-ra
sponge cake or bread covered in a sugary
syrup with eggs & a hint of lemon

barrinhas de pescada ⓕ pl
ba-*rree*-nyash de pesh-*kaa*-da fish sticks

batata doce ⓕ ba-*taa*-ta *do*-se
sweet potato

batatas ⓕ pl ba-*taa*-tash potatoes

— a murro a *moo*-rroo
'punched potatoes' – baked potatoes
with the skin on, smashed & seasoned
with olive oil & garlic

— cozidas koo-zee-dash boiled potatoes

— fritas *free*-tash potato chips or crisps

batido ⓜ ba-*tee*-doo milk or fruit shake

baunilha ⓕ bow-*nee*-lya vanilla

bebida ⓕ be-*bee*-da beverage

— (não) alcoólica (nowng)
aal-koo-o-lee-ka (non)alcoholic beverage

— espirituosa shpee-ree-too-o-za spirit

— fria *free*-a cold beverage

— quente keng-te hot beverage

berbigão ⓜ ber-bee-*gowng* cockle

beringela ⓕ be-reeng-*zhe*-la
aubergine • eggplant

besugo ⓜ be-*zoo*-goo sea bream

beterraba ⓕ be-te-*rraa*-ba beetroot

bica ⓕ *bee*-ka espresso coffee

— cheia *shay*-a
espresso topped with hot water

— com uma pinga kong oo-ma
peeng-ga espresso topped with **água-
ardente** (drunk as a digestive)

bifana no pão ⓕ bee-*fa*-na noo powng
thin pork steak sandwich

bifana no prato ⓕ bee-*fa*-na noo *praa*-too
thin pork steak (not in a sandwich)

bife ⓜ *bee*-fe fillet • steak of beef, other
meats, poultry or fish

— à café aa ka-*fe* thick rump steak served
with sauce of milk, lemon juice & mustard

— à casa aa *kaa*-za 'house-style' – thin,
pan-fried steak with a fried egg on top

— à cerveja aa ser-*ve*-zha
steak with beer-based, buttery sauce

— alto *aal*-too thick steak

— à Marrare aa ma-*rraa*-re thick rump
steak served with cream sauce & pepper

— à pimenta aa pee-*meng*-ta
steak with whole peppercorns

— bem passado beng pa-*saa*-doo
well-done steak

— com ovo a cavalo kong o-voo a
ka-*vaa*-loo fried steak marinated with fresh
garlic, served with a fried egg on top

— da alcatra da aal-*kaa*-tra rump steak

— de atum de a-*toong* tuna steak

— do vazio doo va-*zee*-oo sirloin steak

— mal passado maal pa-*saa*-doo
rare steak

bifinho ⓜ bee-*fee*-nyoo
thin, boneless slices of meat

biscoitos ⓜ pl beesh-*koy*-toosh
biscuits • cookies
— **de Alcanena** de aal-ka-*ne*-na
light, airy biscuit made with olive oil
— **de azeite** de a-*zay*-te
light, airy biscuit made with olive oil
bitoque ⓜ bee-*to*-ke *small steak or fillet
usually served with a fried egg on top*
bola ⓕ *bo*-la *breadroll*
— **de Berlim com/sem creme** de
ber-*leeng* kong/seng *kre*-me *plain dough-
nut with/without custard filling*
— **de carne** de *kaar*-ne
baked meat pie with bread dough pastry
— **de presunto** de pre-*zoong*-too **bola
de carne** *with a layer of prosciutto*
— **de sardinhas** de sar-*dee*-nyash **bola**
with a layer of sardines
bolachas ⓕ pl boo-*laa*-shash
biscuits • cookies • crackers
bolachos ⓜ pl boo-*laa*-shoosh
*pig's blood made into a dumpling, served
with the fatty cooking juices of* **rojões**
boleima ⓕ boo-*lay*-ma
*small cakes made of bread dough filled
with apple slices or chopped walnuts*
bolinhos ⓜ pl boo-*lee*-nyoosh *biscuits*
— **de amêndoa** de a-*meng*-doo-a
*almond marzipan moulded into different
shapes: animals, fruit, vegetables*
— **de Jerimu** de zhe-*ree*-moo
pumpkin cakes flavoured with cinnamon
— **de pinhão** de pee-*nyowng*
pine nut cakes
bolo ⓜ *bo*-loo *pastry • sweet cake*
— **de arroz** de a-*rrosh* *cake made with
rice & wheat flour topped with sugar*
— **de bolacha** de boo-*laa*-sha
*biscuits layered with sweetened
butter-cream frosting to form a cake*
— **de caco** de *kaa*-koo *griddle bread
(bread toasted on an iron sheet on the
stove or coals) served hot with garlic
butter, sometimes cooked with a spicy*
chouriço *inside*
— **de coco** de *ko*-koo *coconut custard-
filled pastry tart • coconut macaroon*
— **de Dom Rodrigo**
de dong rroo-*dree*-goo *candy-like, soft
confection made of real eggs,* **ovos moles**
& *ground almonds*

— **de laranja** de la-*rang*-zha *orange cake*
— **de mel** de mel *rich molasses & spice
cake with candied fruit & almonds*
— **de noz** de nosh *walnut cake*
— **de sertã** de ser-*tang* *corn biscuits
cooked in a frying-pan*
— **do caco** doo *kaa*-koo *flat breadrolls
baked on a stone or cement slab*
— **lêvedo** *le*-ve-doo *light scone cooked in
a frying-pan*
— **real** rree-*aal* *dense cake made with lots
of eggs, grated almonds, pumpkin jam,
cinnamon & lemon*
— **rei** rray *Christmas bread in the shape of
a ring, studded with walnuts & pine nuts,
with a gift and a broad bean inside*
bombons ⓜ pl bong-*bongzh* *bonbons*
bonito ⓜ boo-*nee*-too *bonito (fish)*
borrachões ⓜ pl boo-rra-*shoyngsh*
*fried ring-shaped biscuits flavoured with
brandy or white wine & cinnamon*
borrachos ⓜ pl boo-*rraa*-shoosh
breadcrumb fritters in a syrup of white
vinho verde, *lemon & cinnamon*
borrego ⓜ boo-*rre*-goo *lamb*
— **assado** a-*saa*-doo *roast lamb*
broa ⓕ *bro*-a *sweet potato & almond cakes*
— **de milho** de *mee*-lyoo *corn bread*
— **serrana** se-*rra*-na *highland bread
(corn or rye bread)*
broas de mel ⓕ pl *bro*-ash de mel *soft
biscuit made of honey & flour*
bróculos ⓜ pl *bro*-koo-loosh *broccoli*
broínhas (de Natal) ⓕ pl
bro-*eeng*-nyash (de na-*taal*) *muffin-like
pastry with raisins, pine nuts & walnuts*
bucho de porco ⓜ
boo-shoo de *por*-koo *pig stomach*
bucho recheado ⓜ
boo-shoo rre-shee-*aa*-doo *pig's belly
stuffed with pork, bread or rice & cloves or
cumin – served sliced*
burras ⓕ pl boo-*rrash* *roast pig cheeks*

C

cabeça de xara ⓕ ka-*be*-sa de *shaa*-ra
*pig's head cooked with garlic, herbs &
white wine, served sliced*
de cabidela de ka-bee-*de*-la *any dish made
with blood*

FOOD

170

cabrito ⓜ ka-*bree*-too *kid (goat)*
caça ⓕ *kaa*-sa *game*
cacau ⓜ ka-*kow* cocoa
cacholeira ⓕ ka-shoo-*lay*-ra *pork liver sausage*
café ⓜ ka-*fe* coffee • espresso coffee • café
 — **em grão** eng growng *coffee beans*
 — **instantâneo** eeng-shtang-*taa*-nee-oo *instant coffee*
 — **moído** moo-ee-doo *ground coffee*
 — **torrado** too-*rraa*-doo *roast coffee*
cajú ka-*zhoo* cashew
calda (de açúcar) ⓕ *kaal*-da (a-*soo*-kar) *syrup*
caldeirada ⓕ kaal-day-*raa*-da *soup-like stew, usually with fish*
caldo ⓜ *kaal*-doo *broth • soup • stock*
camarão ⓜ ka-ma-*rowng* *shrimp*
canela ⓕ ka-*ne*-la *cinnamon*
canja/caldo de galinha ⓕ *kaang*-zha/ *kaal*-doo de ga-*lee*-nya *chicken broth*
canja/sopa de conquilhas ⓕ *kaang*-zha/ so-pa de kong-*kee*-lyash *cockle soup*
caracóis ⓜ pl ka-ra-*koysh* snails
caracol ⓜ ka-ra-*kol* *similar to a Danish pastry but with raisins or candied fruit*
caril ⓜ ka-*reel* curry (powder)
carne ⓕ *kaar*-ne *meat*
 — **assada** a-*saa*-da *roast meat*
 — **de cavalo** de ka-*vaa*-loo *horse meat*
 — **de porco** de *por*-koo *pork*
 — **de porco à Portuguesa** de *por*-koo a poor-too-*ge*-za *pork Alentejo-style without baby cockles*
 — **de vaca** de *vaa*-ka *beef*
 — **do alguidar** doo aal-gee-*daar* *chunks of cooked meat preserved in pork lard, served as an appetiser*
 — **picada/passada** pee-*kaa*-da/ pa-*saa*-da *ground meat (mince)*
carneiro ⓜ kar-*nay*-roo *lamb • mutton*
carnes frias ⓕ pl *kaar*-nesh *free*-ash *cold meats*
castanhas ⓕ pl kash-*taa*-nyash *chestnuts*
cavacas ⓕ pl ka-*vaa*-kash *sweet biscuit with white sugar icing*
cavalas ⓕ pl ka-*vaa*-lash *mackerel*
cebola ⓕ se-*bo*-la *onion*
cenoura ⓕ se-*noh*-ra *carrot*

cereja ⓕ se-*re*-zha *cherry*
cerveja ⓕ ser-*ve*-zha *beer*
 — **à pressão** aa pre-*sowng* *beer on tap*
 — **loura** *loh*-ra *'blonde beer' – regular beer, as opposed to stout*
 — **preta** *pre*-ta *dark beer • stout*
chá ⓜ shaa *tea*
 — **de ervas** de er-vash *herbal tea*
 — **de limão** de lee-*mowng* *glass or cup of boiling water with lemon rind*
champanhe ⓜ shang-*pa*-nye *champagne*
chanfana ⓕ shang-*fa*-na *hearty stew with goat or mutton in heavy red wine sauce*
charros alimados ⓜ pl *shaa*-rroosh a-lee-*maa*-doosh *skinned mackerel in olive oil & vinegar (or lemon) dressing – served with sliced onion, garlic & parsley*
chila ⓕ *shee*-la *spaghetti squash*
chispe com feijão branco ⓜ *sheesh*-pe kong fay-*zhowng* brang-koo *trotters with white beans, chouriço, pig's ear, kale & potatoes*
chocolate ⓜ shoo-koo-*laa*-te *chocolate*
chouriço ⓜ shoh-*ree*-soo *garlicky pork sausage flavoured with red pepper paste*
 — **assado** a-*saa*-doo *grilled sausage*
 — **de sangue** de *sang*-ge *blood sausage*
churrasco ⓜ shoo-*rraash*-koo *barbecued – grilled on a spit or skewer*
cidra ⓕ *see*-dra *cider*
coco ⓜ *ko*-koo *coconut*
codorniz ⓕ koo-door-*nees* quail
coelho ⓜ koo-e-lyoo *rabbit*
 — **à caçador** aa ka-sa-*dor* *'hunter's style rabbit' – stewed with wine & tomato*
 — **em vinha d'alho** eng *vee*-nya *daa*-lyoo *baked rabbit with slices of fried bread & onion, drizzled with port or white wine*
coentrada ⓕ kweng-*traa*-da *sauce with abundant amounts of coriander*
coentros ⓜ pl *kweng*-troosh *coriander*
cogumelos ⓜ pl koo-goo-*me*-loosh *mushrooms*
colorau ⓜ koo-loo-*row* *sweet paprika*
cominhos ⓜ pl koo-*mee*-nyoosh *cumin*
com todos kong to-doosh *'with everything' – a dish with the lot*
conquilha ⓕ kong-*kee*-lya *cockle*
cordeiro ⓜ cor-*day*-roo *lamb*

coscurões ⓜ pl koosh·koo·*royngsh* orange- & brandy-flavoured biscuit

costeleta ⓕ koosh·te·*le*·ta chop

couve ⓕ *koh*·ve cabbage
— **de Bruxelas** de broo·*she*·lash Brussels sprout
— **flor** flor cauliflower

coxa de galinha ⓕ *ko*·sha de ga·*lee*·nya fried, savoury chicken thigh

cozido/cozida ⓜ/ⓕ koo·*zee*·doo/koo·*zee*·da boiled

cozido à Portuguesa ⓜ koo·*zee*·doo aa poor·too·ge·za hearty meal made with chunks of different meats & sausages, vegetables, beans & rice

creme (de pasteleiro) ⓜ *kre*·me (de pash·te·*lay*·roo) egg, flour, water & sugar paste used to fill cakes

D

delícia de batata ⓕ de·*lee*·sya de ba·*taa*·ta little cakes of mashed potato mixed with almonds & cinnamon

digestivo ⓜ dee·zhesh·*tee*·voo after-dinner drink, usually a liqueur, brandy or port

dobrada ⓕ doo·*braa*·da tripe with white beans & rice

doce ⓜ *do*·se dessert • jam • sweet
— **de amêndoa** de a·*meng*·doo·a marzipan sweets

duchesse ⓕ doo·*shes* puff pastry filled with whipped cream & topped with fruit or thin threads of sugar & egg paste

E

empada ⓕ eng·*paa*·da miniature pot pie

empadão ⓜ eng·pa·*downg* dish similar to shepherd's pie

encharcada ⓕ eng·shar·*kaa*·da cooked egg yolks in a sugary syrup, decorated with cinnamon

enchido ⓜ eng·*shee*·doo any variety of sausage

engarrafado por ⓜ eng·ga·rra·*faa*·doo poor bottled by (winery name)

enguia ⓕ eng·*gee*·a eel

ensopado ⓜ eng·soo·*paa*·doo stew served on toasted or deep-fried bread

entrecosto ⓜ eng·tre·*kosh*·too pork ribs

ervilhas ⓕ pl er·vee·*lyash* peas
— **com ovos escalfados** kong o·*voosh* shkal·*faa*·doosh peas & sliced chouriço cooked with lard, olive oil, onions & parsley, served with poached eggs
— **de vagem** ⓕ de vaa·zheng snow peas

escabeche ⓕ shka·be·she 'vinegar stew' – raw meat or fish pickled in olive oil, vinegar, garlic & bay leaf

escalfado/escalfada ⓜ/ⓕ shkaal·*faa*·doo/shkaal·*faa*·da poached

escalopes ⓜ pl shka·*lo*·pesh medallion-shaped cuts of boneless meat

espanhola, à shpa·*nyo*·la, aa dish in tomato & onion sauce

espargos ⓜ pl shpar·goosh asparagus

esparguete ⓜ shpar·ge·te spaghetti

espetada ⓕ shpe·*taa*·da kebab

espinafres ⓜ pl shpee·*naa*·fresh spinach

estopeta de atum ⓕ shtoo·*pe*·ta de a·*toong* tuna, onion, tomatoes & green capsicum in an olive oil & vinegar dressing

F

faisão ⓜ fai·zowng pheasant

farinha ⓕ fa·*ree*·nya flour

farinheira ⓕ fa·ree·*nyay*·ra sausage stuffed with spiced, flour-based mixture

farófias ⓕ pl fa·*ro*·fee·ash dessert of beaten egg whites in a custard sauce

farripas de laranja ⓕ pl fa·*rree*·pash de la·*rang*·zha chocolate-covered strips of orange peel

farturas ⓕ pl far·*too*·rash deep-fried dough swirls rolled in sugar & cinnamon, usually found at fairs & local festivities

fataça na telha ⓕ fa·*taa*·sa na *te*·lya mullet seasoned with chopped onion, parsley, paprika & bacon, cooked between two clay roof tiles buried in embers

fatias ⓕ pl fa·*tee*·ash slices
— **da China/Tomar** da *shee*·na/too·*maar* steam-cooked loaf made of whipped egg yolks & sugar
— **douradas** doh·*raa*·dash slices of bread soaked in milk & eggs, fried, smothered in sugar & topped with cinnamon

favada à Portuguesa ① fa-*vaa*-da aa poor-too-*ge*-za *stew of fava beans, sausage & sometimes poached eggs*

fava-rica ① fa-va-*rree*-ka *fava bean soup with garlic and vinegar*

favas ① *faa*-vash *broad bean*
— **à Algarvia** ① *faa*-vash aa aal-gar-*vee*-a *fava beans cooked with blood sausage, bacon, sometimes* **chouriço** *& mint*

febras ① pl *fe*-brash *pork cutlets*

feijão ⓜ fay-*zhowng* *bean*

feijoada ① fay-zhwaa-da *bean stew with sausages or other meat*

ferraduras ① pl fe-rra-*doo*-rash *horseshoe-shaped pastry, sometimes layered with candied fruit*

fiambre ⓜ fee-*ang*-bre *cold meat • ham*

fígado ⓜ *fee*-ga-doo *liver*

figo ⓜ *fee*-goo *fig*

flocos ⓜ pl *flo*-koosh *breakfast cereal*

focinho de porco ⓜ foo-*see*-nyoo de por-*koo* *pig's snout*

folar ⓜ foo-*laar* *brioche dough baked with chicken, spicy sausages &* **presunto**, *eaten at Easter*

folhado ⓜ foo-*lyaa*-doo *puff pastry*

formigos ⓜ pl for-*mee*-goosh *sweetmeats – thick paste of soaked hard bread or biscuit with egg yolks, sugar, honey, milk, cinnamon & wine, cooked slowly over low heat*

framboesa ① frang-*bwe*-za *raspberry*

francesinha ① frang-se-*zee*-nya *ham, sausage & cheese in a tomato-cream sauce, on slices of bread*

frango ⓜ *frang*-goo *chicken*

frito/frita ⓜ/① *free*-too/*free*-ta *fried*

fruta ① *froo*-ta *fruit*

frutas secas ① pl *froo*-tash se-kash *dried fruit*

G

galão ⓜ ga-*lowng* *an espresso with hot milk served in a tall glass*

galinha ① ga-*lee*-nya *hen*
— **do campo** doo *kaang*-poo *free-range chicken*

gambas ① pl *gang*-bash *prawns*

garoto ⓜ ga-ro-*too* *ready-made filter coffee topped with warm or hot milk*

gaspacho ① gash-*paa*-shoo *chilled tomato & garlic bread soup flavoured with olive oil, vinegar & oregano*

gelado ⓜ zhe-*laa*-doo *ice cream*

geleia ① zhe-*lay*-a *jelly*

gelo ⓜ *zhe*-loo *ice*

gengibre ⓜ zheng-*zhee*-bre *ginger*

gila ① *zhee*-la *spaghetti squash*

ginja ① *zheeng*-zha *sour cherry*

goiaba ① goy-*aa*-ba *guava*

grão (de bico) ⓜ *growng* (de *bee*-koo) *chickpeas • garbanzo beans*

guardanapo ⓜ gwar-da-*naa*-poo *'napkin' – a jelly roll cake cut into squares & folded in half, filled with* **creme de pasteleiro**

guisado/guisada ⓜ/① gee-*za*-doo/gee-*za*-da *stewed*

H

hortaliça ① or-ta-*lee*-sa *vegetables*

hortelã ① or-te-*lang* *mint*

I

iogurte ⓜ yo-*goor*-te *yogurt*

iscas ① pl *eesh*-kash *pork liver*

J

jaquinzinhos ⓜ pl zha-keeng-*zee*-nyoosh *small fried horse-mackerel*

jardineira ① zhar-dee-*nay*-ra *hearty beef & vegetable stew*

jardineira, à zhar-dee-*nay*-ra, aa *a type of beef & vegetable stew*

javali ⓜ zha-va-*lee* *wild boar*

jesuítas ⓜ pl zhe-zoo-ee-*tash* *puff pastry with baked meringue icing*

L

lagosta ① la-*gosh*-ta *lobster*

lagostim ⓜ la-goosh-*teeng* *crayfish*

laranja ① la-*rang*-zha *orange*

lebre ① *le*-bre hare
— **com feijão branco** kong fay-*zhowng* brang-koo hare & white bean stew
legumes ⓜ pl le-*goo*-mesh vegetables
leitão ① lay-*towng* roasted suckling pig
leite ① *lay*-te milk
— **condensado** kong-deng-*saa*-doo condensed milk
— **gordo** *gor*-doo whole milk
— **magro** *maa*-groo skim milk
lentilha ① leng-*tee*-lya lentil
licor ⓜ lee-*kor* liqueur
lima ① *lee*-ma lime
limão ⓜ lee-*mowng* lemon
limonada ① lee-moo-*naa*-da lemonade
língua ① *leeng*-gwa tongue
— **de gato** *gaa*-too 'cat's tongue' – very small, hard vanilla biscuit
linguiça ① leeng-*gwee*-sa thin, long garlicky sausage
lombinhos de porco ⓜ pl long-*bee*-nyoosh de *por*-koo thinly sliced pork tenderloin
lombo de porco assado ⓜ *long*-boo de *por*-koo a-*saa*-doo roast pork loin
lulas ① pl *loo*-lash squid
— **à Sevilhana** aa se-vee-*lya*-na fried squid rings served with mayonnaise
— **recheadas** rre-shee-*aa*-dash small squid stuffed with a mixture of rice, tomatoes, **presunto** & parsley

M

maçã ① ma-*sang* apple
Madeirense, à ma-day-*reng*-se, aa Madeira-style – a dish cooked with tomatoes, onion & garlic (and sometimes bananas or Madeira wine)
malagueta ① ma-la-*ge*-ta red hot chilli peppers, also called **piripiri**
mal cozido/cozida ⓜ/① maal koo-*zee*-doo/koo-*zee*-da soft-boiled
manga ① *mang*-ga mango
manjar branco ⓜ mang-*zhaar* brang-koo coconut-milk pudding with prunes, with syrup poured over the top
manteiga ① mang-*tay*-ga butter

mão de vaca guisada ⓜ mowng de *vaa*-ka gee-*zaa*-da stew of cow's feet, chickpeas, tomatoes, onion, garlic **chouriço**, parsley & white wine
maracujá ⓜ ma-ra-koo-*zhaa* passionfruit
maranhos ⓜ ma-*ra*-nyoosh pork belly stuffed with lamb, **presunto**, **chouriço**, wine & rice
marisco ⓜ ma-*reesh*-koo shellfish
marmelada ① mar-me-*laa*-da quince paste
massas ① pl *maa*-sash noodles • pasta
mel ⓜ mel honey
melancia ① me-lang-*see*-a watermelon
melão ⓜ me-*lowng* (honeydew) melon
— **com presunto** kong pre-*zoong*-too slices of honeydew melon topped with slices of **presunto**
meloa ① me-*lo*-a cantaloupe • rockmelon
melosa ① me-*lo*-za mixed drink of brandy & honey
merenda ① me-*reng*-da light lunch • snack
merengue ⓜ me-*reng*-ge meringue
mexido/mexida ⓜ/① me-*shee*-doo/me-*shee*-da scrambled
mexilhões ⓜ pl me-shee-*lyoyngsh* mussels
migas ① pl *mee*-gash a side dish, usually made of bread flavoured with olive oil, garlic & spices & fried
— **de bacalhau** de ba-ka-*lyow* migas made with bread, salt cod, onion, tomatoes, garlic, red capsicum paste & coriander, served with grilled eels
— **de batata** de ba-*taa*-ta a side dish of mashed potatoes flavoured with bacon, sausage & garlic, shaped into round balls
mil folhas ⓜ pl meel *fo*-lyash layers of flaky pastry with custard filling
milho ⓜ *mee*-lyoo corn
— **frito** *free*-too cubes of fried white cornmeal served with skewers of grilled meat or poultry
miolos (de porco) ⓜ pl mee-o-loosh (de *por*-koo) (pork) brains
miudezas ① pl myoo-de-*zash* giblets
moda, à *mo*-da, aa in the style of
moelas ① pl mo-*e*-lash chicken gizzards
molho ⓜ *mo*-lyoo dressing • gravy • sauce
morangos ⓜ pl moo-*rang*-goosh strawberries

morcela ① moor-se-la *blood sausage*

morgados ⓜ pl mor-gaa-doosh *sweetmeats made with almonds & figs*

moscatel ⓜ moosh-ka-tel *topaz-coloured, sweet dessert wine*

mostarda ① moosh-taar-da *mustard*

N

nabiça ① na-bee-sa *turnip greens*

nabo ⓜ naa-boo *turnip*

na púcara ① na poo-ka-ra *chicken or duck cooked in a clay pot with **presunto**, tomatoes, onion, port, brandy, white wine, bay leaves & garlic*

natas ① pl naa-tash *cream (from milk)*

negro ⓜ ne-groo *type of sausage made from blood rather than meat*

nêspera ① nesh-pe-ra *loquat*

novilho ⓜ noo-vee-lyoo *veal*

noz ① nos *walnut*

O

oleaginosa ① o-lee-a-zhee-no-za *nut*

óleo ⓜ o-lee-oo *oil*

orelha de porco de coentrada ① o-re-lya de por-koo de kweng-traa-da *sliced pig's ear seasoned with garlic & coriander, in olive oil & vinegar dressing, served cold*

ostra ① osh-tra *oyster*

ovo ⓜ o-voo *egg*

— **cozido** koo-zee-doo *boiled egg*

— **de chocolate** de shoo-koo-laa-te *chocolate Easter egg*

— **escalfado** shkal-faa-doo *poached egg*

— **estrelado** shtre-laa-doo *fried egg*

— **mexido** me-shee-doo *scrambled egg*

ovos moles ⓜ pl o-voosh mo-lesh *sweetened egg yolks*

ovos verdes ⓜ pl o-voosh ver-desh *boiled eggs stuffed with a mixture of egg yolks, butter & parsley, coated in flour & fried*

P

pá ① paa *front leg of an animal*

paio ⓜ pai-oo *smoked pork tenderloin sausage*

panado ⓜ pa-naa-doo *breaded pork cutlet*

pão ⓜ powng *bread*

— **de centeio** de seng-tay-oo *light rye bread*

— **de leite** de lay-te *sweet roll made with wheat flour, eggs & milk*

— **de milho** de mee-lyoo *corn bread*

— **integral** eeng-te-graal *wholegrain bread*

papas ① pl paa-pash *gruel · porridge*

papos-de-anjo ⓜ pl paa-poosh-de-ang-zhoo *little egg-based puffs in a sugar syrup*

papo-seco ⓜ paa-poo-se-koo *most common type of bread roll*

passas ① pl paa-sash *raisins · sultanas*

pastéis ⓜ pl pash-taysh *pastries*

— **de bacalhau** de ba-ka-lyow *deep-fried savouries made of mashed potato, onion, parsley & salt cod*

— **de feijão** de fay-zhowng *rich lima bean & almond mixture in flaky pastry shells*

— **de massa tenra** de ma-sa teng-ra *meat-filled fried pastries*

— **de nata/Belém** de na-ta/be-leng *egg custard tarts with flaky pastry shell*

— **de Tentúgal** de teng-too-gaal *flaky pastries with a filling of creamy egg yolk & sugar paste*

pastel ⓜ pash-tel *pastry*

pataniscas de bacalhau ① pl pa-ta-neesh-kash de ba-ka-lyow *seasoned salt cod fritters*

paté ⓜ paa-te *paté*

pato ⓜ paa-too *duck*

peito de frango ⓜ pay-too de frang-goo *chicken breast*

peixe ⓜ pay-she *fish*

pepino ⓜ pe-pee-noo *cucumber*

pêra ① pe-ra *pear*

perdiz ① per-deez *partridge*

pernil no forno ⓜ per-neel noo for-noo *roast leg of pork*

peru ⓜ pe-roo *turkey*

pescadinhas de rabo na boca ① pl pesh-ka-dee-nyash de rraa-boo na bo-ka *small whiting fried with their tails in their mouths* pêssego ⓜ pe·se·goo *peach*

petingas ⓕ pl pe·teeng·gash *small sardines*

petiscos ⓜ pl pe·teesh·koosh *appetisers*

pezinhos de porco pe·zee·nyoosh de por·koo *pig's feet flavoured with coriander, garlic & onion*

picante ⓜ&ⓕ pee·kang·te *spicy or hot*

pimenta ⓕ pee·meng·ta *pepper*

pimento ⓜ pee·meng·too *capsicum*

pipis ⓜ pl pee·peesh *stewed chicken giblets, flavoured with garlic, onion, paprika, white wine & chilli*

piri piri pee·ree pee·ree *red hot chilli peppers (also called **malagueta**) · sauce made from red hot chilli peppers*

pito de Santa Luzia ⓜ pee·too de sang·ta loo·zee·a *sweet made from yeast dough filled with sugar, cinnamon & pumpkin*

polvo ⓜ pol·voo *octopus*

porco ⓜ por·koo *pork*

posta ⓕ posh·ta *steak slice*

prato de grão ⓜ praa·too de growng *chickpea stew flavoured with tomato, garlic, bay leaf & cumin*

pratos completos ⓜ pl praa·toosh kong·ple·toosh *'complete plates' – a dish with all the elements that would constitute a meal in itself*

prego no pão ⓜ pre·goo noo powng *small steak sandwich*

presunto ⓜ pre·zoong·too *prosciutto · smoked ham*

pudim ⓜ poo·deeng *pudding*
— de café de ka·fe *coffee-flavoured pudding*
— de leite de lay·te *custard-like pudding with lemon-flavoured caramel sauce*
— de ovos de o·voosh *very eggy, baked custard-like pudding*
— do Abade de Priscos doo a·baa·de de preesh·koosh *pudding made of egg yolks, sliced smoked bacon, port, lemon & cinnamon*
— flan flang *caramel custard*
— molotov mo·lo·tov *poached meringue with caramel sauce*

puré de batata ⓜ poo·re de ba·taa·ta *mashed potatoes*

Q

queijada ⓕ kay·zhaa·da *small tarts with sweet, dense filling*

queijo ⓜ kay·zhoo *cheese*
— da Serra/Estrela da se·rra/shtre·la *popular creamy cheese made from sheep's milk*
— de Azeitão de a·zay·towng *soft, creamy cheese made from sheep's milk near the town of Azeitão*
— de cabra de kaa·bra *goat's milk cheese*
— de ovelha de oo·ve·lya *sheep's milk cheese*
— de vaca de vaa·ka *cow's milk cheese*
— saloio sa·loy·oo *firm cow's milk cheese*
— seco se·koo *dry cheese similar in texture to parmesan*

queimado/queimada ⓜ/ⓕ kay·maa·doo/kay·maa·da *burnt*

queque ke·ke *plain yellow cupcake*

quivi kee·vee *kiwi(fruit)*

R

rabanadas ⓕ pl rra·ba·naa·dash *see* fatias douradas

rabanete ⓜ rra·ba·ne·te *radish*

rancho ⓜ rrang·shoo *hearty stew of chickpeas, onion, potatoes, macaroni, veal trotters, pork belly,* chouriço *& beef*

rebento de feijão ⓕ rre·beng·too de fay·zhowng *bean sprout*

regueifas ⓕ pl rre·gay·fash *cinnamon- & saffron-flavoured biscuit rings*

rendinhas ⓕ pl rreng·dee·nyash *almond nougat which resembles lace*

repolho ⓜ rre·po·lyoo *cabbage*

requeijada ⓕ rre·kay·zhaa·da *tart made with* requeijão

requeijão ⓜ rre·kay·zhowng *fresh, ricotta-style cheese*

rim ⓜ rreeng *kidney · kidney-shaped eclair*

rissol ⓜ rree·sol *fried pastry · rissole*

robalo ⓜ rroo·baa·loo *rock bass (fish)*

rocha ⓕ rro·sha *large, soft spice biscuit*

rojões ⓜ pl rroo·zhoyngsh *spiced & marinated chunks of fried pork*

rolo de carne ⓜ rro-loo de *kaar*-ne
meatloaf

rosbife ⓜ rrosh-*bee*-fe *roast beef*

S

safio ⓜ sa-*fee*-oo conger eel • sea eel

sal ⓜ saal *salt*
— **fino** *fee*-noo refined salt
— **grosso** gro-soo rock salt

salada ⓕ sa-*laa*-da salad
— **de alface** de aal-*fa*-se lettuce salad
— **de atum** de a-*toong* salad of tuna,
potato, peas, carrots & boiled eggs in an
olive oil & vinegar dressing
— **de bacalhau com feijão frade** de
ba-ka-*lyow* kong fay-*zhowng* fraa-de
salad of uncooked salt cod & black-eyed
beans in olive oil & vinegar dressing
— **de feijão frade** de fay-*zhowng*
fraa-de black-eyed bean salad flavoured
with onion, garlic, olive oil & vinegar,
sprinkled with chopped boiled egg &
parsley
— **de frutas** de froo-tash fruit salad
— **de tomate** de too-*maa*-te tomato &
onion salad, often flavoured with oregano
— **mista** meesh-ta tomato, lettuce &
onion salad
— **russa** rroo-sa potato salad with peas,
carrots & mayonnaise

salame de chocolate ⓜ sa-*la*-me de
shoo-koo-*laa*-te dense chocolate fudge roll
studded with bits of biscuits, served sliced

salgadinho ⓜ saal-ga-*dee*-nyoo small
savoury pastry

salgado/salgada ⓜ/ⓕ saal-*gaa*-doo/
saal-*gaa*-da salty • small savoury pastry

salmão ⓜ saal-*mowng* salmon
— **fumado** foo-*maa*-doo smoked salmon

salmonete ⓜ saal-moo-ne-te red mullet

salpicão ⓜ saal-pee-*kowng* smoked pork
sausage flavoured with garlic, bay leaf &
sometimes wine

salsa ⓕ saal-sa flat-leaf parsley • parsley

salsicha ⓕ saal-see-sha sausage
— **fresca** fresh-ka fresh pork sausage

salteado/salteada ⓜ/ⓕ saal-tee-*aa*-doo/
saal-tee-*aa*-da sautéed

sálvia ⓕ saal-vee-a sage

sandes ⓕ sang-desh sandwich

sanduiche ⓕ sang-*dwee*-she sandwich
(see also **sandes**)

sardinha ⓕ sar-dee-nya sardine

sarrabulho ⓜ sa-rra-boo-*lyoo* variety of
meats cooked in pig's blood

sável ⓜ *saa*-vel shad (fish)
— **na telha** na te-lya **fataça na telha**
made with shad

sericá/sericaia ⓕ se-ree-*ka*/se-ree-*kay*-a
soft cake with an almost creamy texture
served with a stewed plum in syrup

simples ⓜ&ⓕ seeng-plesh plain • with no
filling, icing or accompaniments

sobremesa ⓕ soo-bre-me-za dessert •
jam • sweet

sonhos ⓜ pl so-nyoosh sweet fried dough,
sprinkled with sugar & cinnamon

sopa ⓕ so-pa soup
— **de pedra** de pe-dra 'stone soup' –
vegetable soup with red beans, onions,
potatoes, pig's ear, bacon & sausages
— **do dia** doo dee-a soup of the day

sumo ⓜ soo-moo juice
— **de laranja natural** de la-*rang*-zha
na-too-raal freshly squeezed orange juice

T

tâmara ⓕ taa-ma-ra date (fruit)

tangerina ⓕ tang-zhe-ree-na mandarin

tarte ⓕ tar-te pie

tecolameco ⓜ te-koo-la-me-koo rich &
sweet orange & almond cake, well loved
around Portalegre

tigelada ⓕ tee-zhe-laa-da firm egg custard
flavoured with vanilla, lemon or cinnamon

tomate ⓜ too-maa-te tomato

tomilho ⓜ too-mee-lyoo thyme

toranja ⓕ to-*rang*-zha grapefruit

tornedó ⓜ tor-ne-do thick, tender steak

torrada ⓕ too-rraa-da toast

torresmos ⓜ pl too-rrezh-moosh
pork cracklings served as a snack

torta ⓕ tor-ta tart with filling
— **de laranja** de la-*rang*-zha rolled
orange-flavoured tart made with lots of
eggs & little flour
— **de Viana** de vee-*aa*-na tart filled with
jam • tart with egg yolk icing

tortulhos ⓜ pl tor·*too*·lyoosh *sheep's tripe stuffed with more sheep's tripe*

tosta ⓕ *tosh*·ta *pieces of toast*
— **mista** *meesh*·ta *toasted ham & cheese sandwich*

toucinho ⓜ toh·*see*·nyoo *uncured bacon*
— **rançoso** rrang·*so*·zoo *cake made with almonds & egg yolks, sprinkled with sugar & cinnamon*
— **salgado** saal·*gaa*·doo *salt-cured bacon*

trança ⓕ *trang*·sa *pastry topped with coconut mixture & chopped nuts*

Transmontana, à transh·mong·*ta*·na, aa *Trás-os-Montes style – hearty dish usually flavoured with sausages & other meat, garlic & onion*

tremoços ⓜ pl tre·mo·*soosh* *salted, preserved yellow lupins eaten as a snack*

tripas ⓕ pl *tree*·pash *tripe*
— **à moda do Porto** aa *mo*·da doo *por*·too *slow-cooked dried beans, trotters, tripe, chicken, vegetables, sausages & cumin*

trouxas de ovos ⓕ pl *troh*·shash de o·*voosh* *beaten egg poached in sugar syrup*

truta ⓕ *troo*·ta *trout*
— **de escabeche** de shka·*be*·she *trout prepared escabeche, fried & with a garlic, onion & parsley dressing, served cold with boiled potatoes*

túberas com ovos ⓕ pl *too*·be·rash kong o·*voosh* *sliced mushrooms fried with onion, bay leaf & eggs*

U

uvas ⓕ pl *oo*·vash *grapes*

V

veado ⓜ vee·*aa*·doo *venison*

velhoses ⓕ pl ve·*lyo*·zesh *orange- & brandy-flavoured pumpkin fritters*

verde ⓜ&ⓕ *ver*·de *unripe (fruit)*

vinagre ⓜ vee·*naa*·gre *vinegar*

vinha d'alhos ⓕ *vee*·nya *daa*·lyoosh *meat marinated in wine or vinegar, olive oil, garlic & bay leaf*

vinho ⓜ *vee*·nyoo *wine*
— **branco** *brang*·koo *white wine*
— **da casa** da *kaa*·za *house wine*
— **da região** da rre·zhee·*owng* *local wine*
— **do Porto** doo *por*·too *port*
— **do Porto branco** doo *por*·too *brang*·koo *dry white port*
— **espumante** shpoo·*mang*·te *sparkling wine*
— **rosé** rro·*ze* *rosé wine*
— **tinto** *teeng*·too *red wine*
— **verde** *ver*·de *young wine – light sparkling red, white or rosé wine*

vitela (assada) ⓕ vee·*te*·la (a·*saa*·da) *(roast) veal*

X

xerém ⓜ she·*reng* *cornmeal porridge, served with shellfish, **chouriço**, pork or other meat*

emergencies

emergências

English	Portuguese	Pronunciation
Help!	*Socorro!*	soo·*ko*·rroo
Stop!	*Stop!*	stop
Go away!	*Vá-se embora!*	vaa·se eng·*bo*·ra
Thief!	*Ladrão!*	la·*drowng*
Fire!	*Fogo!*	*fo*·goo
Watch out!	*Cuidado!*	kwee·*daa*·doo
Call …	*Chame …*	*shaa*·me …
a doctor	*um médico*	oong *me*·dee·koo
an ambulance	*uma ambulância*	*oo*·ma ang·boo·*lang*·sya
the police	*a polícia*	a poo·*lee*·sya

It's an emergency.
É uma emergência. e *oo*·ma ee·mer·*zheng*·sya

There's been an accident.
Houve um acidente. oh·ve oong a·see·*deng*·te

Could you please help?
Pode ajudar, por favor? *po*·de a·zhoo·*daar* poor fa·*vor*

Can I use your phone?
Posso usar o seu telefone? *po*·soo oo·*zaar* oo *se*·oo te·le·*fo*·ne

signs

Esquadra da Polícia	*shkwaa*·dra da poo·*lee*·sya	Police Station
Hospital	osh·pee·*taal*	Hospital
Polícia	poo·*lee*·sya	Police
Urgências	oor·*zheng*·syash	Emergency Department

Is it safe ...?	É seguro ...?	e se·goo·roo ...
at night	à noite	aa noy·te
for gay people	para gays	pa·ra gaysh
for travellers	para turistas	pa·ra too·reesh·tash
for women	para mulheres	pa·ra moo·lye·resh
on your own	ir sozinho/	eer so·zee·nyoo/
	sozinha m/f	so·zee·nya

I'm lost.
Estou perdido/perdida. m/f shtoh per·dee·doo/per·dee·da

Where are the toilets?
Onde é a casa de banho? ong·de e a kaa·za de ba·nyoo

police

Where's the police station?
Onde é a esquadra ong·de e a shkwaa·dra
da polícia? da poo·lee·sya

I want to report an offence.
Eu quero denunciar e·oo ke·roo de·noong·see·aar
um crime. oong kree·me

It was him/her.
Foi ele/ela. foy e·le/e·la

I have insurance.
Eu estou coberto/coberta e·oo shtoh koo·ber·too/koo·ber·ta
pelo seguro. m/f pe·loo se·goo·roo

I've been ...	Eu fui ...	e·oo fwee ...
He/She has been ...	Ele/Ela foi ...	e·le/e·la foy ...
assaulted	agredido m	a·gre·dee·doo
	agredida f	a·gre·dee·da
raped	violado m	vee·oo·laa·doo
	violada f	vee·oo·laa·da
robbed	roubado m	rroh·baa·doo
	roubada f	rroh·baa·da

He/She tried	Ele/Ela	e·le/e·la
to ... me.	tentou ...	teng·toh ...
assault	agredir-me	a·gre·deer·me
rape	violar-me	vee·o·laar·me
rob	roubar-me	rroh·baar·me

My ... was/	Roubaram ...	rroh·baa·rang ...
were stolen.		
I've lost my ...	Eu perdi ...	e·oo per·dee
backpack	a minha	a meeng·nya
	mochila	moo·shee·la
bag	o meu saco	oo me·oo saa·koo
credit card	o meu cartão	oo me·oo kar·towng
	de crédito	de kre·dee·too
handbag	a minha bolsa	a mee·nya bol·sa
jewellery	as minhas	ash mee·nyash
	jóias	zhoy·ash
money	o meu	oo me·oo
	dinheiro	dee·nyay·roo
papers	os meus	oosh me·oosh
	papeís	pa·paysh
passport	o meu	oo me·oo
	passaporte	paa·sa·por·te
travellers	os meus	oosh me·oosh
cheques	travellers cheques	tra·ve·ler she·kesh
wallet	a minha carteira	a mee·nya kar·tay·ra

I (don't) understand.
Eu (não) compreendo. e·oo (nowng) kong·pree·eng·doo

I didn't realise I was doing anything wrong.
Eu não percebi que e·oo nowng per·se·bee ke
estava a fazer algo shtaa·va a fa·zer aal·goo
errado. e·rraa·doo

I didn't do it.
Eu não fiz isso. e·oo nowng feez ee·soo

I'm sorry.
Peço desculpa. pe·soo desh·kool·pa

What am I accused of?
De que sou acusado/ de ke soh a·koo·zaa·doo/
acusada? m/f a·koo·zaa·da

essentials

181

the police may say ...

É acusado/acusada de ... m/f
e a·koo·*zaa*·doo/
a·koo·*zaa*·da de ... **You're charged with ...**

Ele/Ela é acusado/acusada de ... m/f
e·le/e·la e a·koo·*zaa*·doo/
a·koo·*zaa*·da de ... **He/She is charged with ...**

agressão	a·gre·*sowng*	**assault**
distúrbio da	deesh·*toor*·byoo da	**disturbing**
ordem pública	or·*deng* poo·*blee*·ka	**the peace**
excesso de	aysh·*se*·soo de	**speeding**
velocidade	ve·loo·see·*daa*·de	
multa de	*mool*·ta de	**parking fine**
estacionamento	shta·syoo·na·*meng*·too	
não ter um	nowng ter oong	**not having**
visto legal	*veesh*·too le·*gaal*	**a visa**
pequeno furto	pe·*ke*·noo *foor*·too	**shoplifting**
posse (de	*po*·se (de	**possession**
substâncias	su·be·*shtang*·syash	**(of illegal**
ilegais)	ee·le·*gaish*)	**substances)**
roubo	*rroh*·boo	**theft**
ter visto	ter *veesh*·too	**overstaying**
expirado	aysh·pee·*raa*·doo	**a visa**

I want to contact my embassy.
Eu quero contactar com e·oo *ke*·roo kong·tak·*taar* kong
a minha embaixada. a *mee*·nya eng·bai·*shaa*·da

Can I make a phone call?
Posso fazer um *po*·soo fa·*zer* oong
telefonema? te·le·foo·*ne*·ma

Can I have a lawyer (who speaks English)?
Posso ter acesso a um *po*·soo ter a·*se*·soo a oong
advogado (que fale a·de·voo·*gaa*·doo (que *faa*·le
inglês)? eeng·*glesh*)

I have a prescription for this drug.
Eu tenho uma receita e·oo *ta*·nyoo *oo*·ma rre·*say*·ta
para esta droga. *pa*·ra *esh*·ta *dro*·ga

doctor

médico

Address male doctors and dentists as *Senhor Doutor* se·*nyor* doh·*tor* and female doctors and dentists as *Senhora Doutora* se·*nyo*·ra doh·*to*·ra.

Where's the nearest ...?	*Qual é ...* *mais perto?*	kwaal e ... maish *per*·too
dentist	*o dentista*	oo deng·*teesh*·ta
doctor	*o médico* m	oo me·dee·koo
	a médica f	a me·dee·ka
emergency department	*o serviço de urgência*	oo ser·*vee*·soo de oor·*zheng*·sya
hospital	*o hospital*	oo osh·pee·*taal*
medical centre	*o centro de saúde*	oo *seng*·troo de sa·*oo*·de
optometrist	*o oculista*	oo o·koo·*leesh*·ta
(night) pharmacist	*a farmácia* *(de serviço)*	a far·*maa*·sya (de ser·*vee*·soo)

I need a doctor (who speaks English).
Eu preciso de um médico (que fale inglês).
e·oo pre·*see*·zoo de oong me·dee·koo (que *faa*·le eeng·*glesh*)

Could I see a female doctor?
Posso ser visto/vista por uma médica? m/f
po·soo ser *veesh*·too/*veesh*·ta poor *oo*·ma me·dee·ka

Could the doctor come here?
O médico/a médica podia vir aqui? m/f
oo me·dee·koo/a me·dee·ka poo·*dee*·a veer a·*kee*

Is there an after-hours emergency number?
Há algum telefone para fora das horas de serviço?
aa aal·*goong* te·le·*fo*·ne *pa*·ra *fo*·ra dash *o*·rash de ser·*vee*·soo

I've run out of my medication.

Os meus   oosh me·oosh
medicamentos   me·dee·ka·meng·toosh
acabaram.   a·ka·baa·rowng

This is my usual medicine.

Estes são os meus   esh·tesh sowng oosh me·oosh
medicamentos   me·dee·ka·meng·toosh
habituais.   a·bee·too·aish

My son weighs (20) kilos.

O meu filho   oo me·oo fee·lyoo
pesa (vinte) quilos.   pe·za (veeng·te) kee·loosh

My daughter weighs (20) kilos.

A minha filha   a meeng·nya fee·lya
pesa (vinte) quilos.   pe·za (veeng·te) kee·loosh

What's the correct dosage?

Qual é a dose correcta?   kwaal e a do·ze koo·rre·ta

I don't want a blood transfusion.

Eu não quero uma   e·oo nowng ke·roo oo·ma
transfusão   trangsh·foo·zowng
sanguínea.   sang·gwee·nee·a

Please use a new syringe.

Por favor use uma   poor fa·vor oo·ze oo·ma
seringa nova.   se·reeng·ga no·va

I have my own syringe.

Eu tenho a minha   e·oo ta·nyoo a mee·nya
própria seringa.   pro·pree·a se·reeng·ga

I've been vaccinated against …	*Eu tenho as vacinas de …*	e·oo ta·nyoo ash va·see·nash de …
He/She has been vaccinated against …	*Ele/Ela foi vacinado/ vacinada contra …* m/f	e·le/e·la foy va·see·naa·doo/ va·see·naa·da kong·tra …
hepatitis A/B/C	*hepatite A/B/C*	e·pa·tee·te a/be/se
tetanus	*tétano*	te·ta·noo
typhoid	*febre tifóide*	fe·bre tee·foy·de

I need new ...	Eu preciso de ...	e·oo pre·see·zoo de ...
contact lenses	lentes de	leng·tesh de
	contacto novas	kong·taak·too no·vash
glasses	óculos novos	o·koo·loosh no·voosh

My prescription is ...
A minha receita é ...   a meeng·nya rre·say·ta e ...

How much will it cost?
Quanto é que vai custar?   kwang·too e ke vai koosh·taar

Can I have a receipt for my insurance?
Pode-me dar um recibo   po·de·me daar oong rre·see·boo
para a minha seguradora?   pa·ra a meeng·nya se·goo·ra·do·ra

symptoms & conditions

I'm sick.
Estou doente.   shtoh doo·eng·te

My friend is (very) sick. (male)
O meu amigo está   oo me·oo a·mee·goo shtaa
(muito) doente.   (mweeng·too) doo·eng·te

My friend is (very) sick. (female)
A minha amiga está   a meeng·nya a·mee·ga shtaa
(muito) doente.   (mweeng·too) doo·eng·te

I've been ...	Eu tenho	e·oo ta·nyoo
	estado ...	shtaa·doo ...
He/She has	Ele/Ela tem	e·le/e·la teng
been ...	estado ...	shtaa·doo ...
injured	magoado/	ma·goo·aa·doo/
	magoada m/f	ma·goo·aa·da
vomiting	a vomitar	a voo·mee·taar

the doctor may say ...

Qual é o problema?
kwaal e oo pro·*ble*·ma
What's the problem?

Onde é que dói?
ong·de e ke doy
Where does it hurt?

Tem febre?
teng *fe*·bre
Do you have a temperature?

É alérgico/alérgica a alguma coisa? m/f
e a·*ler*·zhee·koo/a·*ler*·zhee·ka
a aal·*goo*·ma koy·za
Are you allergic to anything?

Está a tomar alguma coisa?
shtaa a too·*maar*
aal·*goo*·ma koy·za
Are you on medication?

Há quanto tempo tem estes sintomas?
aa *kwang*·too *teng*·poo teng
esh·tesh seeng·to·mash
How long have you been like this?

Já teve algo semelhante?
zhaa *te*·ve aal·goo
se·me·*lyang*·te
Have you had this before?

Quanto tempo é que vai viajar?
kwaang·too *teng*·poo e ke
vai vee·a·*zhaar*
How long are you travelling for?

É sexualmente activo/activa? m/f
e sek·soo·al·*meng*·te
a·*tee*·voo/a·*tee*·va
Are you sexually active?

Alguma vez praticou sexo sem protecção?
aal·*goo*·ma vezh pra·tee·*koh*
sek·soo seng proo·te·*sowng*
Have you had unprotected sex?

Bebe?	be·be	**Do you drink?**
Fuma?	foo·ma	**Do you smoke?**
Toma drogas?	to·ma dro·gash	**Do you take drugs?**

the doctor may say ...

Vai precisar de ser internado/internada. m/f
vai pre·see·*zaar* de ser **You need to be**
eeng·ter·*naa*·doo/ **admitted to hospital.**
eeng·ter·*naa*·da

Deve tratar disso quando regressar ao seu país.
de·ve tra·*taar* dee·soo **You should have it checked**
kwang·doo rre·gre·*saar* **when you go home.**
ow se·oo pa·*eesh*

Deve regressar ao seu país para tratamento.
de·ve rre·gre·*saar* ow **You should return home**
se·oo pa·*eesh* pa·ra **for treatment.**
tra·ta·*meng*·too

É hipocondríaco/hipocondríaca. m/f
e ee·po·kong·*dree*·a·koo/ **You're a hypochondriac.**
ee·po·kong·*dree*·a·ka

I feel ...	*Eu sinto-me ...*	e·oo seeng·too·me ...
anxious	*ansioso/*	ang·see·o·zoo/
	ansiosa m/f	ang·see·o·za
better	*melhor*	me·*lyor*
depressed	*deprimido/*	de·pree·*mee*·doo/
	deprimida m/f	de·pree·*mee*·da
dizzy	*tonto/tonta* m/f	*tong*·too/*tong*·ta
hot and cold	*com suores*	kong soo·o·resh
	frios	*free*·oosh
nauseous	*enjoado/*	eng·zhoo·*aa*·doo/
	enjoada m/f	eng·zhoo·*aa*·da
shivery	*a tremer*	a tre·*mer*
strange	*estranho/*	*shtra*·nyoo/
	estranha m/f	*shtra*·nya
weak	*fraco/fraca* m/f	*fraa*·koo/*fraa*·ka
worse	*pior*	pee·*or*

health

187

I'm on medication for …
Eu estou a tomar   e·oo shtoh a too·*maar*
medicamentos para …   me·dee·ka·*meng*·toosh *pa*·ra …

I have (a/an) …
Eu tenho …   e·oo ta·nyoo …

He/She has (a/an) …
Ele/Ela tem …   e·le/e·la teng …

I've recently had (a/an) …
Recentemente   rre·seng·te·*meng*·te
eu tive …   e·oo tee·ve …

He/She has recently had (a/an) …
Recentemente ele/   rre·seng·te·*meng*·te e·le/
ela teve …   e·la te·ve …

AIDS	*SIDA* f	*see*·da
asthma	*asma* f	*ash*·ma
blister	*bolha* f	*bo*·lya
cold	*constipação* f	kong·shtee·pa·*sowng*
constipation	*prisão de ventre* f	pree·*zowng* de *veng*·tre
cough	*tosse* f	*to*·se
diabetes	*diabetes* f	dee·a·*be*·tesh
diarrhoea	*diarreia* f	dee·a·*rray*·a
fever	*febre* f	*fe*·bre
food	*intoxicação*	eeng·tok·see·ka·*sowng*
poisoning	*alimentar* f	a·lee·meng·*taar*
headache	*dor de cabeça* f	dor de ka·*be*·sa
heart	*problemas*	proo·*ble*·mash
condition	*cardíacos* m pl	kar·*dee*·a·koosh
insect bite	*mordida por*	mor·*dee*·da poor
	um insecto	oong eeng·*se*·too
nausea	*náusea* f	*now*·zee·a
pain	*dor* f	dor
sea sickness	*enjoo* m	eng·*zho*·oo
sore throat	*dores de garganta* f pl	*do*·resh de gar·*gang*·ta
stomachache	*dor de estômago* f	dor de *shto*·ma·goo
sunburn	*queimadura solar* f	kay·ma·*doo*·ra soo·*laar*
sunstroke	*insolação* f	eeng·soo·la·*sowng*

It hurts here.
Dói-me aqui.   doy·me a·*kee*

I'm dehydrated.
Estou desidratado/   shtoh de·zee·dra·*taa*·doo/
desidratada. m/f   de·zee·dra·*taa*·da

I can't sleep.
Não consigo   nowng kong·*see*·goo
dormir.   dor·*meer*

I think it's the medication I'm on.
Acho que é da   *aa*·shoo ke e da
medicação.   me·dee·ka·*sowng*

women's health

ginecologia saúde feminina

(I think) I'm pregnant.
(Eu acho que) estou   (e·oo *aa*·shoo ke) shtoh
grávida.   *graa*·vee·da

I haven't had my period for (six) weeks.
Eu já não tenho o   e·oo zha nowng *ta*·nyoo oo
período há (seis)   pe·*ree*·o·doo aa (saysh)
semanas.   se·*ma*·nash

I've noticed a lump here.
Notei um alto aqui.   no·*tay* oong *aal*·too a·*kee*

I'm on the pill.
Eu tomo a pílula.   e·oo *to*·moo a *pee*·loo·la

I need (a/the) …	*Eu preciso …*	e·oo pre·*see*·zoo …
contraception	*de*	de
	contraceptivos	kong·tra·se·*tee*·voosh
morning-after pill	*da pílula do*	da *pee*·loo·la doo
	dia seguinte	*dee*·a se·*geeng*·te
pregnancy test	*de um teste*	de oong *tesh*·te
	de gravidez	de gra·vee·*desh*

period pain	dores do	do·resh doo
	período f pl	pe·ree·o·doo
urinary tract	infecção	eeng·fe·sowng
infection	urinária f	oo·ree·naa·rya
yeast	infecção	eeng·fe·sowng
infection	vaginal f	va·zhee·naal

the doctor may say ...

Está com o período?
shtaa kong oo
pe·ree·o·doo
Are you menstruating?

Quando foi a última vez que teve o período?
kwang·doo foy a
ool·tee·ma vezh ke te·ve
oo pe·ree·oo·doo
**When did you last
have your period?**

Usa contraceptivos?
oo·za
kong·tra·se·tee·voosh
Are you using contraception?

Está grávida?
shtaa graa·vee·da
Are you pregnant?

Está grávida.
shtaa graa·vee·da
You're pregnant.

parts of the body

partes do corpo

My ... hurts. m
O meu ... está a doer-me.
oo me·oo ... shtaa a doo·er·me

My ... hurts. f
*A minha ... está a
doer-me. m*
a meeng·nya ... shtaa a
doo·er·me

I can't move my ... m
*Eu não consigo
mexer o meu ...*
e·oo nowng kong·see·goo
me·sher oo me·oo ...

I can't move my ... f
  Eu não consigo
  mexer a minha ...
  e·oo nowng kong·*see*·goo
  me·*sher* a *meeng*·nya ...

I have a cramp in my ... m
  Eu tenho uma
  cãibra no meu ...
  e·oo ta·nyoo oo·ma
  ka·*eeng*·bra noo *me*·oo ...

I have a cramp in my ... f
  Eu tenho uma
  cãibra na minha ...
  e·oo ta·nyoo oo·ma
  ka·*eeng*·bra na *meeng*·nya ...

My ... is swollen. m
  O meu ... está
  inchado.
  oo *me*·oo ... shtaa
  eeng·*shaa*·doo

My ... is swollen. f
  A minha ... está
  inchada.
  a *meeng*·nya ... shtaa
  eeng·*shaa*·da

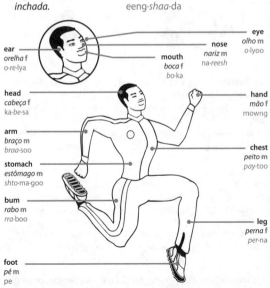

eye
olho m
o·lyoo

nose
nariz m
na·*reesh*

mouth
boca f
bo·ka

ear
orelha f
o·re·lya

head
cabeça f
ka·*be*·sa

arm
braço m
braa·soo

stomach
estômago m
shto·ma·goo

bum
rabo m
rra·boo

hand
mão f
mowng

chest
peito m
pay·too

leg
perna f
per·na

foot
pé m
pe

allergies

I'm allergic to ...
Eu sou alérgico/
alérgica a ... m/f
e·oo soh a·*ler*·zhee·koo/
a·*ler*·zhee·ka a ...

He/She is allergic to ...
Ele/Ela é alérgico/
alérgica a ... m/f
e·le/e·la e a·*ler*·zhee·koo/
a·*ler*·zhee·ka a ...

I have a skin allergy.
Eu tenho uma
alergia da pele.
e·oo *ta*·nyoo *oo*·ma
a·ler·*zhee*·a da *pe*·le

antibiotics	*antibióticos* m pl	ang·tee·bee·*o*·tee·koosh
antihistamines	*anti-*	ang·tee·
	histamínicos m pl	eesh·ta·*mee*·nee·koosh
anti-inflammatories	*anti-*	ang·tee·
	inflamatórios m pl	eeng·fla·ma·*to*·ryoosh
aspirin	*aspirina* f	ash·pee·*ree*·na
bees	*abelhas* f pl	a·*be*·lyash
codeine	*codeína* f	ko·de·*ee*·na
inhaler	*inalador* m	ee·na·la·*dor*
injection	*injecção* f	eeng·zhe·*sowng*
penicillin	*penicilina* f	pe·nee·see·*lee*·na
pollen	*pólen* m	*po*·leng
sulphur-based drugs	*medicamentos* *à base de* *enxofre* m pl	me·dee·ka·*meng*·toosh aa *baa*·ze de eng·*sho*·fre

For food-related allergies, see **special diets & allergies**, page 166.

pharmacist

I need something for (a headache).
Eu preciso de alguma e·oo pre·*see*·zoo de aal·*goo*·ma
coisa para (as dores de *koy*·za pa·ra (ash *do*·resh de
cabeça). ka·*be*·sa)

Do I need a prescription for (antihistamines)?
Necessito de uma ne·se·*see*·too de *oo*·ma
receita para (anti- rre·*say*·ta pa·ra (ang·tee·
histamínicos)? eesh·ta·*mee*·nee·koosh)

I have a prescription.
Eu tenho uma receita. e·oo ta·nyoo *oo*·ma rre·*say*·ta

How many times a day?
Quantas vezes por dia? *kwang*·tash *ve*·zesh poor *dee*·a

Will it make me drowsy?
Vou ficar sonolento/ voh fee·*kaar* soo·noo·*leng*·too/
sonolenta? m/f soo·noo·*leng*·ta

antiseptic	*antiséptico* m	ang·tee·*se*·tee·koo
contraceptives	*contraceptivos* m pl	kong·tra·se·*tee*·voosh
painkillers	*comprimidos*	kong·pree·*mee*·doosh
	para as dores m pl	*pa*·ra ash *do*·resh
rehydration	*sais*	saish
salts	*rehidratantes* m pl	rre·ee·dra·*tang*·tesh
thermometer	*termómetro* m	ter·*mo*·me·troo

---

the pharmacist may say ...

Antes/Depois de comer.
ang·tesh/de·*poysh* de koo·*mer*
Before/After food.

Já tomou isto alguma vez?
zhaa to·*moh* eesh·too
aal·*goo*·ma vezh
Have you taken this before?

Tem que levar o tratamento até ao fim.
teng ke le·*vaar* oo
tra·ta·*meng*·too a·*te* ow feeng
You must complete the course.

health

193

dentist

I have a ...   Eu tenho um ...   e·oo ta·nyoo oong ...
- **broken tooth**   *dente partido*   deng·te par·tee·doo
- **cavity**   *uma cárie*   oo·ma kaa·ree·e
- **toothache**   *uma dor de*   oo·ma dor de
      dentes   deng·tesh

I've lost a filling.
Caiu-me um chumbo.   ka·yoo·me oong shoong·boo

My dentures are broken.
A minha dentadura   a mee·nya deng·ta·doo·ra
está partida.   shtaa par·tee·da

My gums hurt.
As minhas   aash meeng·nyash
gengivas doem-me.   zheng·zhee·vash do·eng·me

I don't want it extracted.
Eu não quero   e·oo nowng ke·roo
extrair o dente.   aysh·tra·eer oo deng·te

I need a/an ...   Eu preciso de ...   e·oo pre·see·zoo de ...
- **anaesthetic**   *anestesia*   a·nesh·te·zee·a
- **filling**   *um chumbo*   oong shoong·boo

the dentist may say ...

Abra bem a boca.
aa·bra beng a bo·ka   **Open wide.**

Isto não dói nada.
eesh·too nowng doy naa·da   **This won't hurt a bit.**

Morda isto.
mor·da eesh·too   **Bite down on this.**

Bocheche.
boo·she·she   **Rinse.**

Venha cá, que eu ainda não terminei.
ve·nya ka ke e·oo a·eeng·da
nowng ter·mee·nay   **Come back,
I haven't finished.**

Portuguese nouns have their gender indicated with ⓜ (masculine) and ⓕ (feminine). Where adjectives or nouns have separate masculine and feminine forms, these are divided by a slash and marked ⓜ/ⓕ. You'll also see words marked as v (verb), n (noun), a (adjective), pl (plural), sg (singular), inf (informal) and pol (polite) where necessary. Verbs are given in the infinitive – for details on how to change verbs for use in a sentence, see the **phrasebuilder**, page 28. For food and drink terms, see the **culinary reader**.

A

aboard *a bordo* a bor·doo
abortion *aborto* ⓜ a·bor·too
about *cerca de* ser·ka de
above *por cima de* poor see·ma de
abroad *no estrangeiro* noo shtrang·zhay·roo
accident *acidente* ⓜ a·see·deng·te
accommodation *hospedagem* ⓕ osh·pe·daa·zheng
account (bill) *conta* ⓕ kong·ta
across *através* a·tra·vesh
activist *activista* ⓜ&ⓕ aa·tee·veesh·ta
actor *actor/actriz* ⓜ/ⓕ aa·tor/aa·treesh
adaptor *adaptador* ⓜ a·da·pe·ta·dor
addiction *vício* ⓜ vee·syoo
address *endereço* ⓜ eng·de·re·soo
administration *administração* ⓕ a·de·mee·neesh·tra·sowng
admission (price) *(preço da) entrada* ⓕ (pre·soo da) eng·traa·da
admit v *admitir* a·de·mee·teer
adult n&a *adulto/adulta* ⓜ/ⓕ a·dool·too/a·dool·ta
advertisement *anúncio* ⓜ a·noong·syoo
advice *conselho* ⓜ kong·se·lyoo
after *depois* de·poysh
afternoon *tarde* ⓕ taar·de
aftershave *aftershave* ⓜ af·ter·shayv
again *novamente* no·va·meng·te
age *idade* ⓕ ee·daa·de
(three days) ago *há (três dias)* aa (tresh dee·ash)
agree *concordar* kong·koor·daar

agriculture *agricultura* ⓕ a·gree·kool·too·ra
ahead *em frente* eng freng·te
AIDS *SIDA* ⓕ see·da
air *ar* ⓜ aar
air conditioning *ar condicionado* ⓜ aar kong·dee·syoo·naa·doo
airline *companhia aérea* ⓕ kong·pa·nyee·a a·e·ree·a
airmail *via aérea* ⓕ vee·a a·e·ree·a
airplane *avião* ⓜ a·vee·owng
airport *aeroporto* ⓜ a·e·ro·por·too
airport tax *taxa de aeroporto* ⓕ taa·sha de a·e·ro·por·too
aisle *coxia* ⓕ koo·shee·a
alarm clock *despertador* ⓜ desh·per·ta·dor
all *todo/toda* ⓜ/ⓕ to·doo/to·da
allergy *alergia* ⓕ a·ler·zhee·a
almost *quase* kwaa·ze
alone *sozinho/sozinha* ⓜ/ⓕ so·zee·nyoo/so·zee·nya
already *já* zhaa
also *também* tang·beng
altitude *altitude* ⓕ aal·tee·too·de
always *sempre* seng·pre
ambassador *embaixador/embaixatriz* ⓜ/ⓕ eng·bai·sha·dor/eng·bai·sha·treesh
ambulance *ambulância* ⓕ ang·boo·lang·sya
American football *futebol americano* ⓜ foo·te·bol a·me·ree·ka·noo
anaemia *anemia* ⓕ a·ne·mee·a
anarchist *anarquista* ⓜ&ⓕ a·nar·keesh·ta
ancient *antigo/antiga* ⓜ/ⓕ ang·tee·goo/ang·tee·ga
and *e* e

angry *zangado/zangada* ⓜ/ⓕ
 zang-*gaa*-doo/zang-*gaa*-da
animal *animal* ⓜ&ⓕ a-nee-*maal*
ankle *tornozelo* ⓜ toor-noo-*ze*-loo
another *um outro/uma outra* ⓜ/ⓕ
 oong oh-*troo*/oo-ma oh-tra
answer *resposta* ⓕ rresh-*posh*-ta
antibiotics *antibióticos* ⓜ pl
 ang-tee-bee-o-tee-koosh
antique *antiguidade* ⓕ
 ang-tee-gwee-*daa*-de
antiseptic *antiséptico* ⓜ ang-tee-se-tee-koo
apartment *apartamento* ⓜ
 a-par-ta-*meng*-too
appendix (body) *apêndice* ⓜ
 a-*peng*-dee-se
appointment *consulta* ⓕ kong-*sool*-ta
archaeological *arqueológico/arque-
 ológica* ⓜ/ⓕ ar-kee-oo-*lo*-zhee-koo/
 ar-kee-oo-*lo*-zhee-ka
architect *arquitecto/arquitecta* ⓜ/ⓕ
 ar-kee-*te*-too/ar-kee-*te*-ta
architecture *arquitectura* ⓕ ar-kee-te-*too*-ra
argue *discutir* deesh-koo-*teer*
arm (body) *braço* ⓜ *braa*-soo
aromatherapy *aromaterapia* ⓕ
 a-ro-ma-te-ra-*pee*-a
arrest *prender* preng-*der*
arrival *chegada* ⓕ she-*gaa*-da
arrive *chegar* she-*gaar*
art *arte* ⓕ *aar*-te
art gallery *galeria de arte* ⓕ
 ga-le-*ree*-a de *aar*-te
artist *artista* ⓜ&ⓕ ar-*teesh*-ta
ashtray *cinzeiro* ⓜ seeng-*zay*-roo
ask (a question) *perguntar* per-goong-*taar*
ask (for something) *pedir* pe-*deer*
aspirin *aspirina* ⓕ ash-pee-*ree*-na
asthma *asma* ⓕ *ash*-ma
at *à* a
athletics *atletismo* ⓜ at-le-*teesh*-moo
atmosphere *atmosfera* ⓕ at-moosh-*fe*-ra
aunt *tia* ⓕ *tee*-a
Australia *Austrália* ⓕ owsh-*traa*-lya
Australian Rules Football
 futebol australiano ⓜ
 foo-te-*bol* owsh-tra-*lya*-noo
automated teller machine (ATM) *caixa
 automático* ⓜ
 kai-sha ow-too-*maa*-tee-koo
avenue *avenida* ⓕ a-ve-*nee*-da
awful *horrível* o-*rree*-vel

196

B

B&W (film) *preto e branco*
 pre-too e *brang*-koo
baby *bebé* ⓜ&ⓕ be-*be*
baby food *comida de bebé* ⓕ
 koo-*mee*-da de be-*be*
baby powder *pó de talco* ⓜ po de *taal*-koo
babysitter *ama* ⓕ *a*-ma
back (body) *costas* ⓕ pl *kosh*-tash
back (position) *atrás* a-*traash*
backpack *mochila* ⓕ moo-*shee*-la
bad *mau/má* ⓜ/ⓕ *ma*-oo/maa
bag *saco* ⓜ *saa*-koo
baggage *bagagem* ⓕ ba-*gaa*-zheng
baggage allowance *limite de peso* ⓜ
 lee-*mee*-te de *pe*-zoo
baggage claim *balcão de bagagens* ⓜ
 bal-*kowng* de ba-*gaa*-zhengsh
bakery *padaria* ⓕ paa-da-*ree*-a
balance (account) *saldo* ⓜ *saal*-doo
balcony *varanda* ⓕ va-*rang*-da
ball (sport) *bola* ⓕ *bo*-la
band (music) *grupo* ⓜ *groo*-poo
bandage *ligadura* ⓕ lee-ga-*doo*-ra
Band-Aid *penso* ⓜ *peng*-soo
bank *banco* ⓜ *bang*-koo
bank account *conta bancária* ⓕ
 kong-ta bang-*kaa*-rya
banknote *nota bancária* ⓕ
 no-ta bang-*kaa*-rya
baptism *baptismo* ⓜ ba-*teezh*-moo
bar *bar* ⓜ baar
barber *barbeiro* ⓜ bar-*bay*-roo
bar work *trabalho num bar* ⓜ
 tra-*baa*-lyoo noong baar
baseball *basebol* ⓜ *bay*-ze-bal
basket *cesto* ⓕ *sesh*-too
basketball *basquetebol* ⓜ bash-ke-te-*bol*
bath *banho* ⓜ *ba*-nyoo
bathroom *casa de banho* ⓕ
 kaa-za de *ba*-nyoo
battery *pilha* ⓕ *pee*-lya
be (ongoing) *ser* ser
be (temporary) *estar* shtaar
beach *praia* ⓕ *prai*-a
beach volleyball *vóleibol de praia* ⓜ
 vo-lay-bol de *prai*-a
beautiful *bonito/bonita* ⓜ/ⓕ
 boo-*nee*-too/boo-*nee*-ta

beauty salon *salão de beleza* ⓜ
sa·*lowng* de be·*le*·za
bed *cama* ⓕ *ka*·ma
bedding *lençóis e mantas* ⓕ pl
leng·*soysh* ee *mang*·tash
bedroom *quarto* ⓜ *kwaar*·too
bee *abelha* ⓕ a·*be*·lya
beer *cerveja* ⓕ ser·*ve*·zha
beer house *cervejaria* ⓕ ser·ve·zha·*ree*·a
before *antes* ang·tesh
beggar *pedinte* ⓜ&ⓕ pe·*deeng*·te
behind *atrás* a·*traash*
below *abaixo* a·*bai*·shoo
beside *ao lado de* ow *laa*·doo de
best *o/a melhor* ⓜ/ⓕ oo/a me·*lyor*
bet *aposta* ⓕ a·*posh*·ta
better *melhor* me·*lyor*
between *entre* *eng*·tre
bicycle *bicicleta* ⓕ bee·see·*kle*·ta
big *grande* *grang*·de
bigger *maior* may·or
bike *bicicleta* ⓕ bee·see·*kle*·ta
biggest *o/a maior* ⓜ/ⓕ oo/a may·or
bike chain *corrente de bicicleta* ⓕ
koo·*rreng*·te de bee·see·*kle*·ta
bike lock *cadeado de bicicleta* ⓜ
ka·dee·*aa*·doo de bee·see·*kle*·ta
bike path *caminho de bicicleta* ⓜ
ka·*mee*·nyoo de bee·see·*kle*·ta
bike shop *loja de ciclismo* ⓕ
lo·zha de see·*kleesh*·moo
bill (restaurant) *conta* ⓕ *kong*·ta
binoculars *binóculos* ⓜ pl
bee·*no*·koo·loosh
bird *pássaro* ⓜ *paa*·sa·roo
birth certificate *certidão de nascimento* ⓕ
ser·tee·*downg* de nash·see·*meng*·too
birthday *aniversário* ⓜ a·nee·ver·*saa*·ryoo
bite (dog) *mordedura* ⓕ moor·de·*doo*·ra
bite (insect) *mordida (por um insecto)* ⓕ
mor·*dee*·da (poor oong eeng·*se*·too)
bitter *amargo/amarga* ⓜ/ⓕ
a·*maar*·goo/a·*maar*·ga
black *preto/preta* ⓜ/ⓕ *pre*·too/*pre*·ta
bladder *bexiga* ⓕ be·*shee*·ga
blanket *cobertor* ⓜ koo·ber·*tor*
blind *cego/cega* ⓜ/ⓕ *se*·goo/*se*·ga
blister *bolha* ⓕ *bo*·lya
blocked *bloqueado/bloqueada* ⓜ/ⓕ
blo·kee·*aa*·doo/blo·kee·*aa*·da
blood *sangue* ⓜ *sang*·ge

blood pressure *tensão arterial* ⓕ
teng·*sowng* ar·te·ree·*aal*
blood test *análise de sangue* ⓕ
a·*naa*·lee·ze de *sang*·ge
blood type *grupo sanguíneo* ⓜ
groo·poo sang·*gwee*·nee·oo
blue *azul* a·*zool*
board *subir a bordo* soo·*beer* a *bor*·doo
boarding house *pensão* ⓕ peng·*sowng*
boarding pass *cartão de embarque* ⓜ
kar·*towng* de eng·*baar*·ke
boat *barco* ⓜ *baar*·koo
body *corpo* ⓜ *kor*·poo
bone *osso* ⓜ *o*·soo
book *livro* ⓜ *lee*·vroo
book (reserve) *reservar* rre·zer·*vaar*
booked out *esgotado/esgotada* ⓜ/ⓕ
shgoo·*taa*·doo/shgoo·*taa*·da
bookshop *livraria* ⓕ lee·vra·*ree*·a
boots *botas* ⓕ *bo*·tash
border (country) *fronteira* ⓕ frong·*tay*·ra
bored *aborrecido/aborrecida* ⓜ/ⓕ
a·boo·rre·*see*·doo/a·boo·rre·*see*·da
boring *chato/chata* ⓜ/ⓕ *shaa*·too/*shaa*·ta
borrow *pedir emprestado* pe·*deer*
eng·presh·*taa*·doo
botanic garden *jardim botânico* ⓜ
zhar·*deeng* boo·*ta*·nee·koo
both *ambos/ambas* ⓜ/ⓕ
ang·boosh/*ang*·bash
bottle *garrafa* ⓕ ga·*rraa*·fa
bottle opener *saca-rolhas* ⓜ
saa·ka·*rro*·lyash
bottle shop *loja de bebidas* ⓕ
lo·zha de be·*bee*·dash
bottom (body) *nádegas* ⓕ pl *naa*·de·gash
bottom (position) *fundo* ⓕ *foong*·doo
bowl *tigela* ⓕ tee·*zhe*·la
box *caixa* ⓕ *kai*·sha
boxing *boxe* ⓜ *bok*·se
boy *menino* ⓜ me·*nee*·noo
boyfriend *namorado* ⓜ na·moo·*raa*·doo
bra *soutien* ⓜ soo·tee·*eng*
brake (car) *travão* ⓜ tra·*vowng*
brave *corajoso/corajosa* ⓜ/ⓕ
koo·ra·*zho*·zoo/koo·ra·*zho*·za
bread *pão* ⓜ powng
break *quebrar* ke·*braar*
break down (car, etc) *avariar* a·va·ree·*aar*
breakfast *pequeno almoço* ⓜ
pe·*ke*·noo aal·*mo*·soo
breast *peito* ⓜ sg *pay*·too

breasts *seios* ⓜ *say*-oosh
breathe *respirar* rresh-pee-*raar*
bribe *suborno* ⓜ soo-*bor*-noo
bridge (structure) *ponte* ⓕ *pong*-te
briefcase *pasta* ⓕ *pash*-ta
bring *trazer* tra-*zer*
brochure *brochura* ⓕ broo-*shoo*-ra
broken *quebrado/quebrada* ⓜ/ⓕ
  ke-*braa*-doo/ke-*braa*-da
broken down (car, etc) *avariado/avariada*
  ⓜ/ⓕ a-va-ree-*aa*-doo/a-va-ree-*aa*-da
bronchitis *bronquite* ⓕ brong-*kee*-te
brother *irmão* ⓜ eer-*mowng*
brown *castanho/castanha* ⓜ/ⓕ
  kash-*ta*-nyoo/kash-*ta*-nya
bruise *nódoa negra* ⓕ *no*-doo-a ne-gra
brush *escova* ⓕ *shko*-va
bucket *balde* ⓜ *baal*-de
Buddhist n&a *budista* ⓜ&ⓕ boo-*deesh*-ta
budget *orçamento* ⓜ or-sa-*meng*-too
buffet *bufete* ⓜ boo-*fe*-te
bug *bicho* ⓜ *bee*-shoo
build *construir* kong-shtroo-*eer*
builder *construtor* ⓜ kong-shtroo-*tor*
building *prédio* ⓜ *pre*-dyoo
bull *touro* ⓜ *toh*-roo
bullfight *tourada* ⓕ toh-*raa*-da
bullfighter *cavaleiro* ⓜ ka-va-*lay*-roo
bullring *praça de touros* ⓕ
  praa-sa de *toh*-roosh
bumbag *bolsa de trás* ⓕ *bol*-sa de traash
burn *queimadura* ⓕ kay-ma-*doo*-ra
bus (city/intercity) *autocarro* ⓜ
  ow-to-*kaa*-roo
business *negócios* ⓜ pl ne-*go*-syoosh
business class *classe executiva* ⓕ
  klaa-se ee-zhe-koo-*te*-e-va
businessperson
  homem/mulher de negócios ⓜ/ⓕ
  o-meng/*moo*-lyer de ne-*go*-syoosh
business trip *viagem de negócios* ⓕ
  vee-*aa*-zheng de ne-*go*-syoosh
busker *artista de rua* ⓜ&ⓕ
  ar-*teesh*-ta de *rroo*-a
bus station/stop *paragem de autocarros* ⓕ
  pa-*raa*-zheng de ow-to-*kaa*-rroosh
busy *ocupado/ocupada* ⓜ/ⓕ
  o-koo-*paa*-doo/o-koo-*paa*-da
but *mas* mash
button *botão* ⓜ boo-*towng*
buy *comprar* kong-*praar*

C

café *café* ⓜ ka-*fe*
cake shop *pastelaria* ⓕ pash-te-la-*ree*-a
calculator *calculadora* ⓕ kaal-koo-la-*do*-ra
calendar *calendário* ⓜ ka-leng-*daa*-ryoo
call (telephone) *telefonar* te-le-foo-*naar*
camera *máquina fotográfica* ⓕ
  maa-kee-na foo-too-*graa*-fee-ka
camera shop *loja de
  equipamentos fotográficos* ⓕ
  lo-zha de e-kee-pa-*meng*-toosh
  foo-too-*graa*-fee-koosh
camp *acampar* a-kang-*paar*
camping ground *acampamento* ⓜ
  a-kang-pa-*meng*-too
camping store *loja de campismo* ⓕ
  lo-zha de kang-*peezh*-moo
camp site *parque de campismo* ⓜ
  paar-ke de kang-*peezh*-moo
can (tin) *lata* ⓕ *laa*-ta
can *poder* poo-*der*
Canada *Canadá* ⓜ ka-na-*daa*
cancel *cancelar* kang-se-*laar*
cancer *cancro* ⓜ *kang*-kroo
candle *vela* ⓕ *ve*-la
can opener *abre latas* ⓜ *aa*-bre *laa*-tash
car *carro* ⓜ *kaa*-rroo
caravan *caravana* ⓕ ka-ra-*va*-na
cards (playing) *cartas* ⓕ pl *kaar*-tash
care (for someone) *gostar* goosh-*taar*
car hire *aluguer de automóvel* ⓜ
  a-loo-*ger* de ow-too-mo-vel
car owner's title *título de registo
  do automóvel* ⓜ *tee*-too-loo de
  rre-*zheesh*-too doo ow-too-mo-vel
car park *parque de estacionamento* ⓜ
  paar-ke de shta-syoo-na-*meng*-too
car registration *registo automóvel* ⓜ
  rre-*zheesh*-too ow-too-mo-vel
carry *carregar* ka-rre-*gaar*
carton *caixa de papelão* ⓕ
  kai-sha de pa-pe-*lowng*
cash *dinheiro* ⓜ dee-*nyay*-roo
cash (a cheque) *levantar (um cheque)*
  le-vang-*taar* (oong *she*-ke)
cash register *caixa registadora* ⓕ
  kai-sha rre-zheesh-ta-*do*-ra
casino *casino* ⓜ ka-*zee*-noo
cassette *cassete* ⓕ *kaa*-se-te
castle *castelo* ⓜ kash-*te*-loo

casual work *trabalho temporário* ⓜ
tra-*baa*-lyoo teng-*poo*-*raa*-ryoo

cat *gato/gata* ⓜ/ⓕ *gaa*-too/*gaa*-ta

cathedral *catedral* ⓕ ka-te-*draal*

Catholic n&a *católico/católica* ⓜ/ⓕ
ka-*to*-lee-koo/ka-*to*-lee-ka

cave *caverna* ⓕ ka-*ver*-na

CD ⓜ CD se-*de*

celebration *comemoração* ⓕ
koo-me-moo-ra-*sowng*

cell phone *telemóvel* ⓜ te-le-*mo*-vel

cemetery *cemitério* ⓜ se-mee-*te*-ryoo

cent *cêntimo* ⓜ *seng*-tee-moo

centimetre *centímetro* ⓜ seng-*tee*-me-troo

centre *centro* ⓜ *seng*-troo

certificate *certificado* ⓜ
ser-tee-fee-*kaa*-doo

chain (bike) *corrente* ⓕ koo-*rreng*-te

chair *cadeira* ⓕ ka-*day*-ra

chairlift (skiing) *teleférico* ⓜ
te-le-*fe*-ree-koo

championships *campeonatos* ⓜ pl
kang-pe-oo-*naa*-toosh

chance *oportunidade* ⓕ
o-poor-too-nee-*daa*-de

change *mudança* ⓕ moo-*dang*-sa

change (coins) *troco* ⓜ *tro*-koo

change (money) *trocar* troo-*kaar*

changing room *sala de provas* ⓕ
saa-la de *pro*-vash

charming *charmoso/charmosa* ⓜ/ⓕ
shar-*mo*-zoo/shar-*mo*-za

chat up *dar conversa* dar kong-*ver*-sa

cheap *barato/barata* ba-*raa*-too/ba-*raa*-ta

cheat *enganar* eng-ga-*naar*

check *verificar* ve-ree-fee-*kaar*

check (banking) *cheque* ⓜ *she*-ke

check (bill) *conta* ⓕ *kong*-ta

check-in (desk) *check-in* ⓜ shek-*eeng*

checkpoint *ponto de controle* ⓜ
pong-too de kong-*tro*-le

chef *cozinheiro/cozinheira chefe* ⓜ/ⓕ
koo-zee-*nyay*-roo/koo-zee-*nyay*-ra *she*-fe

cheque (banking) *cheque* ⓜ *she*-ke

chess *xadrez* ⓜ sha-*dresh*

chess board *tabuleiro de xadrez* ⓜ
ta-boo-*lay*-roo de sha-*dresh*

chest (body) *peito* ⓜ *pay*-too

chewing gum *pastilha elástica* ⓕ
pash-*tee*-lya e-*laash*-tee-ka

chicken *galinha* ⓕ ga-*lee*-nya

chicken pox *bechigas* ⓕ pl be-*shee*-gash

child *criança* ⓜ&ⓕ kree-*ang*-sa

childminding (service) *ama* ⓕ *a*-ma

child seat *cadeira de criança* ⓕ
ka-*day*-ra de kree-*ang*-sa

children *crianças* ⓜ&ⓕ pl kree-*ang*-sash

chiropractor *quiroprático/quiroprática*
ⓜ/ⓕ kee-roo-*praa*-tee-koo/
kee-roo-*praa*-tee-ka

chocolate *chocolate* ⓜ shoo-koo-*laa*-te

choose *escolher* shkoo-*lyer*

Christian n&a *Cristão/Cristã* ⓜ/ⓕ
kreesh-*towng*/kreesh-*tang*

Christian name *primeiro nome* ⓜ
pree-*may*-roo no-me

Christmas *Natal* ⓜ na-*taal*

Christmas Day *Dia de Natal* ⓜ
dee-a de na-*taal*

Christmas Eve *Noite de Natal* ⓕ
noy-te de na-*taal*

church *igreja* ⓕ ee-*gre*-zha

cigar *charuto* ⓜ sha-*roo*-too

cigarette *cigarro* ⓜ see-*gaa*-rroo

cigarette lighter *isqueiro* ⓜ eesh-*kay*-roo

cinema *cinema* ⓜ see-*ne*-ma

circus *circo* ⓜ *seer*-koo

city *cidade* ⓕ see-*daa*-de

city centre *centro da cidade* ⓜ
seng-troo da see-*daa*-de

civil rights *direitos civis* ⓜ pl
dee-*ray*-toosh see-*veesh*

class (category) *classe* ⓕ *klaa*-se

class system *sistema de classes* ⓜ
seesh-*te*-ma de *klaa*-sesh

clean *limpo/limpa* ⓜ/ⓕ
leeng-poo/*leeng*-pa

clean *limpar* leeng-*paar*

cleaning *limpeza* ⓕ leeng-*pe*-za

client *cliente* ⓜ&ⓕ klee-*eng*-te

cliff *penhasco* ⓜ pe-*nyaash*-koo

climb *subir* soo-*beer*

cloakroom *bengaleiro* ⓜ beng-ga-*lay*-roo

clock *relógio* ⓜ rre-*lo*-zhyoo

close *perto* per-*too*

close *fechar* fe-*shaar*

closed *fechado/fechada* ⓜ/ⓕ
fe-*shaa*-doo/fe-*shaa*-da

clothesline *estendal da roupa* ⓕ
shteng-*daal* da *rroh*-pa

clothing *roupas* ⓕ pl *rroh*-pash

clothing store *loja de roupas* ⓕ
lo-zha de *rroh*-pash

cloud *nuvem* ⓕ noo-*veng*

cloudy *nublado/nublada* ⓜ/ⓕ
noo·*blaa*·doo/noo·*blaa*·da
clutch (car) *embraiagem* ⓕ
eng·brai·*aa*·zheng
coach (bus) *autocarro* ⓜ ow·to·*kaa*·rroo
coach (trainer) *treinador/treinadora* ⓜ/ⓕ
tray·na·*dor*/tray·na·*do*·ra
coat *casaco* ⓜ ka·*zaa*·koo
cockroach *barata* ⓕ ba·*raa*·ta
coffee *café* ⓜ ka·*fe*
coins *moedas* ⓕ pl moo·*e*·dash
cold *frio/fria* ⓜ/ⓕ *free*·oo/*free*·a
cold (illness) *constipação* ⓕ
kong·shtee·pa·*sowng*
colleague *colega* ⓜ&ⓕ koo·*le*·ga
collect call *ligação a cobrar* ⓕ
lee·ga·*sowng* a koo·*braar*
college *universidade* ⓕ
oo·nee·ver·see·*daa*·de
colour *cor* ⓕ kor
comb *pente* ⓜ *peng*·te
come *vir* veer
comedy *comédia* ⓕ koo·*me*·dya
comfortable *confortável* kong·for·*taa*·vel
commission *comissão* ⓕ koo·mee·*sowng*
communion *comunhão* ⓕ
koo·moo·*nyowng*
communist n&a *comunista* ⓜ&ⓕ
koo·moo·*neesh*·ta
companion *companheiro/companheira*
ⓜ/ⓕ kong·pa·*nyay*·roo/kong·pa·*nyay*·ra
company (firm) *empresa* ⓕ eng·*pre*·za
compass *bússola* ⓕ *boo*·soo·la
complain *reclamar* rre·kla·*maar*
complaint *reclamação* ⓕ rre·kla·ma·*sowng*
complimentary (free) *grátis* *graa*·teesh
computer *computador* ⓜ kong·poo·ta·*dor*
computer game *jogo de computador* ⓜ
zho·goo de kong·poo·ta·*dor*
concert *concerto* ⓜ kong·*ser*·too
concussion *abalo cerebral* ⓜ
a·*baa*·loo se·re·*braal*
conditioner (hair) *amaciador* ⓜ
a·ma·see·a·*dor*
condom *preservativo* ⓜ pre·zer·va·*tee*·voo
conference (big) *conferência* ⓕ
kong·fe·*reng*·sya
conference (small) *colóquio* ⓜ koo·*lo*·kyoo
confession *confissão* ⓕ kong·fee·*sowng*
confirm (a booking) *confirmar*
kong·feer·*maar*

congratulations *parabéns* ⓜ pl
pa·ra·*bengzh*
conjunctivitis *conjuntivite* ⓕ
kong·zhoong·tee·*vee*·te
connection *ligação* ⓕ lee·ga·*sowng*
constipation *prisão de ventre* ⓕ
pree·*zowng* de *ven*·tre
consulate *consulado* ⓜ kong·soo·*laa*·doo
contact lenses *lentes de contacto* ⓜ pl
leng·tesh de kong·*taak*·too
contact lens solution *líquido para lentes de
contacto* ⓜ *lee*·kee·doo *pa*·ra *leng*·tesh
de kong·*taak*·too
contraceptives *contraceptivo* ⓜ
kong·tra·se·*tee*·voo
contract *contrato* ⓜ kong·*traa*·too
convenience store *loja de conveniência* ⓕ
lo·zha de kong·ve·*nyeng*·sya
cook *cozinheiro/cozinheira* ⓜ/ⓕ
koo·zee·*nyay*·roo/koo·zee·*nyay*·ra
cook *cozinhar* koo·zee·*nyaar*
cooking *cozinha* ⓕ koo·*zee*·nya
cool (cold) *fresco/fresca* ⓜ/ⓕ
fresh·koo/*fresh*·ka
cool (exciting) *fixe* ⓜ&ⓕ *fee*·she
corkscrew *saca-rolhas* ⓜ *saca*·ka·*rro*·lyash
corner *esquina* ⓕ *shkee*·na
corrupt *corrupto/corrupta* ⓜ/ⓕ
koo·*rroop*·too/koo·*rroop*·ta
cost *custar* koosh·*taar*
cotton *algodão* ⓜ aal·goo·*downg*
cotton balls *bolas de algodão* ⓕ pl
bo·lash de aal·goo·*downg*
cotton buds *cotonete* ⓜ ko·to·*ne*·te
cough *tossir* too·*seer*
cough medicine *xarope* ⓜ sha·*ro*·pe
count *contar* kong·*taar*
counter (at bar) *balcão* ⓜ baal·*kowng*
country *país* ⓜ pa·*eesh*
countryside *interior do país* ⓜ
eeng·te·ree·*or* doo pa·*eesh*
coupon *cupão* ⓜ koo·*powng*
court (legal) *tribunal* ⓜ tree·boo·*naal*
court (sport) *campo* ⓜ *kang*·poo
cover charge *consumo obrigatório* ⓜ
kon·soo·moo o·bree·ga·to·ree·oo
cow *vaca* ⓕ *vaa*·ka
crafts *artesanato* ⓜ ar·te·za·*naa*·too
crash (car) *acidente* ⓜ a·see·*deng*·te
crazy *louco/louca* ⓜ/ⓕ *loh*·koo/*loh*·ka
cream (food/lotion) *creme* ⓜ *kre*·me

crèche *infantário* ⓜ eeng·fang·*taa*·ree·oo
credit *crédito* ⓜ *kre*·dee·too
credit card *cartão de crédito* ⓜ
 kar·*towng* de *kre*·dee·too
cricket (sport) *críquet* ⓜ *kree*·ke·te
cross (religious) *cruz* ⓕ kroosh
crowded *cheio/cheia* ⓜ/ⓕ *shay*·oo/*shay*·a
cup *chávena* ⓕ *shaa*·ve·na
cupboard *armário* ⓜ ar·*maa*·ryoo
currency exchange *câmbio* ⓜ *kang*·byoo
current (electricity) *corrente* ⓕ
 koo·*rreng*·te
current affairs *assuntos do dia* ⓜ pl
 a·*soong*·toosh doo *dee*·a
custom *costume* ⓜ koosh·*too*·me
customs *alfândega* ⓕ aal·*fang*·de·ga
cut *cortar* koor·*taar*
cutlery *talheres* ⓜ pl ta·*lye*·resh
CV *CV* ⓜ se·*ve*
cycle *andar de bicicleta*
 ang·*daar* de bee·see·*kle*·ta
cycling *ciclismo* ⓜ see·*kleesh*·moo
cyclist *ciclista* ⓜ&ⓕ see·*kleesh*·ta
cystitis *cistite* ⓕ seesh·*tee*·te

D

daily *diário/diária* ⓜ/ⓕ
 dee·*aa*·ryoo/dee·*aa*·rya
dance *dançar* dang·*saar*
dancing *dança* ⓕ *dang*·sa
dangerous *perigoso/perigosa* ⓜ/ⓕ
 pe·ree·go·*zoo*/pe·ree·go·*za*
dark (colour/night) *escuro/escura* ⓜ/ⓕ
 shkoo·*roo*/shkoo·*ra*
date (appointment) *encontro* ⓜ
 eng·*kong*·troo
date (day) *data* ⓕ *daa*·ta
date (a person) *namorar* na·moo·*raar*
date of birth *data de nascimento* ⓕ
 daa·ta de nash·see·*meng*·too
daughter *filha* ⓕ *fee*·lya
dawn *madrugada* ⓕ ma·droo·*gaa*·da
day *dia* ⓜ *dee*·a
day after tomorrow *depois de amanhã*
 de·*poysh* de aa·ma·*nyang*
day before yesterday *anteontem*
 ang·tee·*ong*·teng
dead *morto/morta* ⓜ/ⓕ *mor*·too/*mor*·ta
deaf *surdo/surda* ⓜ/ⓕ *soor*·doo/*soor*·da
decide *decidir* de·see·*deer*

deep *profundo/profunda* ⓜ/ⓕ
 proo·*foong*·doo/proo·*foong*·da
deforestation *desflorestação* ⓕ
 desh·floo·resh·ta·*sowng*
degrees (temperature) *graus* ⓜ pl growsh
delay *atraso* ⓜ a·*traa*·zoo
delicatessen *charcutaria* ⓕ
 shar·koo·ta·*ree*·a
deliver *entregar* eng·tre·*gaar*
democracy *democracia* ⓕ
 de·moo·kra·*see*·a
demonstration (protest) *manifestação* ⓕ
 ma·nee·fesh·ta·*sowng*
dental dam *protector de borracha* ⓜ
 proo·*te*·tor de boo·*rraa*·sha
dental floss *fio dental* ⓕ *fee*·oo deng·*taal*
dentist *dentista* ⓜ&ⓕ deng·*teesh*·ta
deodorant *desodorizante* ⓜ
 de·zo·doo·ree·*zang*·te
depart *partir* par·*teer*
departure *partida* ⓕ par·*tee*·da
departure gate *porta de partida* ⓕ
 por·ta de par·*tee*·da
deposit (bank) *depósito* ⓜ de·po·zee·too
desert *deserto* ⓜ de·*zer*·too
design *design* ⓜ dee·*zain*
dessert *sobremesa* ⓕ soo·bre·*me*·za
destination *destino* ⓜ desh·*tee*·noo
details *detalhes* ⓜ pl de·*taa*·lyesh
diabetes *diabetes* ⓕ dee·a·*be*·tesh
dial tone *sinal da linha telefónica* ⓕ
 see·*naal* da *lee*·nya te·le·*fo*·nee·ka
diaper *fralda* ⓕ *fraal*·da
diaphragm *diafragma* ⓜ dee·a·*fraa*·ge·ma
diarrhoea *diarreia* ⓕ dee·a·*rray*·a
diary *diário* ⓜ dee·*aa*·ryoo
dice *dados* ⓜ pl *daa*·doosh
dictionary *dicionário* ⓜ dee·syoo·*naa*·ryoo
die *morrer* moo·*rrer*
diet *dieta* ⓕ dee·*e*·ta
different *diferente* dee·fe·*reng*·te
difficult *difícil* dee·*fee*·seel
digital *digital* dee·zhee·*taal*
dining car *vagão restaurante* ⓜ
 va·*gowng* rresh·tow·*rang*·te
dinner *jantar* ⓜ zhang·*taar*
direct *directo/directa* ⓜ/ⓕ
 dee·*re*·too/dee·*re*·ta
direct-dial *ligação directa* ⓕ
 lee·ga·*sowng* dee·*re*·ta
direction *direcção* ⓕ dee·re·*sowng*

director *director/directora* ⓜ/ⓕ
dee-re-tor/dee-re-to-ra

dirty *sujo/suja* ⓜ/ⓕ soo-zhoo/soo-zha

disabled *deficiente* de-fee-see-*eng*-te

disco *disco* ⓜ *deesh*-koo

discount *desconto* ⓜ desh-*kong*-too

discrimination *discriminação* ⓕ
deesh-kree-mee-na-*sowng*

disease *doença* ⓕ doo-*eng*-sa

dish *prato* ⓜ *praa*-too

diving *mergulho* ⓜ mer-*goo*-lyoo

diving equipment *equipamento de
mergulho* ⓜ e-ke-pa-*meng*-too de
mer-*goo*-lyoo

divorced *divorciado/divorciada* ⓜ/ⓕ
dee-vor-see-*aa*-doo/dee-vor-see-*aa*-da

dizzy *tonto/tonta* ⓜ/ⓕ *tong*-too/*tong*-ta

do *fazer* fa-*zer*

doctor *médico/médica* ⓜ/ⓕ
me-dee-koo/*me*-dee-ka

documentary *documentário* ⓜ
doo-koo-meng-*taa*-ryoo

dog *cão* ⓜ kowng

dole (welfare) *assistência social* ⓕ
a-seesh-*teng*-sya soo-see-*aal*

doll *boneco/boneca* ⓜ/ⓕ
boo-ne-koo/boo-ne-ka

double *duplo/dupla* ⓜ/ⓕ
doo-ploo/*doo*-pla

double bed *cama de casal* ⓕ
ka-ma de ka-*zaal*

double room *quarto de casal* ⓜ
kwaar-too de ka-*zaal*

down *baixo* bai-shoo

downhill *para baixo* pa-ra bai-shoo

drama *drama* ⓜ *dra*-ma

dream *sonho* ⓜ so-nyoo

dress *vestido* ⓜ vesh-*tee*-doo

dried *seco/seca* ⓜ/ⓕ *se*-koo/*se*-ka

drink *bebida* ⓕ be-*bee*-da

drink (alcoholic) *bebida alcoólica* ⓕ
be-*bee*-da aal-koo-o-lee-ka

drink *beber* be-*ber*

drive *conduzir* kong-doo-*zeer*

drivers licence *carta de condução* ⓕ
kaar-ta de kong-doo-*sowng*

drug *droga* ⓕ *dro*-ga

drug addiction *vício da droga* ⓜ
vee-syoo da *dro*-ga

drug dealer *traficante de drogas* ⓜ&ⓕ
tra-fee-*kang*-te de *dro*-gash

drug trafficking *tráfico de drogas* ⓜ
traa-fee-koo de *dro*-gash

drug user *toxicodependente* ⓜ&ⓕ
tok-*see*-ko-de-peng-*deng*-te

drunk *bêbado/bêbada* ⓜ/ⓕ
be-ba-doo/be-ba-da

dry *seco/seca* ⓜ/ⓕ *se*-koo/*se*-ka

dry *secar* se-*kaar*

dummy (pacifier) *chupeta* ⓕ shoo-pe-ta

E

each *cada* ka-da

ear *orelha* ⓕ o-re-lya

early *cedo* se-doo

earn *ganhar* ga-*nyaar*

earplugs *tampões para os ouvidos* ⓜ pl
tang-*poyngsh* pa-ra oosh oh-vee-doosh

earrings *brincos* ⓜ pl *breeng*-koosh

Earth *Terra* ⓕ *te*-rra

earthquake *terramoto* ⓜ te-rra-*mo*-too

Easter *Páscoa* ⓕ *paash*-kwa

easy *fácil* *faa*-seel

eat *comer* koo-*mer*

economy class *classe económica* ⓕ
klaa-se ee-koo-no-mee-ka

eczema *eczema* ⓜ e-ke-*ze*-ma

education *educação* ⓕ e-doo-ka-*sowng*

election *eleição* ⓕ e-lay-*sowng*

electrical store *loja de aparelhos
eléctricos* ⓕ *lo*-zha de a-pa-re-lyoosh
ee-*le*-tree-koosh

electricity *electricidade* ⓕ
ee-le-tree-see-*daa*-de

elevator *elevador* ⓜ ee-le-va-*dor*

email *email* ⓜ ee-*mayl*

embarrassed *envergonhado/enver-
gonhada* ⓜ/ⓕ en-ver-goo-*nyaa*-doo/
en-ver-goo-*nyaa*-da

embassy *embaixada* ⓕ eng-bai-*shaa*-da

emergency *emergência* ⓕ
ee-mer-*zheng*-sya

emotional *sensível* seng-*see*-vel

employee *empregado/empregada* ⓜ/ⓕ
eng-pre-*gaa*-doo/eng-pre-*gaa*-da

employer *patrão/patroa* ⓜ/ⓕ
pa-*trowng*/pa-*tro*-a

empty *vazio/vazia* ⓜ/ⓕ va-*zee*-oo/va-*zee*-a

end *fim* ⓜ feeng

engaged (phone) *ocupado* ⓜ
o-koo-*paa*-doo

engaged (to marry) *comprometido/comprometida* ⓜ/ⓕ kong·proo·me·tee·doo/kong·proo·me·tee·da

engagement (to marry) *noivado* ⓜ noy·vaa·doo

engine *motor* ⓜ moo·tor

engineering *engenharia* ⓕ eng·zhe·nya·ree·a

England *Inglaterra* ⓕ eeng·gla·te·rra

English (language) *inglês* ⓜ eeng·glesh

enjoy (oneself) *divertir-se* dee·ver·teer·se

enough *suficiente* soo·fee·see·eng·te

enter *entrar* eng·traar

entertainment guide *guia de espectáculos* ⓜ gee·a de shpe·taa·koo·loosh

entry *entrada* ⓕ eng·traa·da

envelope *envelope* ⓜ eng·ve·lo·pe

environment *ambiente* ⓜ ang·bee·eng·te

epilepsy *epilepsia* ⓕ e·pee·le·pe·see·a

equality *igualdade* ⓕ ee·gwal·daa·de

equal opportunity *igualdade de oportunidades* ⓕ ee·gwal·daa·de de o·poor·too·nee·daa·desh

equipment *equipamento* ⓜ e·kee·pa·meng·too

escalator *escada rolante* ⓕ shkaa·da rroo·lang·te

estate agency *agência de imobiliário* ⓕ a·zheng·sya de ee·mo·bee·lyaa·ryoo

euro *euro* ⓜ e·oo·roo

evening *da noite* ⓜ da noy·te

every *todo/toda* ⓜ/ⓕ to·doo/to·da

everyone *todos/todas* ⓜ/ⓕ to·doosh/to·dash

everything *tudo* ⓜ too·doo

exactly *exactamente* e·za·ta·meng·te

example *exemplo* ⓜ e·zeng·ploo

excellent *excelente* ay·she·leng·te

exchange *câmbio* ⓜ kang·byoo

exchange *trocar* troo·kaar

exchange rate *taxa de câmbio* ⓕ taa·sha de kang·byoo

excluded *excluído/excluída* ⓜ/ⓕ aysh·kloo·ee·doo/aysh·kloo·ee·da

exhaust (car) *exaustor* ⓜ ee·zowsh·tor

exhibition *exposição* ⓕ shpoo·zee·sowng

exit *saída* ⓕ saa·ee·da

expensive *caro/cara* ⓜ/ⓕ kaa·roo/kaa·ra

experience *experiência* ⓕ shpe·ree·eng·sya

exploitation *exploração* ⓕ shplo·ra·sowng

express *expresso/expressa* ⓜ/ⓕ shpre·soo/shpre·sa

express mail *correio azul* ⓜ koo·rray·oo a·zool

extension (visa) *extensão* ⓕ shteng·sowng

eye *olho* ⓜ o·lyoo

eye drops *colírio* ⓕ koo·lee·ree·oo

F

fabric *tecido* ⓜ te·see·doo

face *rosto* ⓜ rrosh·too

face cloth *toalha de rosto* ⓕ twaa·lya de rrosh·too

factory *fábrica* ⓕ faa·bree·ka

factory worker *operário/operária* ⓜ/ⓕ o·pe·raa·ryoo/o·pe·raa·rya

fado (music) *fado* ⓜ faa·doo

fall *cair* ka·eer

family *família* ⓕ fa·mee·lya

family name *apelido* ⓜ a·pe·lee·doo

famous *famoso/famosa* ⓜ/ⓕ fa·mo·zoo/fa·mo·za

fan (machine) *ventoínha* ⓕ veng·too·ee·nya

fan (sport, etc) *adepto/adepta* ⓜ/ⓕ a·de·pe·too/a·de·pe·ta

fanbelt *correia da ventoínha* ⓕ koo·rray·a da veng·too·ee·nya

far *longe* long·zhe

fare *preço da passagem* ⓜ pre·soo da pa·saa·zheng

farm *quinta* ⓕ keeng·ta

farmer *agricultor* ⓜ&ⓕ a·gree·kool·tor

fashion *moda* ⓕ mo·da

fast a *rápido/rápida* ⓜ/ⓕ rraa·pee·doo/rraa·pee·da

fast adv *depressa* de·pre·sa

fat *gordo/gorda* ⓜ/ⓕ gor·doo/gor·da

father *pai* ⓜ pai

father-in-law *sogro* ⓜ so·groo

faucet *torneira* ⓕ toor·nay·ra

fault (someone's) *culpa* ⓕ kool·pa

faulty *defeituoso/defeituosa* ⓜ/ⓕ de·fay·too·o·zoo/de·fay·too·o·za

fax *fax* ⓜ faaks

feed *alimentar* a·lee·meng·taar

feel (touch) *tocar* too·kaar

feeling (physical) *sensação* ⓕ seng·sa·sowng

feelings *sentimentos* ⓜ pl seng·tee·meng·toosh

female a *feminino/feminina* ⓜ/ⓕ
fe·mee·nee·noo/fe·mee·nee·na

fence *cerca* ⓕ ser·ka

ferry *ferryboat* ⓜ fe·rree·boht

festival *festival* ⓜ fesh·tee·vaal

fever *febre* ⓕ fe·bre

few *alguns/algumas* ⓜ/ⓕ pl
aal·goongsh/aal·goo·mash

fiancé/fiancée *noivo/noiva* ⓜ/ⓕ
noy·voo/noy·va

fiction *ficção* ⓕ feek·sowng

fight *luta* ⓕ loo·ta

fill *encher* eng·sher

film (camera/cinema) *filme* ⓜ feel·me

film speed *velocidade do filme* ⓕ
ve·loo·see·daa·de doo feel·me

filtered *filtrado/filtrada* ⓜ/ⓕ
feel·traa·doo/feel·traa·da

find *encontrar* eng·kong·traar

fine (payment) *multa* ⓕ mool·ta

fine *bom/boa* ⓜ/ⓕ bong/bo·a

finger *dedo* ⓜ de·doo

finish *terminar* ter·mee·naar

fire *fogo* ⓜ fo·goo

firewood *lenha* ⓕ le·nya

first *primeiro/primeira* ⓜ/ⓕ
pree·may·roo/pree·may·ra

first-aid kit *estojo de primeiros socorros* ⓜ
shto·zhoo de pree·may·roosh
so·ko·rroosh

first class *primeira classe* ⓕ
pree·may·ra klaa·se

fish *peixe* ⓜ pay·she

fishing *pesca* ⓕ pesh·ka

fishmonger (person) *peixeiro/peixeira*
ⓜ/ⓕ pay·shay·roo/pay·shay·ra

fish shop *peixaria* ⓕ pay·sha·ree·a

flag *bandeira* ⓕ bang·day·ra

flannel (face cloth) *toalha de rosto* ⓜ
twaa·lya de rrosh·too

flash (camera) *flash* ⓜ flaash

flashlight (torch) *luz do flash* ⓕ
loosh doo flaash

flat (apartment) *apartamento* ⓜ
a·par·ta·meng·too

flat a *plano/plana* ⓜ/ⓕ pla·noo/pla·na

flea *pulga* ⓕ pool·ga

fleamarket *feira da ladra* ⓕ
fay·ra da laa·dra

flight *voo* ⓜ vo·oo

flood *inundação* ⓕ ee·noong·da·sowng

floor *chão* ⓜ showng

floor (storey) *andar* ⓜ ang·daar

florist (shop) *florista* ⓕ floo·reesh·ta

flower *flor* ⓕ flor

flu *gripe* ⓕ gree·pe

fly *voar* voo·aar

foggy *enevoado/enevoada* ⓜ/ⓕ
e·ne·voo·aa·doo/e·ne·voo·aa·da

folk music *música popular* ⓕ
moo·zee·ka poo·poo·laar

follow *seguir* se·geer

food *comida* ⓕ koo·mee·da

foot *pé* ⓜ pe

football (soccer) *futebol* ⓜ foo·te·bol

footpath *caminho* ⓜ ka·mee·nyoo

foreign *estrangeiro/estrangeira* ⓜ/ⓕ
shtrang·zhay·roo/shtrang·zhay·ra

forest *floresta* ⓕ floo·resh·ta

forever *para sempre* pa·ra seng·pre

forget *esquecer* shke·ser

forgive *perdoar* per·doo·aar

fork *garfo* ⓜ gaar·foo

fortnight *quinzena* ⓕ keeng·ze·na

fortune teller *vidente* ⓜ&ⓕ vee·deng·te

foyer *sala de estar* ⓕ saa·la de shtaar

fragile *frágil* fraa·zheel

France *França* ⓕ fraang·sa

free (available) a *disponível*
deesh·po·nee·vel

free (gratis) a *grátis* graa·teesh

free (not bound) a *livre* lee·vre

freeze *congelar* kong·zhe·laar

fresh *fresco/fresca* ⓜ/ⓕ fresh·koo/fresh·ka

fridge *frigorífico* ⓜ free·goo·ree·fee·koo

friend *amigo/amiga* ⓜ/ⓕ
a·mee·goo/a·mee·ga

from *de* de

frost *geada* ⓕ zhee·aa·da

frozen *gelado/gelada* ⓜ/ⓕ
zhe·laa·doo/zhe·laa·da

fruit-picking *colheita de frutas* ⓕ
koo·lyay·ta de froo·tash

full *cheio/cheia* ⓜ/ⓕ shay·oo/shay·a

full-time *tempo inteiro*
teng·poo eeng·tay·roo

fun *divertido/divertida* ⓜ/ⓕ
dee·ver·tee·doo/dee·ver·tee·da

funeral *funeral* ⓜ foo·ne·raal

funny *engraçado/engraçada* ⓜ/ⓕ
eng·gra·saa·doo/eng·gra·saa·da

furniture *móveis* ⓜ pl mo·vaysh

future *futuro* ⓜ foo·too·roo

G

game (sport) *jogo* ⓜ *zho*-goo
garage *garagem* ⓕ ga-*raa*-zheng
garbage *lixo* ⓜ *lee*-shoo
garbage can *caixote do lixo* ⓜ
  kai-*sho*-te doo *lee*-shoo
garden *jardim* ⓜ zhar-*deeng*
gardening *jardinagem* ⓕ
  zhar-dee-*naa*-zheng
gas (cooking) *gás* ⓜ gaash
gas (petrol) *gasolina* ⓕ ga-zoo-*lee*-na
gas cartridge *botija de gás* ⓜ
  boo-*tee*-zha de gaash
gastroenteritis *gastrenterite* ⓕ
  gash-treng-te-*ree*-te
gate (airport) *portão/porta* ⓜ/ⓕ
  por-*towng/por*-ta
gauze *gaze* ⓕ *gaa*-ze
gay n&a *gay* ⓜ&ⓕ gay
gearbox *caixa de velocidades* ⓕ
  kai-sha de ve-loo-see-*daa*-desh
get *agarrar* a-ga-*rraar*
get off (bus, train) *descer* desh-*ser*
gift *presente* ⓜ pre-*zeng*-te
girl *menina* ⓕ me-*nee*-na
girlfriend *namorada* ⓕ na-moo-*raa*-da
give *dar* daar
glandular fever *febre glandular* ⓕ
  fe-bre glang-doo-*laar*
glass (drinking) *copo* ⓜ *ko*-poo
glasses (spectacles) *óculos* ⓜ pl
  o-koo-loosh
gloves *luvas* ⓕ pl *loo*-vash
gloves (latex) *luvas de borracha* ⓕ pl
  loo-vash de boo-*rraa*-sha
glue *cola* ⓕ *ko*-la
go *ir* eer
goal (sport) *golo* ⓜ *go*-loo
goalkeeper *guarda-redes*
  gwaar-da-*rre*-desh
goat *cabra* ⓕ *kaa*-bra
God (general) *Deus* ⓜ *de*-oosh
goggles (skiing) *óculos de esqui* ⓜ pl
  o-koo-loosh de shkee
goggles (swimming) *óculos de natação*
  ⓜ pl *o*-koo-loosh de na-ta-*sowng*
gold *ouro* ⓜ *oh*-roo
golf ball *bola de golfe* ⓕ *bo*-la de *gol*-fe
golf course *campo de golfe* ⓜ
  kang-poo de *gol*-fe

good *bom/boa* ⓜ/ⓕ bong/*bo*-a
go out *sair* sa-*eer*
go out with *sair com* sa-*eer* kong
go shopping *fazer compras*
  fa-*zer* kong-*prash*
government *governo* ⓜ goo-*ver*-noo
gram *grama* ⓜ *graa*-ma
grandchild *neto/neta* ⓜ/ⓕ *ne*-too/*ne*-ta
grandfather *avô* ⓜ a-*voh*
grandmother *avó* ⓕ a-*vo*
grass (lawn) *relva* ⓕ *rrel*-va
grateful *grato/grata* ⓜ/ⓕ *graa*-too/*graa*-ta
grave *túmulo* ⓜ *too*-moo-loo
great (fantastic) *óptimo/óptima* ⓜ/ⓕ
  o-tee-moo/*o*-tee-ma
green *verde* *ver*-de
greengrocer *vendedor de hortaliças* ⓜ
  veng-*de*-dor de or-ta-*lee*-sash
grey a *cinzento/cinzenta* ⓜ/ⓕ
  seeng-*zeng*-too/seeng-*zeng*-ta
grocery *mercearia* ⓕ mer-see-a-*ree*-a
grow *crescer* kresh-*ser*
guaranteed *garantido/garantida* ⓜ/ⓕ
  ga-rang-*tee*-doo/ga-rang-*tee*-da
guess *adivinhar* a-dee-vee-*nyaar*
guesthouse *casa de hóspedes* ⓕ
  kaa-za de *osh*-pe-desh
guide (audio) *guia auditivo* ⓜ
  gee-a ow-dee-*tee*-voo
guide (person) *guia* ⓜ *gee*-a
guidebook *guia de viagem* ⓜ
  gee-a de vee-*aa*-zheng
guide dog *cão-guia* ⓜ kowng-*gee*-a
guided tour *excursão guiada* ⓕ
  shkoor-*sowng* gee-*aa*-da
guilty *culpado/culpada* ⓜ/ⓕ
  kool-*paa*-doo/kool-*paa*-da
guitar *guitarra* ⓕ gee-*taa*-rra
gun *pistola* ⓕ peesh-*to*-la
gym (place) *ginásio* ⓜ zhee-*naa*-zyoo
gynaecologist *ginecologista* ⓜ&ⓕ
  zhee-ne-koo-loo-*zheesh*-ta

H

hair *cabelo* ⓜ ka-*be*-loo
hairbrush *escova* ⓕ shko-va
haircut *corte de cabelo* ⓜ
  kor-te de ka-*be*-loo
hairdresser *cabeleireiro/cabeleireira* ⓜ/ⓕ
  ka-be-lay-*ray*-roo/ka-be-lay-*ray*-ra

half *a* metade ① a me-*taa*-de
hallucination *alucinação* ①
a-loo-see-na-*sowng*
hammer *martelo* ⓜ mar-*te*-loo
hammock *cama de rede* ① *ka*-ma de *rre*-de
hand *mão* ① mowng
handbag *mala de mão* ①
maa-la de mowng
handicrafts *artesanato* ⓜ ar-te-za-*naa*-too
handkerchief *lenço de mão* ⓜ *leng*-soo
de mowng
handlebars *guiador* ⓜ gee-a-*dor*
handmade *feito/feita à mão* ⓜ/①
fay-too/*fay*-ta aa mowng
handsome *bonito/bonita* ⓜ/①
bo-*nee*-too/bo-*nee*-ta
happy *feliz* fe-*leesh*
harassment *assédio* ⓜ a-se-dyoo
harbour *porto* ⓜ *por*-too
hard (not soft) *duro/dura* ⓜ/①
doo-roo/*doo*-ra
hardware store *loja de ferramentas* ①
lo-zha de fe-rra-*meng*-tash
hat *chapéu* ⓜ sha-*pe*-oo
have *ter* ter
have a cold *estar constipado/constipada*
ⓜ/① shtaar kong-shtee-*paa*-doo/
kong-shtee-*paa*-da
have fun *divertir-se* dee-ver-*teer*-se
hay fever *febre dos fenos* ①
fe-bre doosh fe-*noosh*
he *ele* *e*-le
head *cabeça* ① ka-*be*-sa
headache *dor de cabeça* ① dor de ka-*be*-sa
headlights *faróis* ⓜ pl fa-*roysh*
health *saúde* ① sa-oo-de
hear *escutar* shkoo-*taar*
hearing aid *aparelho auditivo* ⓜ
a-pa-re-lyoo ow-dee-*tee*-voo
heart *coração* ⓜ koo-ra-*sowng*
heart attack *ataque de coração* ⓜ
a-*taa*-ke de koo-ra-*sowng*
heart condition *problema de coração* ⓜ
proo-*ble*-ma de koo-ra-*sowng*
heat *calor* ⓜ ka-*lor*
heated *aquecido/aquecida* ⓜ/①
a-ke-*see*-doo/a-ke-*see*-da
heater *aquecedor* ⓜ a-ke-se-*dor*
heating *aquecimento* ⓜ a-ke-see-*meng*-too
heavy *pesado/pesada* ⓜ/①
pe-*zaa*-doo/pe-*zaa*-da
helmet *capacete* ⓜ ka-pa-*se*-te

help *ajuda* ① a-*zhoo*-da
help *ajudar* a-zhoo-*daar*
hepatitis *hepatite* ① e-pa-*tee*-te
her (possessive) *dela* *de*-la
herb *erva* ① *er*-va
here *aqui* a-*kee*
high *alto/alta* ⓜ/① *aal*-too/*aal*-ta
highchair *cadeira de refeição para bebé* ①
ka-*day*-ra de rre-fay-*sowng* pa-ra be-*be*
high school *escola secundária* ①
shko-la se-koong-*daa*-ree-a
highway *autoestrada* ① ow-to-*shtraa*-da
hike *caminhar* ka-mee-*nyaar*
hiking *caminhada* ① ka-mee-*nyaa*-da
hiking boots *botas para caminhadas* ① pl
bo-tash pa-ra ka-mee-*nyaa*-dash
hiking route *rota de caminhada* ①
rro-ta de ka-mee-*nyaa*-da
hill *colina* ① koo-*lee*-na
Hindu n&a *hindu* ⓜ&① eeng-*doo*
hire *alugar* a-loo-*gaar*
his (possessive) *dele* *de*-le
historical *histórico/histórica* ⓜ/①
shto-ree-koo/shto-ree-ka
history *história* ① shto-rya
hitchhike *apanhar boleia*
a-pa-*nyaar* boo-*lay*-a
HIV *VIH* ① ve ee a-*gaa*
hockey *hóquei* ⓜ o-*kay*
holiday *feriado* ⓜ fe-ree-*aa*-doo
holidays *férias* ① pl fe-ryash
home *casa* ① *kaa*-za
homeless *sem abrigo* seng a-*bree*-goo
homemaker *dona de casa* ①
do-na de *kaa*-za
homesick *com saudades* kong sow-*da*-desh
homosexual n&a *homosexual* ⓜ&①
o-mo-sek-soo-*aal*
honeymoon *lua de mel* ① *loo*-a de mel
horoscope *horóscopo* ⓜ o-*rosh*-koo-poo
horse *cavalo* ⓜ ka-*vaa*-loo
horseriding *hipismo* ⓜ ee-*peezh*-moo
hospital *hospital* ⓜ osh-pee-*taal*
hospitality *hospitalidade* ①
osh-pee-ta-lee-*daa*-de
hot *quente* *keng*-te
hotel *hotel* ⓜ o-tel
hot water *água quente* ① *aa*-gwa *keng*-te
hour *hora* ① o-ra
house *casa* ① *kaa*-za
housework *trabalho doméstico* ⓜ
tra-*baa*-lyoo doo-*mesh*-tee-koo

how *como* ko·moo
hug *abraçar* a·bra·saar
huge *enorme* m&f ee·nor·me
human resources *recursos humanos* m pl rre·koor·soosh oo·ma·noosh
human rights *direitos humanos* m pl dee·ray·toosh oo·ma·noosh
hungry *faminto/faminta* m/f fa·meeng·too/fa·meeng·ta
hurt *aleijar* a·lay·zhaar
husband *marido* m ma·ree·doo

I

I *eu* e·oo
Iberian Peninsula *Península Ibérica* f pe·neeng·soo·la ee·be·ree·ka
ice *gelo* m zhe·loo
ice axe *machado de gelo* m ma·shaa·doo de zhe·loo
ice hockey *hóquei sobre o gelo* m o·kay so·bre oo zhe·loo
identification *identificação* f ee·deng·tee·fee·ka·sowng
identification card (ID) *bilhete de identidade* m bee·lye·te de ee·deng·tee·daa·de
idiot *idiota* m&f ee·dee·o·ta
if *se* se
ill *doente* doo·eng·te
immigration *imigração* f ee·mee·gra·sowng
important *importante* eeng·por·tang·te
impossible *impossível* eeng·po·see·vel
in *em* eng
in a hurry *com pressa* kong pre·sa
included *incluído/incluída* m/f eeng·kloo·ee·doo/eeng·kloo·ee·da
income tax *imposto de rendimentos* m eeng·posh·too de rreng·dee·meng·toosh
indigestion *indigestão* f eeng·dee·zhesh·towng
indoors *no interior* noo eeng·te·ree·or
industry *indústria* f eeng·doosh·trya
infection *infecção* f eeng·fe·sowng
inflammation *inflamação* f eeng·fla·ma·sowng
influenza *gripe* f gree·pe
information *informação* f eeng·for·ma·sowng
in front of *na frente de* na freng·te de

ingredient *ingrediente* m eeng·gre·dee·eng·te
inject *injectar* eeng·zhe·taar
injection *injecção* f eeng·zhe·sowng
injured *ferido/ferida* m/f fe·ree·doo/fe·ree·da
injury *ferimento* m fe·ree·meng·too
inner tube *câmara de ar* f ka·ma·ra de aar
innocent *inocente* ee·noo·seng·te
insect repellant *repelente* m rre·pe·leng·te
inside *dentro* deng·troo
instructor *instrutor/instrutora* m/f eeng·shtroo·tor/eeng·shtroo·to·ra
insurance *seguro* m se·goo·roo
interesting *interessante* eeng·te·re·sang·te
intermission *intervalo* m eeng·ter·vaa·loo
international *internacional* eeng·ter·naa·syoo·naal
Internet *internet* f eeng·ter·net
Internet café *café da internet* m ka·fe da eeng·ter·ne·te
interpreter *intérprete* m&f eeng·ter·pre·te
interview *entrevista* f eng·tre·veesh·ta
invite *convidar* kong·vee·daar
Ireland *Irlanda* f eer·lang·da
iron (clothes) *ferro de engomar* m fe·rroo de eng·goo·maar
island *ilha* f ee·lya
it *ele/ela* m/f e·le/e·la
IT *informática* f eeng·for·maa·tee·ka
itch *comichão* f koo·mee·showng
itinerary *itinerário* m ee·tee·ne·raa·ryoo
IUD *DIU* m de·ee·oo

J

jacket *casaco* m ka·zaa·koo
jail *prisão* f pree·zowng
jam *compota* f kong·po·ta
jar *frasco* m fraash·koo
jaw (human) *maxilar* m maak·see·laar
jealous *ciumento/ciumenta* m/f see·oo·meng·too/see·oo·meng·ta
jeep *jipe* m zhee·pe
jewellery *ourivesaria* f oh·ree·ve·za·ree·a
Jewish *Judeu/Judia* m/f zhoo·de·oo/zhoo·dee·a
job *emprego* m eng·pre·goo
jogging *corrida* f koo·rree·da
joke *piada* f pee·aa·da

journalist *jornalista* ⓜ&ⓕ zhor-na-*leesh*-ta
journey *viagem* ⓕ vee-*aa*-zheng
judge *juiz/juiza* ⓜ/ⓕ zhoo-*eesh*/zhoo-*ee*-za
jump *saltar* saal-*taar*
jumper (sweater) *camisola* ⓕ ka-mee-*zo*-la
jumper leads *recarregador de bateria* ⓜ rre-ka-rre-ga-*dor* de ba-te-*ree*-a

K

key *chave* ⓕ *shaa*-ve
keyboard *teclado* ⓜ te-*klaa*-doo
kick *chutar* shoo-*taar*
kidney *rim* ⓜ rreeng
kill *matar* ma-*taar*
kilogram *quilograma* ⓜ kee-loo-*graa*-ma
kilometre *quilómetro* ⓜ kee-*lo*-me-troo
kind (nice) *amável* ⓜ&ⓕ a-*maa*-vel
kindergarten *jardim de infância* ⓜ zhar-*deeng* de eeng-*fang*-sya
king *rei* ⓜ rray
kiosk *quiosque* ⓜ kee-*osh*-ke
kiss *beijo* ⓜ *bay*-zhoo
kiss *beijar* bay-*zhaar*
kitchen *cozinha* ⓕ koo-*zee*-nya
knee *joelho* ⓜ zhoo-e-*lyoo*
knife *faca* ⓕ *faa*-ka
know *saber* sa-*ber*
kosher *kosher* ko-*sher*

L

labourer *trabalhador/trabalhadora* ⓜ/ⓕ tra-ba-lya-*dor*/tra-ba-lya-*do*-ra
lace *renda* ⓕ *reng*-da
lake *lago* ⓜ *laa*-goo
lamb (animal) *cordeiro* ⓜ koor-*day*-roo
land *terra* ⓕ *te*-rra
landlady *senhoria* se-nyoo-*ree*-a
landlord *senhorio* se-nyoo-*ree*-oo
language *língua* ⓕ *leeng*-gwa
laptop *computador portátil* ⓜ kong-poo-ta-*dor* por-*taa*-teel
large *grande* *grang*-de
last (final) *último/última* ⓜ/ⓕ *ool*-tee-moo/*ool*-tee-ma
last (previous) *passado/passada* ⓜ/ⓕ pa-*saa*-doo/pa-*saa*-da
late *atrasado/atrasada* ⓜ/ⓕ a-tra-*zaa*-doo/a-tra-*zaa*-da
later *mais tarde* maish *tar*-de

laugh *rir* rreer
laundry (clothes/place) *lavandaria* ⓕ la-vang-da-*ree*-a
law *lei* ⓕ lay
law (study/profession) *Direito* ⓜ dee-*ray*-too
lawyer *advogado/advogada* ⓜ/ⓕ a-de-voo-*gaa*-doo/a-de-voo-*gaa*-da
laxative *laxante* ⓜ la-*shang*-te
lazy *preguiçoso/preguiçosa* ⓜ/ⓕ pre-gee-so-zoo/pre-gee-so-za
leader *líder* ⓜ&ⓕ *lee*-der
leaf *folha* ⓕ *fo*-lya
learn *aprender* a-preng-*der*
leather *couro* ⓜ *koh*-roo
lecturer *professor/professora* ⓜ/ⓕ proo-fe-*sor*/proo-fe-*so*-ra
ledge *parapeito* ⓜ pa-ra-*pay*-too
left (direction) *esquerda* ⓕ *shker*-da
left luggage *perdidos e achados* ⓜ pl per-*dee*-doosh ee aa-*shaa*-doosh
leg (body) *perna* ⓕ *per*-na
legal *legal* le-*gaal*
lens (camera) *lente* ⓕ *leng*-te
lesbian n&a *lésbica* ⓕ *lezh*-bee-ka
less *menos* me-noosh
letter (mail) *carta* ⓕ *kaar*-ta
liar *mentiroso/mentirosa* ⓜ/ⓕ meng-tee-ro-zoo/meng-tee-ro-za
library *biblioteca* ⓕ bee-blee-oo-*te*-ka
lice *piolhos* ⓜ pl pee-o-*lyoosh*
licence *licença* ⓕ lee-*seng*-sa
license plate number *número da matrícula* ⓜ *noo*-me-roo da ma-*tree*-koo-la
lie (not stand) *deitar-se* day-*taar*-se
lie (not tell the truth) *mentir* meng-*teer*
life *vida* ⓕ *vee*-da
life jacket *colete salva-vidas* ⓜ koo-*le*-te saal-va-*vee*-dash
lift (elevator) *elevador* ⓜ ee-le-va-*dor*
light (sun) *luz* ⓕ loosh
light (colour) *claro/clara* ⓜ/ⓕ *klaa*-roo/*klaa*-ra
light (weight) *leve* *le*-ve
light bulb *lâmpada* ⓕ *lang*-pa-da
lighter (cigarette) *isqueiro* ⓜ eesh-*kay*-roo
light meter *fotómetro* ⓜ foo-*to*-me-troo
like *gostar* goosh-*taar*
linen (material) *linho* ⓜ *lee*-nyoo
lip balm *bálsamo para os lábios* ⓜ *baal*-sa-moo *pa*-ra oosh *laa*-byoosh
lips *lábios* ⓜ pl *laa*-byoosh

lipstick *batom* ⓜ ba-*tong*

liquor store *loja de bebidas* ⓕ
lo-zha de be-*bee*-dash

listen *escutar* shkoo-*taar*

little (quantity) *pouco/pouca* ⓜ/ⓕ
poh-koo/*poh*-ka

little (size) *pequeno/pequena* ⓜ/ⓕ
pe-*ke*-noo/pe-*ke*-na

live (somewhere) *morar* moo-*raar*

liver *fígado* ⓜ *fee*-ga-doo

lizard *lagarto* ⓜ la-*gaar*-too

local ⓐ *local* loo-*kaal*

lock *tranca* ⓕ *trang*-ka

lock *trancar* trang-*kaar*

locked *trancado/trancada* ⓜ/ⓕ
trang-*kaa*-doo/trang-*kaa*-da

long *longo/longa* ⓜ/ⓕ *long*-goo/*long*-ga

look *olhar* oo-*lyaar*

look after *cuidar* kwee-*daar*

look for *procurar* pro-koo-*raar*

lookout *miradouro* ⓜ mee-ra-*doh*-roo

loose *solto/solta* ⓜ/ⓕ *sol*-too/*sol*-ta

loose change *trocos* ⓜ pl *tro*-koosh

lose *perder* per-*der*

lost *perdido/perdida* ⓜ/ⓕ
per-*dee*-doo/per-*dee*-da

lost-property office *gabinete de*
perdidos e achados ⓜ gaa-bee-*ne*-te
de per-*dee*-doosh ee a-*shaa*-doosh

(a) lot *muito/muita* ⓜ/ⓕ
mweeng-too/*mweeng*-ta

loud *alto/alta* ⓜ/ⓕ *aal*-too/*aal*-ta

love *amor* ⓜ a-*mor*

love *amar* a-*maar*

lover *amante* ⓜ&ⓕ a-*maang*-te

low *baixo/baixa* ⓜ/ⓕ *bai*-shoo/*bai*-sha

lubricant *lubrificante* ⓜ
loo-bree-fee-*kang*-te

luck *sorte* ⓕ *sor*-te

lucky *afortunado/afortunada* ⓜ/ⓕ
a-foor-too-*naa*-doo/a-foor-too-*naa*-da

luggage *bagagem* ⓕ ba-*gaa*-zheng

luggage locker *depósito de bagagens* ⓜ
de-*po*-zee-too de ba-*gaa*-zhengsh

luggage tag *etiqueta de bagagem* ⓕ
e-tee-*ke*-ta de ba-*gaa*-zheng

lump *nódulo* ⓜ *no*-doo-loo

lunch *almoço* ⓜ *aal*-mo-soo

lung *pulmão* ⓜ pool-*mowng*

luxury *luxo* ⓜ *loo*-shoo

M

machine *máquina* ⓕ *maa*-kee-na

magazine *revista* ⓕ rre-*veesh*-ta

mail *enviar* eng-vee-*aar*

mail (letters/postal system) *correio* ⓜ
koo-*rray*-oo

mailbox *caixa do correio* ⓕ *kai*-sha doo
koo-*rray*-oo

main *principal* preeng-see-*paal*

main road *rua principal* ⓕ
rroo-a preeng-see-*paal*

make *fazer* fa-*zer*

make-up *maquilhagem* ⓕ
ma-kee-*lyaa*-zheng

mammogram *mamograma* ⓜ
ma-moo-*graa*-ma

man *homem* ⓜ *o*-meng

manager (business) *gerente* zhe-*reng*-te

manager (sport) *treinador/treinadora*
ⓜ/ⓕ tray-na-*dor*/tray-na-*do*-ra

Manueline (art) *Manuelino/Manuelina*
ⓜ/ⓕ man-wel-ee-*noo*/man-wel-ee-*na*

manual worker *trabalhador/trabalhadora*
ⓜ/ⓕ tra-ba-lya-*dor*/tra-ba-lya-*do*-ra

many *vários/várias* ⓜ/ⓕ
vaa-ryoosh/*vaa*-ryash

map *mapa* ⓜ *maa*-pa

marital status *estado civil* ⓜ
shtaa-doo see-*veel*

market *mercado* ⓜ mer-*kaa*-doo

marriage *casamento* ⓜ ka-za-*meng*-too

married *casado/casada* ⓜ/ⓕ
ka-*zaa*-doo/ka-*zaa*-da

marry *casar* ka-*zaar*

martial arts *artes marciais* ⓕ pl
ar-tesh mar-see-*aish*

mass (Catholic) *missa* ⓕ *mee*-sa

massage *massagem* ⓕ ma-*saa*-zheng

masseur/masseuse *massagista* ⓜ&ⓕ
ma-sa-*zheesh*-ta

mat *capacho* ⓜ ka-*paa*-shoo

match (sport) *partida* ⓕ par-*tee*-da

matches (for lighting) *fósforos* ⓜ pl
fosh-foo-roosh

mattress *colchão* ⓜ kol-*showng*

maybe *talvez* tal-*vesh*

mayor *presidente da câmara* ⓜ&ⓕ
pre-zee-*deng*-te da *ka*-ma-ra

me *mim* ⓜ&ⓕ meeng

meal *refeição* ⓕ rre-fay-*sowng*

measles *sarampo* ⓜ sa-*rang*-poo
mechanic *mecânico/mecânica* ⓜ/ⓕ
  me-*ka*-nee-koo/me-*ka*-nee-ka
media *os meios de comunicação* ⓜ pl oosh
  may-oosh de koo-moo-nee-ka-*sowng*
medicine (medication) *medicamentos*
  ⓜ pl me-dee-ka-*meng*-toosh
medicine (study/profession) *medicina* ⓕ
  me-dee-*see*-na
meditation *meditação* ⓕ me-dee-ta-*sowng*
meet *encontrar* eng-kong-*traar*
meet (first time) *conhecer* koo-nye-*ser*
member *membro* ⓜ&ⓕ *meng*-broo
memory card *memória* ⓕ me-mo-ree-a
menstruation *menstruação* ⓕ
  meng-shtroo-a-*sowng*
menu *ementa* ⓕ ee-*meng*-ta
message *mensagem* ⓕ meng-*saa*-zheng
metal *metal* ⓜ me-*taal*
metre *metro* ⓜ *me*-troo
metro (train) *metropolitano* ⓜ
  me-troo-poo-lee-*ta*-noo
metro station *estação de metropolitano* ⓕ
  shta-*sowng* de me-troo-poo-lee-*ta*-noo
microwave oven *microondas* ⓜ pl
  mee-kro-*ong*-dash
midday *meio-dia* ⓜ *may*-oo-dee-a
midnight *meia-noite* ⓕ *may*-a-*noy*-te
migraine *enxaqueca* ⓕ eng-sha-*ke*-ka
military *forças armadas* ⓕ pl
  for-sash ar-*maa*-dash
milk *leite* ⓜ *lay*-te
millimetre *milímetro* ⓜ mee-lee-me-troo
minute *minuto* ⓜ mee-*noo*-too
mirror *espelho* ⓜ shpe-*lyoo*
miscarriage *aborto espontâneo* ⓜ
  a-*bor*-too shpong-*ta*-nee-oo
Miss (title) *Menina* ⓕ me-*nee*-na
miss (feel absence of) *ter saudades*
  ter sow-*daa*-desh
mistake *erro* ⓜ e-rroo
mix *misturar* meesh-too-*raar*
mobile phone *telemóvel* ⓜ te-le-*mo*-vel
modem *modem* ⓜ *mo*-deng
modern *moderno/moderna* ⓜ/ⓕ
  moo-*der*-noo/moo-*der*-na
moisturiser *hidratante* ⓜ ee-dra-*tang*-te
monastery *mosteiro* ⓜ moosh-*tay*-roo
money *dinheiro* ⓜ dee-*nyay*-roo
month *mês* ⓜ mesh
monument *monumento* ⓜ
  moo-noo-*meng*-too

moon *lua* ⓕ *loo*-a
Moorish *mourisco/mourisca* ⓜ/ⓕ
  moh-*reesh*-koo/moh-*reesh*-ka
more *mais* maish
morning *manhã* ⓕ ma-*nyang*
morning sickness *enjoo matinal* ⓜ
  eng-*zho*-oo ma-tee-*naal*
mosque *mesquita* ⓕ mesh-*kee*-ta
mosquito *mosquito* ⓜ moosh-*kee*-too
mosquito coil *repelente em espiral* ⓜ
  rre-pe-*leng*-te eng shpee-*raal*
mosquito net *mosquiteiro* ⓜ
  moosh-kee-*tay*-roo
motel *motel* ⓜ mo-*tel*
mother *mãe* ⓕ maing
mother-in-law *sogra* ⓕ *so*-gra
motorbike *mota* ⓕ *mo*-ta
motorboat *barco a motor* ⓜ
  baar-koo a moo-*tor*
motorway (tollway) *autoestrada* ⓕ
  ow-to-*shtraa*-da
mountain *montanha* ⓕ mong-*ta*-nya
mountain bike *bicicleta de montanha* ⓕ
  bee-see-*kle*-ta de mong-*ta*-nya
mountaineering *montanhismo* ⓜ
  mong-ta-*nyeezh*-moo
mountain path *trilho de montanha* ⓜ
  tree-lyoo de mong-*ta*-nya
mountain range *cordilheira* ⓕ
  koor-dee-*lyay*-ra
mouse *rato* ⓜ *rraa*-too
mouth *boca* ⓕ *bo*-ka
movie *filme* ⓜ *feel*-me
Mr *Senhor* se-*nyor*
Mrs/Ms *Senhora* se-*nyo*-ra
mud *lama* ⓕ *la*-ma
mumps *papeira* ⓕ pa-*pay*-ra
murder *assassinato* ⓜ a-sa-see-*naa*-too
murder *assassinar* a-sa-see-*naar*
muscle *músculo* ⓜ *moosh*-koo-loo
museum *museu* ⓜ moo-ze-oo
music *música* ⓕ *moo*-zee-ka
(university) music group *tuna* ⓕ *too*-na
musician *músico/música* ⓜ/ⓕ
  moo-zee-koo/*moo*-zee-ka
music shop *loja de música* ⓕ
  lo-zha de *moo*-zee-ka
Muslim n&a *muçulmano/muçulmana*
  ⓜ/ⓕ moo-sool-*ma*-noo/moo-sool-*ma*-na
mute *mudo/muda* ⓜ/ⓕ *moo*-doo/*moo*-da
my *meu/minha* ⓜ/ⓕ *me*-oo/*mee*-nya

N

nail clippers *corta-unhas* ⓜ
kor·ta-oong-nyash
name *nome* ⓜ no·me
napkin *guardanapo* ⓜ gwar·da-*naa*-poo
nappy (diaper) *fralda* ⓕ *fraal*·da
nappy rash *irritação por causa da fralda* ⓕ
ee·rree·ta·*sowng* por *kow*·sa da *fraal*·da
nationality *nacionalidade* ⓕ
na·syoo·na·lee·*daa*·de
national park *parque nacional* ⓜ
paar·ke na·syoo·*naal*
nature *natureza* ⓕ na·too·*re*·za
nausea *náusea* ⓕ *now*·zee·a
near *perto* per·too
nearby *próximo/próxima* ⓜ/ⓕ
pro·see·moo/*pro*·see·ma
nearby *por perto* poor *per*·too
nearest *o/a mais perto* ⓜ/ⓕ
oo/a maish *per*·too
necessary *necessário/necessária*
ⓜ/ⓕ ne·se·*saa*·ryoo/ne·se·*saa*·rya
neck *pescoço* ⓜ pesh·*ko*·soo
necklace *colar* ⓜ koo·*laar*
need *precisar* pre·see·*zaar*
needle (sewing) *agulha* ⓕ a·*goo*·lya
needle (syringe) *seringa* ⓕ se·*reeng*·ga
negatives (film) *negativos* ⓜ pl
ne·ga·*tee*·voosh
neither *nenhum/nenhuma* ⓜ/ⓕ
neng·*yoong*/neng·*yoo*·ma
net/network *rede* ⓕ *rre*·de
never *nunca* noong·ka
new *novo/nova* ⓜ/ⓕ *no*·voo/*no*·va
news *notícias* ⓕ pl noo·*tee*·syash
newspaper *jornal* ⓜ zhor·*naal*
newsstand *quiosque* ⓜ kee·*osh*·ke
New Year's Day *Dia de Ano Novo* ⓜ
dee·a de a·noo *no*·voo
New Year's Eve *Passagem de Ano* ⓕ
pa·*saa*·zheng de a·noo
New Zealand *Nova Zelândia* ⓕ
no·va ze·*lang*·dya
next *próximo/próxima* ⓜ/ⓕ
pro·see·moo/*pro*·see·ma
next to *ao lado de* ow *laa*·doo de
nice *simpático/simpática* ⓜ/ⓕ
seeng·*paa*·tee·koo/seeng·*paa*·tee·ka
nickname *alcunha* ⓕ aal·*koo*·nya
night *noite* ⓕ *noy*·te

nightclub *discoteca* ⓕ deesh·koo·*te*·ka
night out *saída à noite* ⓕ
sa·*ee*·da aa *noy*·te
no *não* nowng
noisy *barulhento/barulhenta* ⓜ/ⓕ
ba·roo·*lyeng*·too/ba·roo·*lyeng*·ta
none *nenhum/nenhuma* ⓜ/ⓕ
neng·*yoong*/neng·*yoo*·ma
nonsmoking *não-fumador*
nowng·foo·ma·*dor*
noon *meio-dia* ⓜ *may*·oo·*dee*·a
nose *nariz* ⓜ na·*reesh*
not *não* nowng
notebook *bloco-notas* ⓜ *blo*·koo·*no*·tash
nothing *nada* ⓜ *naa*·da
now *agora* a·go·ra
nuclear energy *energia nuclear* ⓕ
ee·ner·*zhee*·a noo·klee·*aar*
nuclear testing *teste nuclear* ⓜ
tesh·te noo·klee·*aar*
nuclear waste *resíduos nucleares* ⓜ pl
rre·*zee*·doo·oosh noo·klee·*aar*·esh
number *número* ⓜ *noo*·me·roo
numberplate *número de matrícula* ⓕ
noo·me·roo de ma·*tree*·koo·la
nurse *enfermeiro/enfermeira* ⓜ/ⓕ
eng·fer·*may*·roo/eng·fer·*may*·ra

O

oats *aveia* ⓕ sg a·*vay*·a
ocean *oceano* ⓜ o·see·*a*·noo
off (spoiled) *estragado/estragada* ⓜ/ⓕ
shtra·*gaa*·doo/shtra·*gaa*·da
off (power) *desligado/desligada* ⓜ/ⓕ
desh·lee·*gaa*·doo/desh·lee·*gaa*·da
office *escritório* ⓜ shkree·*to*·ryoo
office worker *empregado/empregada
de escritório* ⓜ/ⓕ eng·pre·*gaa*·doo/
eng·pre·*gaa*·da de shkree·*to*·ryoo
often *frequentemente* fre·kweng·te·*meng*·te
oil (food) *óleo* ⓜ o·lyoo
oil (petrol) *petróleo* ⓜ pe·*tro*·lyoo
old (age) *velho/velha* ⓜ/ⓕ *ve*·lyoo/*ve*·lya
old (former) *antigo/antiga* ⓜ/ⓕ
ang·*tee*·goo/ang·*tee*·ga
on *sobre* *so*·bre
on (power) *ligado/ligada* ⓜ/ⓕ
lee·*gaa*·doo/lee·*gaa*·da
once *uma vez* oo·ma vezh
one-way (ticket) *só de ida* so de *ee*·da

only *somente* so·*meng*·te
on time *a horas* a o·rash
open a *aberto/aberta* ⓜ/ⓕ
a·*ber*·too/a·*ber*·ta
open *abrir* a·*breer*
opening hours *horário de expediente* ⓜ
o·*raa*·ryoo de shpe·dee·*eng*·te
operation (medical) *cirurgia* ⓕ
see·*roor*·zhee·a
operator (telephone) *telefonista* ⓜ&ⓕ
te·le·foo·*neesh*·ta
opinion *opinião* ⓕ o·pee·nee·*owng*
opposite *oposto/oposta* ⓜ/ⓕ
o·*posh*·too/o·*posh*·ta
optometrist *optometrista* ⓜ&ⓕ
o·to·me·*treesh*·ta
or *ou* oh
orange (colour) *cor de laranja*
kor de la·*rang*·zha
orchestra *orquestra* ⓕ or·*kesh*·tra
order *pedido* ⓜ pe·*dee*·doo
order *pedir* pe·*deer*
ordinary *comum* koo·*moong*
orgasm *orgasmo* ⓜ or·*gaazh*·moo
original ⓐ *original* o·ree·zhee·*naal*
other n&a *outro/outra* ⓜ/ⓕ
oh·troo/*oh*·tra
our (one thing) *nosso/nossa* ⓜ/ⓕ
no·soo/*no*·sa
our (more than one thing) *nossos/nossas*
ⓜ/ⓕ *no*·soosh/*no*·sash
out of order *avariado/avariada* ⓜ/ⓕ
a·va·ree·*aa*·doo/a·va·ree·*aa*·da
outside *fora* *fo*·ra
ovarian cyst *cisto no ovário* ⓜ
seesh·too noo o·*vaa*·ryoo
ovary *ovário* ⓜ o·*vaa*·ryoo
oven *forno* ⓜ *for*·noo
overcoat *sobretudo* ⓜ soo·bre·*too*·doo
overdose *dose excessiva* ⓕ
do·ze she·*see*·va
overnight *de noite* de *noy*·te
overseas *no estrangeiro*
noo shtrang·*zhay*·roo
owe *dever* de·*ver*
owner *dono/dona* ⓜ/ⓕ *do*·noo/*do*·na
oxygen *oxigénio* ⓜ ok·see·*zhe*·nyoo
ozone layer *camada de ozono* ⓕ
ka·*maa*·da de o·*zo*·noo

P

pacemaker *pacemaker* ⓜ pays·*may*·ker
package *embrulho* ⓜ eng·*broo*·lyoo
packet *pacote* ⓜ pa·*ko*·te
padlock *cadeado* ⓜ ka·dee·*aa*·doo
page *página* ⓕ *paa*·zhee·na
pain *dor* ⓕ dor
painkiller *analgésico* ⓜ a·nal·*zhe*·zee·koo
painted tile *azulejo* ⓜ a·zoo·*le*·zhoo
painter *pintor/pintora* ⓜ/ⓕ
peeng·*tor*/peeng·*to*·ra
painting *pintura* ⓕ peeng·*too*·ra
pair (couple) *casal* ⓜ ka·*zaal*
palace *palácio* ⓜ pa·*laa*·syoo
pan *panela* ⓕ pa·*ne*·la
pants (trousers) *calças* ⓕ pl *kaal*·sash
pantyhose *collants* ⓜ pl ko·*langsh*
panty liner *penso higiénico* ⓜ
peng·soo ee·zhee·e·*nee*·koo
paper *papel* ⓜ pa·*pel*
paperwork *papelada* ⓕ pa·pe·*laa*·da
pap smear *exame papa nicolau* ⓜ
e·*za*·me *paa*·pa nee·koo·*low*
paraplegic n&a *paraplégico/paraplégica*
ⓜ/ⓕ pa·ra·pe·*le*·zhee·koo/
pa·ra·pe·*le*·zhee·ka
parcel *encomenda* ⓕ eng·koo·*meng*·da
parents *pais* ⓜ pl *paish*
park *parque* ⓜ *paar*·ke
park (a car) *estacionar* shta·syoo·*naar*
parliament *parlamento* ⓜ par·la·*meng*·too
part (component) *parte* ⓕ *paar*·te
part-time *meio tempo* *may*·oo *teng*·poo
party (night out) *festa* ⓕ *fesh*·ta
party (politics) *partido* ⓜ par·*tee*·doo
passenger *passageiro/passageira*
pa·sa·*zhay*·roo/pa·sa·*zhay*·ra
passport *passaporte* ⓜ paa·sa·*por*·te
passport number *número do passaporte* ⓜ
noo·me·roo doo paa·sa·*por*·te
past *passado* ⓜ pa·*saa*·doo
pastry shop *pastelaria* ⓕ pash·te·la·*ree*·a
path *caminho* ⓜ ka·*mee*·nyoo
pay *pagar* pa·*gaar*
payment *pagamento* ⓜ pa·ga·*meng*·too
peace *paz* ⓕ pash
peak (mountain) *pico* ⓜ *pee*·koo
pedal *pedal* ⓜ pe·*daal*
pedestrian *peão* ⓜ pee·*owng*
pen *caneta* ⓕ ka·*ne*·ta

pencil *lápis* ⓜ *laa*·peesh
penis *pénis* ⓜ *pe*·neesh
penknife *canivete* ⓜ ka·nee·*ve*·te
pensioner *pensionista* ⓜ&ⓕ
  peng·syoo·*neesh*·ta
people *pessoas* ⓕ pl pe·*so*·ash
per (day) *por* poor
per cent *por cento* poor *seng*·too
perfect *perfeito/perfeita* ⓜ/ⓕ
  per·*fay*·too/per·*fay*·ta
performance *actuação* ⓕ a·too·a·*sowng*
perfume *perfume* ⓜ per·*foo*·me
period pain *dor menstrual* ⓕ
  dor meng·shtroo·*aal*
permission *licença* ⓕ lee·*seng*·sa
permit *licença* ⓕ lee·*seng*·sa
person *pessoa* ⓕ pe·*so*·a
petition *petição* ⓕ pe·tee·*sowng*
petrol *gasolina* ⓕ ga·zoo·*lee*·na
petrol station *posto de gasolina* ⓜ
  posh·too de ga·zoo·*lee*·na
pharmacist *farmacêutico/farmacêutica*
  ⓜ/ⓕ far·ma·se·oo·tee·koo/
  far·ma·se·oo·tee·ka
pharmacy *farmácia* ⓕ far·*maa*·sya
phone book *lista telefónica* ⓕ
  leesh·ta te·le·*fo*·nee·ka
phone box *telefone público* ⓜ
  te·le·*fo*·ne *poo*·blee·koo
phonecard *cartão telefónico* ⓜ
  kar·*towng* te·le·*fo*·nee·koo
photo *fotografar* foo·too·gra·*faar*
photographer *fotógrafo/fotógrafa* ⓜ/ⓕ
  foo·*to*·gra·foo/foo·*to*·gra·fa
photography *fotografia* ⓕ
  foo·too·gra·*fee*·a
phrasebook *livro de frases* ⓜ
  lee·vroo de *fraa*·zesh
pickaxe *picareta* ⓕ pee·ka·*re*·ta
picnic *piquenique* ⓜ pee·ke·*nee*·ke
piece *pedaço* ⓜ pe·*daa*·soo
pig *porco/porca* ⓜ/ⓕ *por*·koo/*por*·ka
pill *comprimido* ⓜ kong·pree·*mee*·doo
the pill *pílula* ⓕ *pee*·loo·la
pillory (stone column) *pilar* ⓜ pee·*laar*
pillow *almofada* ⓕ al·moo·*faa*·da
pillowcase *fronha* ⓕ *fro*·nya
pink *cor-de-rosa* kor·de·*rro*·za
place *lugar* ⓜ loo·*gaar*
place of birth *local de nascimento* ⓜ
  loo·*kaal* de nash·see·*meng*·too
plane *avião* ⓜ a·vee·*owng*

plant *planta* ⓕ *plang*·ta
plate *prato* ⓜ *praa*·too
plateau *planalto* pla·*naal*·too
platform *plataforma* ⓕ pla·ta·*for*·ma
play (theatre) *peça* ⓕ *pe*·sa
play (cards, etc) *jogar* zhoo·*gaar*
play (guitar, etc) *tocar* too·*kaar*
plug (bath) *tampão* ⓜ tang·*powng*
plug (electricity) *tomada* ⓕ too·*maa*·da
pocket *bolso* ⓜ *bol*·soo
pocketknife *canivete* ⓜ ka·nee·*ve*·te
poetry *poesia* ⓕ po·e·*zee*·a
point *ponto* ⓜ *pong*·too
point *apontar* a·pong·*taar*
poisonous *venenoso/venenosa* ⓜ/ⓕ
  ve·ne·no·zoo/ve·ne·no·za
police *polícia* ⓕ poo·*lee*·sya
police officer *polícia* poo·*lee*·sya
police station *esquadra da polícia* ⓕ
  shkwaa·dra da poo·*lee*·sya
policy *política* ⓕ poo·*lee*·tee·ka
politician *político/política* ⓜ/ⓕ
  poo·*lee*·tee·koo/poo·*lee*·tee·ka
politics *política* ⓕ poo·*lee*·tee·ka
pollen *pólen* ⓜ *po*·leng
pollution *poluição* ⓕ poo·loo·ee·*sowng*
pool (game) *bilhar* ⓜ bee·*lyaar*
pool (swimming) *piscina* ⓕ pesh·*see*·na
poor *pobre* *po*·bre
popular *popular* poo·poo·*laar*
port (river/sea) *porto* ⓜ *por*·too
Portugal *Portugal* ⓜ poor·too·*gaal*
Portuguese (language) *português* ⓜ
  poor·too·*gesh*
positive *positivo/positiva* ⓜ/ⓕ
  poo·zee·*tee*·voo/poo·zee·*tee*·vaa
possible *possível* poo·*see*·vel
post *enviar* eng·vee·*aar*
postage *tarifa postal* ⓕ ta·*ree*·fa poosh·*taal*
postcode *código postal* ⓜ *ko*·dee·goo
  poosh·*taal*
poster *cartaz* ⓜ kar·*taash*
post office *correio* ⓜ koo·*rray*·oo
pot (cooking) *panela* ⓕ pa·*ne*·la
pottery *cerâmica* ⓕ se·*raa*·mee·ka
pound (weight) *libra* ⓕ *lee*·bra
poverty *pobreza* ⓕ poo·*bre*·za
powder *pó* ⓜ po
power *poder* ⓜ poo·*der*
prayer *oração* ⓕ o·ra·*sowng*
prefer *preferir* pre·fe·*reer*

pregnancy test kit *teste de gravidez* ⓜ
tesh-te de gra-vee-desh
pregnant *grávida* graa-vee-da
premenstrual tension *tensão
pré-menstrual* ⓕ teng-sowng
pre-meng-shtroo-aal
prepare *preparar* pre-pa-raar
prescription *receita médica* ⓕ
rre-say-ta me-dee-ka
present (gift/time) *presente* ⓜ pre-zeng-te
president *presidente* ⓜ&ⓕ
pre-zee-deng-te
pressure (tyre) *pressão* ⓕ pre-sowng
pretty *bonito/bonita* ⓜ/ⓕ
boo-nee-too/boo-nee-ta
price *preço* ⓜ pre-soo
priest *padre* ⓜ paa-dre
prime minister *primeiro ministro/
primeira ministra* ⓜ/ⓕ pree-may-roo
mee-nee-shtroo/pree-may-ra
mee-nee-shtra
printer (computer) *impressora* ⓕ
eeng-pre-so-ra
prison *prisão* ⓕ pree-zowng
private *privado/privada* ⓜ/ⓕ
pree-vaa-doo/pree-vaa-da
produce *produzir* proo-doo-zeer
profit *lucro* ⓜ loo-kroo
program *programa* ⓜ proo-gra-ma
projector *projector* ⓜ proo-zhe-tor
promise *prometer* proo-me-ter
prostitute *prostituto/prostituta* ⓜ/ⓕ
proosh-tee-too-too/proosh-tee-too-ta
protect *proteger* proo-te-zher
protected (species) *protegido/protegida*
ⓜ/ⓕ proo-te-zhee-doo/proo-te-zhee-da
protest *manifestação* ⓕ
ma-nee-fesh-ta-sowng
protest *protestar* proo-tesh-taar
provisions *provisões* ⓕ pl
proo-vee-zoyngsh
pub (bar) *bar* ⓜ baar
public gardens *jardins públicos* ⓜ pl
zhar-deengzh poo-blee-koosh
public relations *relações públicas* ⓕ pl
rre-la-soyngsh poo-blee-kash
public telephone *telefone público* ⓜ
te-le-fo-ne poo-blee-koo
public toilet *casa de banho pública* ⓕ
kaa-za de ba-nyoo poo-blee-ka
pull *puxar* poo-shaar
pump *bomba* ⓕ bong-ba

puncture *furo* ⓜ foo-roo
pure *puro/pura* ⓜ/ⓕ poo-roo/poo-ra
purple *roxo/roxa* ⓜ/ⓕ rro-shoo/rro-sha
purse *bolsa* ⓕ bol-sa
push *empurrar* eng-poo-rraar
put *colocar* koo-loo-kaar

Q

quadriplegic n&a *quadraplégico/quad-
raplégica* ⓜ/ⓕ kwa-dra-ple-zhee-koo/
kwa-dra-ple-zhee-ka
qualifications *qualificações* ⓕ pl
kwa-lee-fee-ka-soyngsh
quality *qualidade* ⓕ kwa-lee-daa-de
quarantine *quarentena* ⓕ kwa-reng-te-na
queen *rainha* ⓕ rra-ee-nya
question *pergunta* ⓕ per-goong-ta
queue *fila* ⓕ fee-la
quick *rápido/rápida* ⓜ/ⓕ
rraa-pee-doo/rraa-pee-da
quiet *calado/calada* ⓜ/ⓕ
ka-laa-doo/ka-laa-da
quit *desistir* de-zeesh-teer

R

rabbit *coelho* ⓜ koo-e-lyoo
race (sport) *corrida* ⓕ koo-rree-da
racetrack *pista de corridas* ⓕ
peesh-ta de koo-rree-dash
racing bike *bicicleta de corrida* ⓕ
bee-see-kle-ta de koo-rree-da
racism *racismo* ⓜ rra-seezh-moo
racquet *raquete* ⓕ rra-ke-te
radiator *radiador* ⓜ rra-dee-a-dor
radio *rádio* rraa-dyoo
railway station *estação de caminhos de
ferro* ⓕ shta-sowng de ka-mee-nyoosh
de fe-rroo
rain *chuva* ⓕ shoo-va
raincoat *gabardina* ⓕ gaa-baar-dee-na
rape *violação* ⓕ vee-oo-la-sowng
rare (uncommon) *raro/rara* ⓜ/ⓕ
rraa-roo/rraa-ra
rash *irritação da pele* ⓕ
ee-rree-ta-sowng da pe-le
rat *ratazana* ⓜ&ⓕ rra-ta-za-na
raw *cru/crua* ⓜ/ⓕ kroo/kroo-a
razor *gilete* ⓕ zhee-le-te

razor blade *lâmina de barbear* ①
  la·mee·na de bar·bee·*aar*
read *ler* ler
reading *leitura* ① lay·*too*·ra
ready *pronto/pronta* ⓜ/①
  prong·too/*prong*·ta
real estate agent *agente imobiliário* ⓜ&①
  a·*zheng*·te ee·moo·bee·*lyaa*·ryoo
realistic *realista* rree·a·*leesh*·ta
reason *razão* ① rra·*zowng*
receipt *recibo* ⓜ rre·*see*·boo
recently *recentemente* rre·seng·te·*meng*·te
recommend *recomendar*
  rre·koo·meng·*daar*
record *gravar* gra·*vaar*
recording *gravação* ① gra·va·*sowng*
recyclable *reciclável* rre·see·*klaa*·vel
recycle *reciclar* rre·see·*klaar*
red *vermelho/vermelha* ⓜ/①
  ver·me·*lyoo*/ver·me·*lya*
referee *juiz/juíza* ⓜ/①
  zhoo·*eesh*/zhoo·ee·za
reference *referência* ① rre·fe·*reng*·sya
refrigerator *frigorífico* ⓜ
  free·goo·*ree*·fee·koo
refugee *refugiado/refugiada* ⓜ/①
  rre·foo·zhee·*aa*·doo/rre·foo·zhee·*aa*·da
refund *reembolso* ⓜ rre·eng·*bol*·soo
refuse *recusar* rre·koo·*zaar*
regional *regional* rre·zhyoo·*naal*
registered mail *correio registado* ⓜ
  koo·*rray*·oo re·zhee·*shtaa*·doo
rehydration salts *sais de hidratação* ⓜ pl
  saish de ee·dra·ta·*sowng*
relationship *relacionamento* ⓜ
  rre·la·syoo·na·*meng*·too
relax *relaxar* rre·laa·*shaar*
relic *relíquia* ① rre·*lee*·kya
religion *religião* ① rre·lee·zhee·*owng*
religious *religioso/religiosa* ⓜ/①
  rre·lee·zhee·o·zoo/rre·lee·zhee·o·za
remote *remoto/remota* ⓜ/①
  rre·mo·too/rre·mo·ta
remote control *telecomando* ⓜ
  te·le·koo·*mang*·doo
rent *alugar* a·loo·*gaar*
repair *consertar* kong·ser·*taar*
reservation *reserva* ① rre·*zer*·va
rest *descansar* desh·kang·*saar*
restaurant *restaurante* ⓜ rresh·tow·*rang*·te
résumé *currículo* ⓜ koo·*rree*·koo·loo

retired *aposentado/aposentada* ⓜ/①
  a·poo·zeng·*taa*·doo/a·poo·zeng·*taa*·da
return (ticket) ⓐ *ida e volta* ee·da ee *vol*·ta
return *voltar* vol·*taar*
review *revisão* ① rre·vee·*zowng*
rhythm *ritmo* ⓜ *rreet*·moo
rib *costela* ① koosh·*te*·la
rich (wealthy) *rico/rica* ⓜ/①
  rree·koo/*rree*·ka
ride (car) *boleia* ① boo·*lay*·a
ride *andar*
ride a bike *andar de bicicleta*
  ang·*daar* de bee·see·*kle*·ta
ride a horse *andar a cavalo*
  ang·*daar* a ka·*vaa*·loo
right (correct) ⓐ *correcto/correcta* ⓜ/①
  koo·*rre*·too/koo·*rre*·ta
right (direction) *(à) direita* (aa) dee·*ray*·ta
ring (jewellery) *anel* ⓜ a·*nel*
rip-off *roubo* ⓜ *rroh*·boo
risk *risco* ⓜ *rreesh*·koo
river *rio* ⓜ *rree*·oo
road *estrada* ① *shtraa*·da
road map *mapa de estradas* ⓜ
  maa·pa de *shtraa*·dash
rob *roubar* rroh·*baar*
rock *pedra* ① *pe*·dra
rock (music) *rock* ⓜ *rro*·ke
rock climbing *alpinismo* ⓜ
  aal·pee·*neezh*·moo
rock group *banda de rock* ①
  baang·da de *rro*·ke
rollerblading *patins em linha* ⓜ pl
  pa·*teengzh* eng *lee*·nya
romantic *romântico/romântica* ⓜ/①
  rroo·*maang*·tee·koo/rroo·*maang*·tee·ka
room *quarto* ⓜ *kwaar*·too
room number *número do quarto* ⓜ
  noo·me·roo doo *kwaar*·too
rope *corda* ① *kor*·da
round *redondo/redonda* ⓜ/①
  rre·*dong*·doo/rre·*dong*·da
roundabout *rotunda* ① rroo·*toong*·da
route *rota* ① *rro*·ta
rubbish *lixo* ⓜ *lee*·shoo
rubella *rubéola* ① rroo·*be*·o·la
rug *tapete* ⓜ ta·*pe*·te
rugby *ráguebi* ⓜ *rra*·ge·bee
ruins *ruínas* ① pl rroo·ee·nash
rule *regra* ① *rre*·gra
run *correr* koo·*rrer*

running *corrida* ① koo-*rree*-da
runny nose *nariz a pingar* ⓜ na-*reesh* a peeng-*gaar*

S

sad *triste* *treesh*-te
safe *cofre* ⓜ *ko*-fre
safe *seguro/segura* ⓜ/① se-*goo*-roo/se-*goo*-ra
safe sex *sexo protegido* ⓜ *sek*-soo proo-te-*zhee*-doo
sailboarding *windsurf* ① *weend*-sarf
saint n *santo/santa* ⓜ/① *sang*-too/*sang*-ta
salary *salário* ① sa-*laa*-ryoo
sale *liquidação* ① lee-kee-da-*sowng*
sales tax *IVA* ⓜ *ee*-va
same *mesmo/mesma* ⓜ/① *mezh*-moo/*mezh*-ma
sand *areia* ① a-*ray*-a
sandal *sandália* ① sang-*daa*-lya
sanitary napkin *penso higiénico* ⓜ *peng*-soo ee-zhee-e-*nee*-koo
sauna *sauna* ① *sow*-na
say *dizer* dee-*zer*
scalp *couro cabeludo* ⓜ *koh*-roo ka-be-*loo*-doo
scarf *lenço* ⓜ *leng*-soo
school *escola* ① *shko*-la
science *ciências* ① pl see-*eng*-syash
scientist *cientista* ⓜ&① see-eng-*teesh*-ta
scissors *tesoura* ① sg te-*zoh*-ra
score (a goal) *marcar* mar-*kaar*
scoreboard *placar* ⓜ pla-*kaar*
Scotland *Escócia* ① *shko*-sya
sculpture *escultura* ① shkool-*too*-ra
sea *mar* ⓜ maar
seasick *enjoado/enjoada* ⓜ/① eng-zhoo-*aa*-doo/eng-zhoo-*aa*-da
seaside *beira mar* ① *bay*-ra maar
season *estação* ① shta-*sowng*
seat *assento* ⓜ a-*seng*-too
seatbelt *cinto de segurança* ⓜ *seeng*-too de se-goo-*raang*-sa
second (time) *segundo* ⓜ se-*goong*-doo
second *segundo/segunda* ⓜ/① se-*goong*-doo/se-*goong*-da
second class *segunda classe* ① se-*goong*-da *klaa*-se
second-hand *em segunda mão* eng se-*goong*-da mowng

second-hand shop *loja de segunda mão* ① *lo*-zha de se-*goon*-da mowng
secretary *secretário/secretária* ⓜ/① se-kre-*taa*-ryoo/se-kre-*taa*-rya
see *ver* ver
self-employed person *empregado/empregada por conta própria* ⓜ/① eng-pre-*gaa*-doo/eng-pre-*gaa*-da poor *kong*-ta *pro*-pree-a
selfish *egoísta* e-goo-*eesh*-ta
sell *vender* veng-*der*
send *enviar* eng-vee-*aar*
sensible *razoável* rra-zoo-*aa*-vel
sensual *sensual* seng-soo-*aal*
separate *separado/separada* ⓜ/① se-pa-*raa*-doo/se-pa-*raa*-da
serious *sério/séria* ⓜ/① *se*-ryoo/*se*-rya
service *serviço* ⓜ ser-*vee*-soo
service charge *taxa de serviço* ① *taa*-sha de ser-*vee*-soo
serviette *guardanapo* ⓜ gwar-da-*naa*-poo
several *vários/várias* ⓜ/① pl *vaa*-ryoosh/*vaa*-ryash
sew *coser* koo-*zer*
sex *sexo* ⓜ *sek*-soo
sexism *machismo* ⓜ ma-*sheezh*-moo
sexy *sexy* sek-see
shadow *sombra* ① *song*-bra
shampoo *champô* ⓜ shang-*poo*
shape *forma* ① *for*-ma
share (room, etc) *partilhar* par-tee-*lyaar*
shave *fazer a barba* fa-zer a *baar*-ba
shaving cream *creme de barbear* ⓜ *kre*-me de bar-bee-*aar*
she *ela* e-la
sheep *ovelha* ① oo-*ve*-lya
sheet (bed) *lençol* ⓜ leng-*sol*
shingles (illness) *zona* ① *zo*-na
ship *navio* ⓜ na-*vee*-oo
shirt *camisa* ① ka-*mee*-za
shoe *sapato* ⓜ sa-*paa*-too
shoe shop *sapataria* ① sa-pa-ta-*ree*-a
shoot *atirar* a-tee-*raar*
shop *loja* ① *lo*-zha
shop *fazer compras* fa-zer kong-*prash*
shopping *compras* ① pl kong-*prash*
shopping centre *centro comercial* ⓜ *seng*-troo koo-mer-see-*aal*
short (length) *curto/curta* ⓜ/① *koor*-too/*koor*-ta
shorts *calções* ⓜ pl kaal-*soyngsh*
shoulder *ombro* ⓜ *ong*-broo

shout *gritar* gree-*taar*
show *espectáculo* ⓜ shpe-*taa*-koo-loo
show *mostrar* moosh-*traar*
shower *chuveiro* ⓜ shoo-*vay*-roo
shrine *santuário* ⓜ sang-too-*aa*-ryoo
shut *fechado/fechada* ⓜ/①
  fe-*shaa*-doo/fe-*shaa*-da
shy *tímido/tímida* ⓜ/①
  tee-mee-doo/*tee*-mee-da
sick *doente* doo-*eng*-te
side *lado* ⓜ *laa*-doo
sign *sinal* ⓜ see-*naal*
signature *assinatura* ① a-see-na-*too*-ra
silk *seda* ① *se*-da
silver *prata* ① *praa*-ta
SIM card *cartão SIM* ⓜ kar-*towng* seeng
similar *parecido/parecida* ⓜ/①
  pa-re-*see*-doo/pa-re-*see*-da
simple *simples* *seeng*-plesh
since (time) *desde* *dezh*-de
singer *cantor/cantora* ⓜ/①
  kang-*tor*/kang-*to*-ra
single (person) ⓐ *solteiro/solteira* ⓜ/①
  sol-*tay*-roo/sol-*tay*-ra
single room *quarto de solteiro* ⓜ
  kwaar-too de sol-*tay*-roo
sister *irmã* ① eer-*mang*
sit *sentar* seng-*taar*
size *tamanho* ⓜ ta-*ma*-nyoo
skate *patinar* pa-tee-*naar*
skateboarding *skate* ⓜ *skay*-te
ski *esquiar* shkee-*aar*
skiing *esqui* ⓜ shkee
skim milk *leite magro* ⓜ *lay*-te *maa*-groo
skin *pele* ① *pe*-le
skirt *saia* ① *sai*-a
skull *crânio* ⓜ *kra*-nyoo
sky *céu* ⓜ se-oo
sleep *dormir* door-*meer*
sleeping bag *saco de dormir* ⓜ
  saa-koo de dor-*meer*
sleeping car *vagão cama* ⓜ
  va-*gowng ka*-ma
sleeping pills *pílula para dormir* ①
  pee-loo-laa *pa*-ra door-*meer*
sleepy *sonolento/sonolenta* ⓜ/①
  soo-noo-*leng*-too/soo-noo-*leng*-ta
slice *fatia* ① fa-*tee*-a
slide (transparency) *diapositivo* ⓜ
  dee-a-po-zee-*tee*-voo
slide film *filme de diapositivos* ⓜ
  feel-me de dee-a-po-zee-*tee*-voosh

slow (down) *devagar* de-va-*gaar*
slowly *vagarosamente* va-ga-ro-za-*meng*-te
small *pequeno/pequena* ⓜ/①
  pe-*ke*-noo/pe-*ke*-na
smaller *menor* me-*nor*
smallest *o/a menor* ⓜ/① oo/a me-*nor*
smell *cheiro* ⓜ *shay*-roo
smile *sorrir* so-*rreer*
smoke *fumar* foo-*maar*
snack *refeição ligeira* ①
  rre-fay-*sowng* lee-*zhay*-ra
snake *cobra* ① *ko*-bra
snorkelling *snorkel* ⓜ *snor*-kel
snow *neve* ① *ne*-ve
snowboarding *snowboarding* ⓜ
  snow-*bor*-deeng
soap *sabonete* ⓜ sa-boo-*ne*-te
soap opera *telenovela* ① te-le-noo-*ve*-la
soccer *futebol* ⓜ foo-te-*bol*
socialist n&a *socialista* ⓜ&①
  soo-see-a-*leesh*-ta
sock *meia* ① *may*-a
soft drink *refrigerante* ⓜ
  rre-free-zhe-*rang*-te
soldier *soldado* ⓜ&① sol-*daa*-doo
some *uns/umas* ⓜ/① pl oongsh/*oo*-mash
someone *alguém* ⓜ&① aal-*geng*
something *alguma coisa* ①
  aal-*goo*-ma *koy*-za
sometimes *às vezes* aash *ve*-zesh
son *filho* ⓜ *fee*-lyoo
song *canção* ① kang-*sowng*
soon *em breve* eng *bre*-ve
sore ⓐ *dorido/dorida* ⓜ/①
  doo-*ree*-doo/doo-*ree*-da
souvenir *lembrança* ① leng-*brang*-sa
souvenir shop *loja de lembranças* ①
  lo-zha de leng-*brang*-sash
soy milk *leite de soja* ⓜ *lay*-te de *so*-zha
space (room) *espaço* ⓜ shpaa-soo
Spain *Espanha* ① shpa-nya
Spanish (language) *espanhol* ⓜ shpa-*nyol*
speak *falar* fa-*laar*
special *especial* shpe-see-*aal*
specialist *especialista* ⓜ&①
  shpe-see-a-*leesh*-ta
speed (velocity) *velocidade* ①
  ve-loo-see-*daa*-de
speed limit *limite de velocidade* ①
  lee-*mee*-te de ve-loo-see-*daa*-de
speedometer *mostrador de velocidade* ⓜ
  moosh-tra-*dor* de ve-loo-see-*daa*-de

spider *aranha* ① a·ra·nya
spoilt (person) *mimado/mimada* ⑩/①
mee·*maa*·doo/mee·*maa*·da
spoke *raio de roda* ⑩ *rraa*·yoo de *rro*·da
spoon *colher* ① koo·*lyer*
sport *desporto* ⑩ desh·*por*·too
sportsperson *desportista* ⑩&①
desh·*poor·teesh*·ta
sports store *loja de desporto* ①
lo·zha de desh·*por*·too
sprain *entorse* ① eng·*tor*·se
spring (coil) *molas* ① pl mo·lash
square (town) *praça* ① *praa*·sa
stadium *estádio* ⑩ shtaa·*dyoo*
stairway *escadaria* ① shka·da·*ree*·a
stale *seco/seca* ⑩/① *se*·koo/se·ka
stamp (postage) *selo* ⑩ *se*·loo
stand-by ticket *bilhete sem garantia* ⑩
bee·*lye*·te seng ga·rang·*tee*·a
star *estrela* ① *shtre*·la
(four-)star *(quatro) estrelas* ① pl
(kwaa·troo) *shtre*·lash
start *começo* ⑩ koo·*me*·soo
start *começar* koo·me·*saar*
station *estação* ① shta·*sowng*
stationery shop *papelaria* ① pa·pe·la·*ree*·a
statue *estátua* ① shtaa·*too*·a
stay *ficar* fee·*kaar*
steal *roubar* rroh·*baar*
steep *íngreme* eeng·*gre*·me
step *passo* ⑩ *paa*·soo
stereo *estéreo* ⑩ shte·*ree*·oo
stockings *meias de vidro* ① pl
may·ash de *vee*·droo
stolen *roubado/roubada* ⑩/①
rroh·*baa*·doo/rroh·*baa*·da
stomach *estômago* ⑩ shto·ma·goo
stomachache *dor de estômago* ①
dor de *shto*·ma·goo
stone *pedra* ① *pe*·dra
stoned (drugged) *drogado/drogada* ⑩/①
droo·*gaa*·doo/droo·*gaa*·da
stop *parar* pa·*raar*
storm *tempestade* ① teng·*pesh·taa*·de
story *história* ① *shto*·rya
stove *fogão* ⑩ foo·*gowng*
straight *directo/directa* ⑩/①
dee·*re*·too/dee·*re*·ta
strange *estranho/estranha* ⑩/①
shtra·nyoo/*shtra*·nya
stranger *estranho/estranha* ⑩/①
shtra·nyoo/*shtra*·nya

stream *ribeiro* ⑩ rree·*bay*·roo
street *rua* ① *rroo*·a
street market *feira* ① *fay*·ra
street party *festa na rua* ① *fesh*·ta na *rroo*·a
strike *greve* ① *gre*·ve
string *cordel* ⑩ koor·*del*
stroke (health) *trombose* ① trong·*bo*·ze
strong *forte* *for*·te
stubborn *teimoso/teimosa* ⑩/①
tay·*mo*·zoo/tay·*mo*·za
student *estudante* ⑩&① shtoo·*dang*·te
studio *estúdio* ⑩ shtoo·*dyoo*
stupid *burro/burra* ⑩/① boo·*rroo*/boo·rra
style *estilo* ⑩ *shtee*·loo
subtitles *legendas* ① pl le·*zheng*·dash
suburb *bairro nos arredores da cidade*
⑩ *bai*·rroo noosh a·rre·do·resh da
see·*daa*·de
subway (train) *metropolitano* ⑩
me·troo·poo·lee·*ta*·no
suit bag *saco de fatos* ⑩
saa·koo de *faa*·toosh
suitcase *mala de viagem* ①
maa·la de vee·*aa*·zheng
sun *sol* ⑩ sol
sunblock *protecção anti-solar* ①
proo·te·*sowng* ang·tee·soo·*laar*
sunburnt *queimado/queimada do sol* ⑩/①
kay·*maa*·doo/kay·*maa*·da doo sol
sunglasses *óculos de sol* ⑩ pl
o·koo·loosh de sol
sunny *ensolarado/ensolarada* ⑩/①
eng·soo·la·*raa*·doo/eng·soo·la·*raa*·da
sunrise *nascer do sol* ⑩ *nash*·ser doo sol
sunset *pôr do sol* ⑩ por doo sol
sunstroke *insolação* ① eeng·soo·la·*sowng*
supermarket *supermercado* ⑩
soo·per·mer·*kaa*·doo
superstition *superstição* ①
soo·persh·tee·*sowng*
supporter (politics) *partidário/partidária*
⑩/① par·tee·*daa*·ryoo/par·tee·*daa*·rya
supporter (sport) *adepto/adepta* ⑩/①
a·*de*·pe·too/a·*de*·pe·ta
surf *fazer surf* fa·*zer* sarf
surface mail (land) *correspondência por
via terrestre* ① koo·rresh·pong·*deng*·sya
poor *vee*·a te·*rresh*·tre
surface mail (sea) *correspondência por via
marítima* ① koo·rresh·pong·*deng*·sya
poor *vee*·a ma·*ree·tee*·ma

surfboard *prancha de surf* ① *prang*-sha de surf

surfing *surf* ⓜ sarf

surname *apelido* ⓜ a-pe-*lee*-doo

surprise *surpresa* ① soor-*pre*-za

sweater *camisola* ① ka-mee-*zo*-la

sweet ⓐ *doce* *do*-se

swelling *inchaço* ⓜ eeng-*shaa*-soo

swim *nadar* na-*daar*

swimming *natação* ① na-ta-*sowng*

swimming pool *piscina* ① pesh-*see*-na

swimsuit *fato de banho* ⓜ *faa*-too de *ba*-nyoo

synagogue *sinagoga* ① see-na-*go*-ga

synthetic *sintético/sintética* ⓜ/① seeng-*te*-tee-koo/seeng-*te*-tee-ka

syringe *seringa* ① se-*reeng*-ga

T

table *mesa* ① *me*-za

tablecloth *toalha de mesa* ① *twaa*-lya de *me*-za

table tennis *ténis de mesa* ⓜ *te*-neesh de *me*-za

tail *cauda* ① *kow*-da

tailor *alfaiate* ⓜ aal-fai-*aa*-te

take *levar* le-*vaar*

take a photo *tirar uma foto* tee-*raar* *oo*-ma *fo*-too

talk *falar* fa-*laar*

tall *alto/alta* ⓜ/① *aal*-too/*aal*-ta

tampon *tampão* ⓜ tang-*powng*

tap *torneira* ① toor-*nay*-ra

tasty *gostoso/gostosa* ⓜ/① goosh-*to*-zoo/goosh-*to*-za

tax *imposto* ⓜ eeng-*posh*-too

taxi *táxi* ⓜ *taak*-see

taxi rank *praça de táxis* ① *praa*-sa de *taak*-seesh

tea *chá* ⓜ shaa

teacher *professor/professora* ⓜ/① proo-fe-*sor*/proo-fe-*so*-ra

tea house *casa de chá* ① *kaa*-za de shaa

team *equipa* ① e-*kee*-pa

teaspoon *colher de chd* ① koo-*lyer* de shaa

technique *técnica* ① *tek*-nee-ka

teeth *dentes* ⓜ pl *deng*-tesh

telephone *telefone* ⓜ te-le-*fo*-ne

telephone *telefonar* te-le-foo-*naar*

telescope *telescópio* ⓜ te-lesh-*ko*-pyoo

television *televisão* ① te-le-vee-*zowng*

tell *dizer* dee-*zer*

temperature (fever) *febre* ① *fe*-bre

temperature (weather) *temperatura* ① teng-pe-ra-*too*-ra

tennis *ténis* ⓜ *te*-neesh

tennis court *campo de ténis* ⓜ *kang*-poo de *te*-neesh

tent *tenda* ① *teng*-da

tent peg *estaca* ① *shtaa*-ka

terrible *terrível* te-*rree*-vel

terrorism *terrorismo* ⓜ te-rroo-*reezh*-moo

test *teste* ⓜ *tesh*-te

thank *agradecer* a-gra-de-*ser*

that *aquele/aquela* ⓜ/① a-*ke*-le/a-*ke*-la

theatre *teatro* ⓜ te-*aa*-troo

their *deles* de-*lesh*

there (where neither of us is) *lá* laa

there (where you are) *aí* a-*ee*

they *eles/elas* ⓜ/① e-*lesh*/e-*lash*

thick *grosso/grossa* ⓜ/① *gro*-soo/*gro*-sa

thief *ladrão/ladra* ⓜ/① la-*drowng*/*laa*-dra

thin *fino/fina* ⓜ/① *fee*-noo/*fee*-na

think *pensar* peng-*saar*

thirsty *sedento/sedenta* ⓜ/① se-*deng*-too/se-*deng*-ta

this *este/esta* ⓜ/① *esh*-te/*esh*-ta

thread *linha de coser* ① *lee*-nya de koo-*zer*

throat *garganta* ① gar-*gang*-ta

thrush (health) *corrimento* ⓜ koo-rree-*meng*-too

thunderstorm *trovoada* ① troo-voo-*aa*-da

ticket *bilhete* ⓜ bee-*lye*-te

ticket collector *cobrador* ⓜ koo-bra-*dor*

ticket machine *máquina de vender bilhetes* ① *maa*-kee-na de veng-*der* bee-*lye*-tesh

ticket office *bilheteira* ① bee-lye-*tay*-ra

tide *maré* ① ma-*re*

tight *apertado/apertada* ⓜ/① a-per-*taa*-doo/a-per-*taa*-da

time *tempo* ⓜ *teng*-poo

time difference *diferença horária* ① dee-fe-*reng*-sa o-*raa*-rya

timetable *horário* ⓜ o-*raa*-ryoo

tin (can) *lata* ① *laa*-ta

tin opener *abre latas* ⓜ *aa*-bre *laa*-tash

tiny *minúsculo/minúscula* ⓜ/① mee-*noosh*-koo-loo/mee-*noosh*-koo-la

tip (gratuity) *gorjeta* ① gor-*zhe*-ta

tire *pneu* ⓜ pe-*ne*-oo

tired *cansado/cansada* ⓜ/① kang-*saa*-doo/kang-*saa*-da

tissue *lenço de papel* ⓜ leng·soo de pa·*pel*

to *a* a

toaster *torradeira* ⓕ too·rra·*day*·ra

tobacco *tabaco* ⓜ ta·*ba*·koo

tobacconist *tabacaria* ⓕ ta·ba·ka·*ree*·a

tobogganing *tobogã* ⓜ to·bo·*gang*

today *hoje* o·zhe

toe *dedo do pé* de·doo doo pe

together *junto/junta* ⓜ/ⓕ zhoong·too/zhoong·ta

toilet *casa de banho* ⓕ *kaa*·za de *ba*·nyoo

toilet paper *papel higiénico* ⓜ pa·*pel* ee·zhee·e·nee·koo

toiletry bag *necessaire* ⓕ ne·se·*ser*

tomorrow *amanhã* aa·ma·*nyang*

tomorrow afternoon *amanhã à tarde* aa·ma·*nyang* aa *taar*·de

tomorrow evening *amanhã à noite* aa·ma·*nyang* aa *noy*·te

tomorrow morning *amanhã de manhã* aa·ma·*nyang* de ma·*nyang*

tonight *hoje à noite* o·zhe aa *noy*·te

too (also) *também* tang·*beng*

too (much) *demais* de·*maish*

tooth *dente* ⓜ *deng*·te

toothache *dor de dentes* ⓕ dor de *deng*·tesh

toothbrush *escova de dentes* ⓕ shko·va de *deng*·tesh

toothpaste *pasta de dentes* ⓕ *paash*·ta de *deng*·tesh

toothpick *palito* ⓜ pa·*lee*·too

torch (flashlight) *lanterna eléctrica* ⓕ lang·*ter*·na ee·*le*·tree·ka

touch *tocar* too·*kaar*

tour *excursão* ⓕ shkoor·*sowng*

tourist *turista* ⓜ&ⓕ too·*reesh*·ta

tourist office *escritório de turismo* ⓜ shkree·to·ryoo de too·*reezh*·moo

towel *toalha* ⓕ *twaa*·lya

tower *torre* ⓕ to·rre

toy shop *loja de brinquedos* ⓕ lo·zha de breeng·ke·doosh

track (path) *caminho* ⓜ ka·*mee*·nyoo

track (sport) *pista* ⓕ *peesh*·ta

tradesperson *comerciante* ⓜ&ⓕ koo·mer·see·*aang*·te

traffic *tráfico* ⓜ *traa*·fee·koo

traffic light *semáforo* ⓜ se·*maa*·foo·roo

trail *atalho* ⓜ a·*taa*·lyoo

train *comboio* ⓜ kong·*boy*·oo

train station *estação de caminhos de ferro* ⓕ shta·*sowng* de ka·*mee*·nyoosh de *fe*·rroo

tram *eléctrico* ⓜ ee·*le*·tree·koo

transit lounge *sala de trânsito* ⓕ *saa*·la de *trang*·zee·too

translate *traduzir* tra·doo·*zeer*

transport *transporte* ⓜ trangsh·*por*·te

travel *viajar* vee·a·*zhaar*

travel agency *agência de viagens* ⓕ a·*zheng*·sya de vee·*aa*·zhengsh

travellers cheques *travellers cheques* ⓜ pl *tra*·ve·ler she·kesh

travel sickness *enjoo de viagem* ⓜ eng·*zho*·oo de vee·*aa*·zheng

tree *árvore* ⓕ *aar*·vo·re

trip (journey) *viagem* ⓕ vee·*aa*·zheng

trolley *carrinho* ⓜ ka·*rree*·nyoo

trousers *calças* ⓕ pl *kaal*·sash

truck *camião* ⓜ ka·mee·*yowng*

trust *confiar* kong·fee·*aar*

try (attempt) *tentar* teng·*taar*

tube (tyre) *câmara* ⓕ *ka*·ma·ra

tumour *tumor* ⓜ too·*mor*

tune *melodia* ⓕ me·loo·*dee*·a

turn *virar* vee·*raar*

TV *televisão* ⓕ te·le·vee·*zowng*

tweezers *pinça* ⓕ *peeng*·sa

twice *duas vezes* doo·ash *ve*·zesh

twin beds *camas gémeas* ⓕ pl *ka*·mash zhe·me·ash

twins *gémeos/gémeas* ⓜ/ⓕ zhe·mee·oosh/zhe·mee·ash

type *tipo* ⓜ *tee*·poo

typical *típico/típica* ⓜ/ⓕ *tee*·pee·koo/*tee*·pee·ka

tyre *pneu* ⓜ pe·ne·oo

U

ultrasound *ultrasom* ⓜ ool·tra·*song*

umbrella *guarda-chuva* ⓜ *gwaar*·da·*shoo*·va

uncomfortable *desconfortável* desh·kong·foor·*taa*·vel

understand *compreender* kong·pree·eng·*der*

underwear *roupa interior* ⓕ *rroh*·pa eeng·te·*ree*·or

unemployed *desempregado/desempregada* ⓜ/ⓕ
de-zeng-pre-*gaa*-doo/de-zeng-pre-*gaa*-da

unfair *injusto/injusta* ⓜ/ⓕ
eeng-*zhoosh*-too/eeng-*zhoosh*-ta

uniform *farda* ⓕ *faar*-da

universe *universo* ⓜ oo-nee-*ver*-soo

university *universidade* ⓕ
oo-nee-ver-see-*daa*-de

unsafe *inseguro/insegura* ⓜ/ⓕ
eeng-se-goo-roo/eeng-se-goo-ra

until *até* a-*te*

unusual *invulgar* eeng-vool-*gaar*

up *para cima* pa-ra *see*-ma

urgent *urgente* oor-*zheng*-te

urinary infection *infecção urinária* ⓕ
eeng-fek-*sowng* oo-ree-*naa*-rya

USA *EUA* ⓜ ple-oo-*aa*

useful *útil* oo-teel

V

vacancy *vaga* ⓕ *vaa*-ga

vacant *vago/vaga* ⓜ/ⓕ *vaa*-goo/*vaa*-ga

vacation *férias* ⓕ pl fe-ree-ash

vaccination *vacina* ⓕ va-*see*-na

vagina *vagina* ⓕ va-zhee-na

validate *validar* va-lee-*daar*

valley *vale* ⓜ *vaa*-le

valuable *valioso/valiosa* ⓜ/ⓕ
va-lee-o-zoo/va-lee-o-za

value *valor* ⓜ va-*lor*

van *carrinha* ⓕ ka-*rree*-nya

vegetarian n&a *vegetariano/vegetariana*
ⓜ/ⓕ ve-zhe-ta-ree-*a*-noo/
ve-zhe-ta-ree-*a*-na

vein *veia* ⓕ *vey*-a

venereal disease *doença venérea* ⓕ
do-*eng*-sa ve-ne-ree-a

venue *local* ⓜ loo-*kaal*

very *muito* *mweeng*-too

video camera *câmara de vídeo* ⓕ
ka-ma-ra de *vee*-dee-oo

video recorder *gravador de vídeo* ⓜ
gra-va-*dor* de *vee*-dee-oo

video tape *cassete de vídeo* ⓕ
ka-*se*-te de *vee*-dee-oo

view *vista* ⓕ *veesh*-ta

village *aldeia* ⓕ aal-*day*-a

vineyard *vinha* ⓕ *vee*-nya

virus *vírus* ⓜ *vee*-roosh

visa *visto* ⓜ *veesh*-too

visit *visitar* vee-zee-*taar*

vitamin *vitamina* ⓕ vee-ta-*mee*-na

voice *voz* ⓕ vosh

volleyball (sport) *vóleibol* ⓜ *vo*-lay-bol

volume *volume* ⓜ voo-*loo*-me

vote *votar* voo-*taar*

W

wage *salário* ⓜ sa-*laa*-ryoo

wait (for) *esperar* shpe-*raar*

waiter *criado/criada de mesa* ⓜ/ⓕ
kree-*aa*-doo/kree-*aa*-da de *me*-za

waiting room *sala de espera* ⓕ
saa-la de shpe-ra

wake (someone) up *acordar* a-koor-*daar*

Wales *País de Gales* ⓜ pa-*eesh* de *gaa*-lesh

walk *caminhar* ka-mee-*nyaar*

wall (outer) *parede* ⓕ pa-*re*-de

want *querer* ke-*rer*

war *guerra* ⓕ *ge*-rra

wardrobe *guarda-roupa* ⓜ
gwaar-da-*rroh*-pa

warm *morno/morna* ⓜ/ⓕ
mor-noo/*mor*-na

warn *avisar* a-vee-*zaar*

wash *lavar* la-*vaar*

wash (oneself) *lavar-se* la-*vaar*-se

washing machine *máquina de lavar roupa*
ⓕ *maa*-kee-na de la-*vaar* rroh-pa

watch *relógio* ⓜ rre-lo-zhyoo

watch (look after) *vigiar* vee-zhee-*aar*

watch (television, etc) *ver* ver

water *água* ⓕ *aa*-gwa

water bottle *garrafa de água* ⓕ
ga-*rraa*-fa de *aa*-gwa

waterfall *cascata* ⓕ kash-*kaa*-ta

waterproof *à prova d'água*
aa *pro*-va *daa*-gwa

water-skiing *esqui aquático* ⓜ
shkee a-*kwaa*-tee-koo

wave (ocean) *onda* ⓕ *ong*-da

way *caminho* ⓜ ka-*mee*-nyoo

we *nós* nosh

weak *fraco/fraca* ⓜ/ⓕ *fraa*-koo/*fraa*-ka

wealthy *rico/rica* ⓜ/ⓕ *rree*-koo/*rree*-ka

wear *usar* oo-*zaar*

weather *tempo* ⓜ *teng*-poo

wedding *casamento* ⓜ ka-za-*meng*-too

week *semana* ⓕ se-*ma*-na

weekend *fim-de-semana* ⓜ
feeng-de-se-*ma*-na
weigh *pesar* pe-*zaar*
weight *peso* ⓜ pe-*zoo*
welcome *receber* rre-se-*ber*
welfare *seguro social* ⓜ
se-*goo*-roo soo-*see*-aal
well *bem* beng
wet *molhado/molhada* ⓜ/ⓕ
moo-*lyaa*-doo/moo-*lyaa*-da
what *que* ke
wheel *roda* ⓕ *rro*-da
wheelchair *cadeira de rodas* ⓕ
ka-*day*-ra de *rro*-dash
when *quando* kwang-doo
where *onde* ong-de
which *qual* kwaal
white *branco/branca* ⓜ/ⓕ
brang-koo/brang-ka
who *quem* keng
why *porquê* poor-*ke*
wide *largo/larga* ⓜ/ⓕ *laar*-goo/*laar*-ga
wife *esposa* ⓕ *shpo*-za
win *ganhar* ga-*nyaar*
wind *vento* ⓜ *veng*-too
window *janela* ⓕ zha-*ne*-la
windscreen (windshield) *pára-brisas* ⓜ pl
pa-ra-*bree*-zash
wine *vinho* ⓜ *vee*-nyoo
winner *vencedor/vencedora* ⓜ/ⓕ
veng-se-*dor*/veng-se-*do*-ra
wish *desejar* de-ze-*zhaar*
with *com* kong
within (time) *dentro de* deng-troo de
without *sem* seng
woman *mulher* ⓕ moo-*lyer*
wonderful *maravilhoso/maravilhosa* ⓜ/ⓕ
ma-ra-vee-*lyo*-zoo/ma-ra-vee-*lyo*-za
wood *madeira* ⓕ ma-*day*-ra
wool *lã* ⓕ lang
word *palavra* ⓕ pa-*laa*-vra

work *trabalho* ⓜ tra-*baa*-lyoo
work *trabalhar* tra-ba-*lyaar*
work experience *experiência de trabalho*
ⓕ shpe-ree-*eng*-sya de tra-*baa*-lyoo
workout *treinamento* ⓜ tre-na-*meng*-too
work permit *licença de trabalho* ⓕ
lee-*seng*-sa de tra-*baa*-lyoo
workshop *oficina* ⓕ o-fe-*see*-na
world *mundo* ⓜ moong-doo
World Cup *Taça Mundial de Futebol* ⓕ
taa-sa moong-dee-*aal* de foo-te-*bol*
worms (intestinal) *lombrigas* ⓕ pl
long-*bree*-gash
worried *preocupado/preocupada* ⓜ/ⓕ
pree-o-koo-*paa*-doo/pree-o-koo-*paa*-da
worship *reverenciar* rre-ve-reng-see-*aar*
wrist *pulso* ⓜ *pool*-soo
write *escrever* shkre-*ver*
writer *escritor/escritora* ⓜ/ⓕ
shkre-*tor*/shkre-*to*-ra
wrong *errado/errada* ⓜ/ⓕ
e-*rraa*-doo/e-*rraa*-da

Y

year *ano* ⓜ *a*-noo
yellow *amarelo/amarela* ⓜ/ⓕ
a-ma-*re*-loo/a-ma-*re*-la
yes *sim* seeng
yesterday *ontem* ong-teng
you inf sg/pl *tu/vocês* too/vo-*sesh*
you pol sg/pl *você/vós* vo-se/vosh
young *jovem* zho-veng
youth hostel *pousada de juventude* ⓕ
poh-*zaa*-da de zhoo-veng-*too*-de

Z

zip (zipper) *fecho écler* ⓜ *fe*-shoo e-*kler*
zoo *jardim zoológico* ⓜ
zhar-*deeng* zoo-oo-lo-zhee-koo

Portuguese nouns have their gender indicated with ⓜ (masculine) and ⓕ (feminine). Where adjectives or nouns have separate masculine and feminine forms, these are divided by a slash and marked ⓜ/ⓕ. You'll also see words marked as v (verb), n (noun), a (adjective), pl (plural), sg (singular), inf (informal) and pol (polite) where necessary. Verbs are given in the infinitive – for details on how to change verbs for use in a sentence, see the **phrasebuilder**, page 28. For food and drink terms, see the **culinary reader**.

A

a a *to*

à a *at*

abaixo a-*bai*-shoo *below*

abalo cerebral ⓜ
a-*baa*-loo se-re-*braal concussion*

abelha ⓕ a-*be*-lya *bee*

aberto/aberta ⓜ/ⓕ a-*ber*-too/a-*ber*-ta
open a

a bordo a *bor*-doo *aboard*

aborrecido/aborrecida ⓜ/ⓕ
a-boo-rre-*see*-doo/a-boo-rre-*see*-da *bored*

aborto ⓜ a-*bor*-too *abortion*
— **espontâneo** shpong-*ta*-nee-oo
miscarriage

abraçar a-bra-*saar hug*

abrir a-*breer open*

acampamento ⓜ a-kang-pa-*meng*-too
camping ground

acampar a-kang-*paar camp*

acidente ⓜ a-see-*deng*-te
accident • crash (car)

acordar a-koor-*daar wake (someone) up*

actor/actriz ⓜ/ⓕ aa-*tor*/aa-*treesh actor*

actuação ⓕ a-too-a-*sowng performance*

adepto/adepta ⓜ/ⓕ a-*de*-pe-too/
a-*de*-pe-ta *supporter (sport)*

adivinhar a-dee-vee-*nyaar guess*

administração ⓕ
a-de-mee-neesh-tra-*sowng
administration*

admitir a-de-mee-*teer
acknowledge • let in*

adulto/adulta ⓜ/ⓕ a-*dool*-too/a-*dool*-ta
adult n&a

advogado/advogada a-de-voo-*gaa*-doo/
a-de-voo-*gaa*-da *lawyer*

aeroporto ⓜ a-e-ro-*por*-too *airport*

afortunado/afortunada ⓜ/ⓕ
a-foor-too-*naa*-doo/a-foor-too-*naa*-da
lucky

agarrar a-ga-*rraar get*

agência ⓕ a-*zheng*-sya *agency*
— **de imobiliário** de
ee-mo-bee-*lyaa*-ryoo *real estate agency*
— **de viagens** de vee-*aa*-zhengsh
travel agency
— **noticiosa** noo-tee-see-*o*-za
newsagency

agora a-*go*-ra *now*

agradecer a-gra-de-*ser thank*

agricultor ⓜ&ⓕ a-gree-kool-*tor farmer*

agricultura ⓕ a-gree-kool-*too*-ra
agriculture

água ⓕ *aa*-gwa *water*

agulha ⓕ a-*goo*-lya *needle (sewing)*

a horas a *o*-rash *on time*

aí a-*ee there (where you are)*

ajuda ⓕ a-*zhoo*-da *help*

ajudar a-zhoo-*daar help*

alcunha ⓕ aal-*koo*-nya *nickname*

aldeia ⓕ aal-*day*-a *village*

aleijar a-lay-*zhaar hurt*

alfândega ⓕ aal-*fang*-de-ga *customs*

algodão ⓜ aal-goo-*downg cotton*

alguém ⓜ&ⓕ aal-*geng someone*

alguma coisa ⓕ aal-*goo*-ma *koy*-za
something

alguns/algumas ⓜ/① pl aal-*goongsh*/
aal-*goo*-mash *few • some*

alimentar a-lee-meng-*taar* *feed*

almoço ⓜ aal-*mo*-soo *lunch*

almofada ① al-moo-*faa*-da *pillow*

alto/alta ⓜ/① aal-too/aal-ta
high • loud • tall

alugar a-loo-*gaar* *hire (rent)*

aluguer de automóvel ⓜ
a-loo-*ger* de ow-too-mo-vel *car hire*

ama ① a-ma *babysitter • childminding*

amaciador ⓜ a-ma-see-a-*dor*
hair conditioner

amanhã aa-ma-*nyang* *tomorrow*
— **à noite** aa *noy*-te *tomorrow evening*
— **à tarde** aa *taar*-de
tomorrow afternoon
— **de manhã** de ma-*nyang*
tomorrow morning

amante ⓜ&① a-*maang*-te *lover*

amar a-*maar* *love*

amarelo/amarela ⓜ/①
a-ma-re-loo/a-ma-re-la *yellow*

amável ⓜ&① a-*maa*-vel *kind (nice)*

ambiente ⓜ ang-bee-*eng*-te *environment*

ambos/ambas ⓜ/①
ang-boosh/ang-bash *both*

ambulância ①
ang-boo-*lang*-sya *ambulance*

amigo/amiga ⓜ/①
a-*mee*-goo/a-*mee*-ga *friend*

amor ⓜ a-*mor* *love*

analgésico a-nal-*zhe*-zee-koo *painkiller*

análise de sangue ①
a-*naa*-lee-ze de *sang*-ge *blood test*

andar ⓜ ang-*daar* *floor (storey)*

andar ang-*daar* *ride*
— **a cavalo** a ka-*vaa*-loo *ride a horse*
— **de bicicleta** de bee-see-*kle*-ta
ride a bicycle

anel a-*nel* *ring (jewellery)*

anemia ① a-ne-*mee*-a *anaemia*

aniversário ⓜ a-nee-ver-*saa*-ryoo *birthday*

ano ⓜ a-noo *year*

anteontem ang-tee-*ong*-teng
day before yesterday

antes ang-*tesh* *before*

antibióticos ⓜ pl ang-tee-bee-o-te-koosh
antibiotics

antigo/antiga ⓜ/① ang-*tee*-goo/
ang-*tee*-ga *ancient • antique • old (former)*

antiguidade ① ang-tee-gwee-*daa*-de
antique

antiséptico ⓜ ang-tee-*se*-tee-koo *antiseptic*

anúncio ⓜ a-*noong*-syoo *advertisement*

ao ow *at*

ao lado de ow *laa*-doo de *beside • next to*

apanhar boleia a-pa-*nyaar* boo-*lay*-a
hitchhike

aparelho auditivo ⓜ a-pa-*re*-lyoo
ow-dee-*tee*-voo *hearing aid*

apelido ⓜ a-pe-*lee*-doo *family name*

apêndice ⓜ a-*peng*-dee-se *appendix (body)*

apertado/apertada ⓜ/①
a-per-*taa*-doo/a-per-*taa*-da *tight*

apontar a-pong-*taar* *point*

aposentado/aposentada ⓜ/①
a-poo-zeng-*taa*-doo/a-poo-zeng-*taa*-da
retired

aposta ① a-*posh*-ta *bet*

aprender a-preng-*der* *learn*

à prova d'água aa *pro*-va *daa*-gwa
waterproof

aquecedor ⓜ a-ke-se-*dor* *heater*

aquecido/aquecida ⓜ/①
a-ke-*see*-doo/a-ke-*see*-da *heated*

aquecimento ⓜ a-ke-see-*meng*-too
heating

aquele/aquela ⓜ/① a-*ke*-le/a-*ke*-la *that*

aqui a-*kee* *here*

ar ⓜ aar *air*
— **condicionado**
kong-dee-syoo-*naa*-doo *air conditioning*

aranha ① a-*ra*-nya *spider*

areia ① a-*ray*-a *sand*

arqueológico/arqueológica
ⓜ/① ar-kee-oo-*lo*-zhee-koo/
ar-kee-oo-*lo*-zhee-ka *archaeological*

arquitectura ① ar-kee-te-*too*-ra *architecture*

arte ① *aar*-te *art*

artesanato ⓜ ar-te-za-*naa*-too *crafts*

artes marciais ① pl *ar*-tesh mar-see-*aish*
martial arts

árvore ① *aar*-vo-re *tree*

asma ① *ash*-ma *asthma*

aspirina ① ash-pee-*ree*-na *aspirin*

assassinato ⓜ a-sa-see-*naa*-too *murder*

assédio ⓜ a-se-*dyoo* *harassment*

assento ⓜ a-*seng*-too *seat*

assinar a-see-*naar* *sign*

assinatura ① a-see-na-*too*-ra *signature*

assistência social ① a-seesh-*teng*-sya
soo-see-*aal* *dole (welfare)*

às vezes aash ve-zesh *sometimes*
atalho ⓜ a-*taa*-lyoo *trail*
ataque de coração ⓜ
  a-*taa*-ke de koo-ra-*sowng heart attack*
até a-*te until*
atirar a-tee-*raar shoot*
atmosfera ① at-moosh-*fe*-ra *atmosphere*
atrás a-*traash back (position)* • *behind*
atrasado/atrasada ⓜ/①
  a-tra-*zaa*-doo/a-tra-*zaa*-da *late*
atraso ⓜ a-*traa*-zoo *delay*
através a-tra-*vesh across*
autocarro ⓜ ow-to-*kaa*-roo *bus* • *coach*
autoestrada ① ow-to-*shtraa*-da
  highway • *motorway (tollway)*
avariado/avariada ⓜ/① a-va-ree-*aa*-doo/
  a-va-ree-*aa*-da *broken down (car, etc)* •
  out of order
avariar a-va-ree-*aar break down (car, etc)*
avenida ① a-ve-*nee*-da *avenue*
avião ⓜ a-vee-*owng airplane*
avisar a-vee-*zaar warn*
avó ① a-*vo grandmother*
avô ⓜ a-*voh grandfather*
azul a-*zool blue*
azulejo ① a-zoo-*le*-zhoo *painted tile*

B

bagagem ① ba-*gaa*-zheng *baggage*
bairro nos arredores da cidade ⓜ *bai*-rroo
  noosh a-rre-*do*-resh da see-*daa*-de *suburb*
baixo *bai*-shoo *down*
baixo/baixa ⓜ/① *bai*-shoo/*bai*-sha *low*
balcão ⓜ bal-*kowng counter (at bar)*
  — de bagagens de ba-*gaa*-zhengsh
  baggage claim
balde ⓜ *baal*-de *bucket*
bálsamo para os lábios ⓜ *baal*-sa-moo
  pa-ra oosh *laa*-byoosh *lip balm*
banco ⓜ *bang*-koo *bank*
bandeira ① bang-*day*-ra *flag*
banho ⓜ *ba*-nyoo *bath*
baptismo ⓜ ba-*teezh*-moo *baptism*
barata ① ba-*raa*-ta *cockroach*
barato/barata ⓜ/① ba-*raa*-too/ba-*raa*-ta
  cheap
barbeiro ⓜ bar-*bay*-roo *barber*
barco ⓜ *baar*-koo *boat*
  — a motor a moo-*tor motorboat*

barulhento/barulhenta ⓜ/①
  ba-roo-*lyeng*-too/ba-roo-*lyeng*-ta *noisy*
basquetebol ⓜ bash-ke-te-*bol basketball*
batom ⓜ ba-*tong lipstick*
bêbado/bêbada ⓜ/① be-ba-doo/be-ba-da
  drunk
bebé ⓜ&① be-*be baby*
beber be-*ber drink*
bechigas ① pl be-*shee*-gash *chicken pox*
beijo ⓜ *bay*-zhoo *kiss*
beira mar ① *bay*-ra maar *seaside*
bem beng *well*
bengaleiro ⓜ beng-ga-*lay*-roo *cloakroom*
bexiga ① be-*shee*-ga *bladder*
biblioteca ① bee-blee-oo-*te*-ka *library*
bicho ⓜ *bee*-shoo *bug*
bicicleta ① bee-see-*kle*-ta *bicycle*
  — de corrida de koo-*rree*-da *racing bike*
  — de montanha de mong-*ta*-nya
  mountain bike
bilhar ⓜ bee-*lyaar pool (game)*
bilhete ⓜ bee-*lye*-te *ticket*
  — de identidade de ee-deng-tee-*daa*-de
  identification card (ID)
  — sem garantia seng ga-rang-*tee*-a
  stand-by ticket
bilheteira ① bee-lye-*tay*-ra *ticket office*
binóculos ⓜ pl bee-*no*-koo-loosh
  binoculars
bloco-notas ⓜ blo-koo-no-tash *notebook*
bloqueado/bloqueada ⓜ/①
  blo-kee-*aa*-doo/blo-kee-*aa*-da *blocked*
boca ① *bo*-ka *mouth*
bola ① *bo*-la *ball (sport)*
bolas de algodão ① pl *bo*-lash de
  aal-goo-*downg cotton balls*
boleia ① boo-*lay*-a *ride (car, etc)*
bolha ① *bo*-lya *blister*
bolo ⓜ *bo*-loo *cake*
bolsa ① *bol*-sa *purse*
  — de trás de traash *bumbag*
bolso ⓜ *bol*-soo *pocket*
bom/boa ⓜ/① bong/*bo*-a *fine* • *good*
bomba ① *bong*-ba *pump*
boneco/boneca ⓜ/①
  boo-ne-koo/boo-ne-ka *doll*
bonito/bonita ⓜ/① boo-*nee*-too/
  boo-*nee*-ta *beautiful* • *handsome* • *pretty*
botão ⓜ boo-*towng button*
botas ① *bo*-tash *boots*
  — para caminhadas
  pa-ra ka-mee-*nyaa*-dash *hiking boots*

botija de gás ⓜ boo-tee-zha de gaash *gas cartridge*
boxe ⓜ bok-se *boxing*
braço ⓜ braa-soo *arm (body)*
branco/branca ⓜ/ⓕ brang-koo/brang-ka *white*
brincos ⓜ pl breeng-koosh *earrings*
brochura ⓕ broo-shoo-ra *brochure*
bronquite ⓕ brong-kee-te *bronchitis*
budista ⓜ&ⓕ boo-deesh-ta *Buddhist* n&a
bufete ⓜ boo-fe-te *buffet*
burro/burra ⓜ/ⓕ boo-rroo/boo-rra *stupid*
bússola ⓕ boo-soo-la *compass*

C

cabeça ⓕ ka-be-sa *head*
cabeleireiro/cabeleireira ⓜ/ⓕ ka-be-lay-ray-roo/ka-be-lay-ray-ra *hairdresser*
cabelo ⓜ ka-be-loo *hair*
cabra ⓕ kaa-bra *goat*
caça ⓕ kaa-sa *hunting*
cada ka-da *each*
cadeado ⓜ ka-dee-aa-doo *padlock*
cadeira ⓕ ka-day-ra *chair*
  — **de criança** de kree-ang-sa *child seat*
  — **de refeição para bebé** de rre-fay-sowng pa-ra be-be *highchair*
  — **de rodas** de rro-dash *wheelchair*
café ⓜ ka-fe *café • coffee*
cair ka-eer *fall*
caixa ⓕ kai-sha *box*
  — **automático** ow-too-maa-tee-koo *automated teller machine (ATM)*
  — **de papelão** de pa-pe-lowng *carton*
  — **de velocidades** de ve-loo-see-daa-desh *gearbox*
  — **do correio** doo koo-rray-oo *mailbox*
  — **registadora** rre-zheesh-ta-do-ra *cash register*
caixote do lixo ⓜ kai-sho-te doo lee-shoo *garbage can • rubbish bin*
calado/calada ⓜ/ⓕ ka-laa-doo/ka-laa-da *quiet*
calças ⓕ pl kaal-sash *trousers*
calções ⓜ pl kaal-soyngsh *shorts*
calculadora ⓕ kaal-koo-la-do-ra *calculator*
calendário ⓜ ka-leng-daa-ryoo *calendar*
calor ⓜ ka-lor *heat*

cama ⓕ ka-ma *bed*
  — **de casal** de ka-zaal *double bed*
  — **de rede** de rre-de *hammock*
câmara ⓕ ka-ma-ra *tube (tyre)*
câmara de vídeo ⓕ ka-ma-ra de vee-dee-oo *video camera*
camas gémeas ⓕ pl ka-mash zhe-me-ash *twin beds*
câmbio ⓜ kang-byoo *currency exchange*
camião ⓜ ka-mee-yowng *truck*
caminhada ⓕ ka-mee-nyaa-da *hiking*
caminhar ka-mee-nyaar *hike • walk*
caminho ⓜ ka-mee-nyoo *footpath • path • way*
camisa ⓕ ka-mee-za *shirt*
camisola ⓕ ka-mee-zo-la *sweater*
campeonatos ⓜ pl kang-pe-oo-naa-toosh *championships*
campo de golfe ⓜ kang-poo de gol-fe *golf course*
campo de ténis ⓜ kang-poo de te-neesh *tennis court*
canção ⓕ kang-sowng *song*
cancelar kang-se-laar *cancel*
cancro ⓜ kang-kroo *cancer*
caneta ⓕ ka-ne-ta *pen*
canivete ⓜ ka-nee-ve-te *pocketknife*
cansado/cansada ⓜ/ⓕ kang-saa-doo/kang-saa-da *tired*
cantor/cantora ⓜ/ⓕ kang-tor/kang-to-ra *singer*
cão ⓜ kowng *dog*
cão-guia ⓜ kowng-gee-a *guide dog*
capacete ⓜ ka-pa-se-te *helmet*
capacho ⓜ ka-paa-shoo *mat*
caro/cara ⓜ/ⓕ kaa-roo/kaa-ra *expensive*
carregar ka-rre-gaar *carry*
carrinha ⓕ ka-rree-nya *van*
carrinho ⓜ ka-rree-nyoo *trolley*
  — **de bebé** de be-be *stroller*
carro ⓜ kaa-rroo *car*
carta ⓕ kaar-ta *letter (mail)*
carta de condução ⓕ kaar-ta de kong-doo-sowng *drivers licence*
cartão ⓜ kar-towng *card*
  — **de crédito** de kre-dee-too *credit card*
  — **de embarque** de eng-baar-ke *boarding pass*
  — **telefónico** te-le-fo-nee-koo *phonecard*
cartas ⓕ pl kaar-tash *playing cards*
cartaz ⓜ kar-taash *poster*

casa ① *kaa·*za home • house
— **de banho** de *ba·*nyoo
bathroom • toilet
— **de banho pública** de *ba·*nyoo
*poo·blee·*ka *public toilet*
— **de chá** de shaa *tea house*
— **de fados** de *faa·*doosh *fado house*
— **de hóspedes** de *osh·*pe·desh
guesthouse
casaco ⓜ ka·*zaa·*koo *coat • jacket*
casado/casada ⓜ/① ka·*zaa·*doo/ka·*zaa·*da
married
casal ⓜ ka·*zaal pair (couple)*
casamento ⓜ ka·za·*meng·*too
marriage • wedding
casar ka·*zaar marry*
cascata ① kash·*kaa·*ta *waterfall*
cassete ① kaa·*se·*te *cassette*
— **de vídeo** de *vee·*dee·oo *video tape*
castanho/castanha ⓜ/①
kash·*ta·*nyoo/kash·*ta·*nya *brown*
castelo ⓜ kash·*te·*loo *castle*
catedral ① ka·te·*draal cathedral*
católico/católica ⓜ/①
ka·to·lee·koo/ka·to·lee·ka *Catholic* n&a
cauda ① *kow·*da *tail*
cavaleiro ⓜ ka·va·*lay·*roo *bullfighter*
cavalo ⓜ ka·*vaa·*loo *horse*
caverna ① ka·*ver·*na *cave*
cedo *se·*doo *early*
cego/cega ⓜ/① *se·*goo/*se·*ga *blind*
cemitério ⓜ se·mee·*te·*ryoo *cemetery*
centímetro ⓜ seng·*tee·*me·troo *centimetre*
cêntimo ⓜ *seng·*tee·moo *cent*
centro ⓜ *seng·*troo *centre*
— **comercial** koo·mer·see·*aal*
shopping centre
— **da cidade** da see·*daa·*de *city centre*
cerâmica ① se·*raa·*mee·ka *pottery*
cerca ① *ser·*ka *fence*
cerca de *ser·*ka de *about*
certidão de nascimento ① ser·tee·*downg*
de nash·see·*meng·*too *birth certificate*
cesto ① *sesh·*too *basket*
céu ⓜ *se·*oo *sky*
champô ⓜ shang·*poo shampoo*
chão ⓜ showng *floor*
chapéu ⓜ sha·*pe·*oo *hat*
charcutaria ① shar·koo·ta·*ree·*a
delicatessen
charmoso/charmosa ⓜ/①
shar·*mo·*zoo/shar·*mo·*za *charming*

charuto ⓜ sha·*roo·*too *cigar*
chato/chata ⓜ/① shaa·too/shaa·ta *boring*
chave ① *shaa·*ve *key*
chávena ① *shaa·*ve·na *cup*
chegada ① she·*gaa·*da *arrival*
chegar she·*gaar arrive*
cheio/cheia ⓜ/① *shay·*oo/*shay·*a
crowded • full
cheiro ⓜ *shay·*roo *smell*
chupeta ① shoo·*pe·*ta *dummy (pacifier)*
chutar shoo·*taar kick*
chuva ① *shoo·*va *rain*
chuveiro ⓜ shoo·*vay·*roo *shower*
ciclismo ⓜ see·*kleesh·*moo *cycling*
cidadania ① see·da·da·*nee·*a *citizenship*
cidade ① see·*daa·*de *city*
ciências ① pl see·*eng·*syash *science*
cigarro ⓜ see·*gaa·*rroo *cigarette*
cinema ⓜ see·*ne·*ma *cinema*
cinto de segurança ⓜ *seeng·*too de
se·goo·*raang·*sa *seatbelt*
cinzeiro ⓜ seeng·*zay·*roo *ashtray*
cinzento/cinzenta ⓜ/①
seeng·*zeng·*too/seeng·*zeng·*ta *grey*
circo ⓜ *seer·*koo *circus*
cirurgia ① see·roor·*zhee·*a
operation (medical)
ciumento/ciumenta ⓜ/①
see·oo·*meng·*too/see·oo·*meng·*ta *jealous*
claro/clara ⓜ/① *klaa·*roo/*klaa·*ra
light (colour)
classe ① *klaa·*se *class (category)*
— **económica** ee·koo·*no·*mee·ka
economy class
— **executiva** ee·zhe·koo·*tee·*va
business class
— **primeira** pree·*may·*ra *first class*
— **segunda** se·*goong·*da *second class*
cliente ⓜ&① klee·*eng·*te *client*
cobertor ⓜ koo·ber·*tor blanket*
cobra ① *ko·*bra *snake*
cobrador ⓜ koo·bra·*dor ticket collector*
código postal ⓜ *ko·*dee·goo poosh·*taal*
postcode
coelho ⓜ koo·*e·*lyoo *rabbit*
cofre ⓜ *ko·*fre *safe*
cola ① *ko·*la *glue*
colar ⓜ koo·*laar necklace*
colchão ⓜ kol·*showng mattress*
colega ⓜ&① koo·*le·*ga *colleague*
colete salva-vidas ⓜ koo·*le·*te
*saal·*va·vee·dash *life jacket*

C

colher ① koo-*lyer* spoon
— **de chá** de shaa *teaspoon*
colina ① koo-*lee*-na hill
colírio ⑩ koo-*lee*-ree-oo eye drops
collants ⑪ pl ko-*langsh* pantyhose
colocar koo-loo-*kaar* put
colóquio ⑩ koo-*lo*-kyoo small conference
com kong with
— **pressa** pre-sa in a hurry
— **saudades** sow-*daa*-desh homesick
comboio ⑩ kong-*boy*-oo train
começar koo-me-*saar* start
começo ⑩ koo-*me*-soo start
comédia ① koo-*me*-dya comedy
comemoração ① koo-me-moo-ra-*sowng* celebration
comer koo-*mer* eat
comerciante ⑩&① koo-mer-see-*aang*-te tradesperson
comércio ⑩ koo-*mer*-syoo trade
comichão ① koo-mee-*showng* itch
comida ① koo-*mee*-da food
— **de bebé** de be-*be* baby food
comissão ① koo-mee-*sowng* commission
como *ko*-moo how
companheiro/companheira ⑩/① kong-pa-*nyay*-roo/kong-pa-*nyay*-ra companion
companhia aérea ① kong-pa-*nyee*-a a-e-ree-a airline
compota ① kong-*po*-ta jam
comprar kong-*praar* buy
compras ⑪ pl kong-*prash* shopping
compreender kong-pree-eng-*der* understand
comprimido ⑩ kong-pree-*mee*-doo pill
comprometido/comprometida ⑩/① kong-proo-me-*tee*-doo/kong-proo-me-*tee*-da engaged (to marry)
computador ⑩ kong-poo-ta-*dor* computer
— **portátil** por-*taa*-teel laptop
comum koo-*moong* ordinary
comunhão ① koo-moo-*nyowng* communion
concerto ⑩ kong-*ser*-too concert
concordar kong-koor-*daar* agree
conduzir kong-doo-*zeer* drive
conferência ① kong-fe-*reng*-sya big conference
confiar kong-fee-*aar* trust
confirmar kong-feer-*maar* confirm
confissão ① kong-fee-*sowng* confession

confortável kong-for-*taa*-vel comfortable
congelar kong-zhe-*laar* freeze
conhecer koo-nye-*ser* meet (first time)
conjuntivite ① kong-zhoong-tee-*vee*-te conjunctivitis
conselho ⑩ kong-se-*lyoo* advice
consertar kong-ser-*taar* repair
conservador/conservadora ⑩/① kong-ser-va-*dor*/kong-ser-va-*do*-ra conservative n&a
constipação ① kong-shtee-pa-*sowng* cold (illness)
construir kong-shtroo-*eer* build
construtor ⑩ kong-shtroo-*tor* builder
consulado ⑩ kong-soo-*laa*-doo consulate
consulta ① kong-*sool*-ta appointment
consumo obrigatório ⑩ kon-soo-moo o-bree-ga-*to*-ree-oo cover charge
conta ① *kong*-ta bill (restaurant) • account
— **bancária** bang-*kaa*-rya bank account
contar kong-*taar* count
contraceptivo ⑩ kong-tra-se-*tee*-voo contraceptives
contrato ⑩ kong-*traa*-too contract
convidar kong-vee-*daar* invite
copo ⑩ *ko*-poo glass (drinking)
cor ① kor colour
— **de laranja** de la-*rang*-zha orange (colour)
coração ⑩ koo-ra-*sowng* heart
corajoso/corajosa ⑩/① koo-ra-*zho*-zoo/koo-ra-*zho*-za brave
corda ① *kor*-da rope
cordeiro ⑩ koor-*day*-roo lamb (animal)
cordel ⑩ koor-*del* string
cor-de-rosa kor-de-*rro*-za pink
cordilheira ① koor-dee-*lyay*-ra mountain range
corpo ⑩ *kor*-poo body
correcto/correcta ⑩/① koo-*rre*-too/koo-*rre*-ta right (correct)
correia da ventoinha ① koo-*rray*-a da veng-too-ee-nya fanbelt
correio ⑩ koo-*rray*-oo mail (letters/postal system) • post office
— **azul** a-*zool* express mail
— **registado** re-zhee-*shtaa*-doo registered mail
corrente ① koo-*rreng*-te current (electricity)
corrente de bicicleta ① koo-*rreng*-te de bee-see-*kle*-ta bike chain
correr koo-*rrer* run

228

correspondência ①
koo-rresh-pong-*deng*-sya *mail (letters)*
— **por via marítima** poor *vee*-a
ma-*ree*-tee-ma *surface mail (sea)*
— **por via terrestre** poor *vee*-a
te-*rresh*-tre *surface mail (land)*
corrida ① koo-*rree*-da *jogging · race (sport)*
corrimento ⓜ koo-rree-*meng*-too
thrush (health)
corrupto/corrupta ⓜ/①
koo-*rroop*-too/koo-*rroop*-ta *corrupt*
cortar koor-*taar* *cut*
corta-unhas ⓜ *kor*-ta-oong-nyash
nail clippers
corte de cabelo ⓜ *kor*-te de ka-*be*-loo
haircut
coser koo-*zer* *sew*
costas ① pl *kosh*-tash *back (body)*
costela ① koosh-*te*-la *rib (body)*
costume ⓜ koosh-*too*-me *custom*
cotonete ⓜ ko-to-*ne*-te *cotton buds*
couro cabeludo ⓜ koh-roo ka-be-*loo*-doo
scalp
couro ⓜ *koh*-roo *leather*
coxia ① koo-*shee*-a *aisle*
cozinha ① koo-*zee*-nya *cooking · kitchen*
cozinhar koo-zee-*nyaar* *cook*
cozinheiro/cozinheira ⓜ/①
koo-zee-*nyay*-roo/koo-zee-*nyay*-ra *cook*
crânio ⓜ *kra*-nyoo *skull*
crédito ⓜ *kre*-dee-too *credit*
creme ⓜ *kre*-me *cream (food/lotion)*
— **de barbear** de bar-bee-*aar*
shaving cream
crescer kresh-*ser* *grow*
criado/criada de mesa ⓜ/①
kree-*aa*-doo/kree-*aa*-da de *me*-za *waiter*
criança ⓜ&① kree-*ang*-sa *child*
Cristão/Cristã ⓜ/①
kreesh-*towng*/kreesh-*tang* *Christian* n&a
cru/crua ⓜ/① kroo/*kroo*-a *raw*
cruz ① kroosh *cross (religious)*
cuidar kwee-*daar* *look after*
culpa ① *kool*-pa *fault (someone's)*
culpado/culpada ⓜ/①
kool-*paa*-doo/kool-*paa*-da *guilty*
cupão ⓜ koo-*powng* *coupon*
currículo ⓜ koo-*rree*-koo-loo
curriculum vitae · résumé
curto/curta ⓜ/① *koor*-too/*koor*-ta
short (length)
custar koosh-*taar* *cost*

D

dança ① *dang*-sa *dance · dancing*
dançar dang-*saar* *dance*
da noite da *noy*-te *evening*
dar daar *give · deal (cards)*
dar conversa daar kong-*ver*-sa *chat up (flirt)*
data ① *daa*-ta *date (day)*
— **de nascimento**
de nash-see-*meng*-too *date of birth*
de de *from*
decidir de-see-*deer* *decide*
dedo ⓜ *de*-doo *finger*
— **do pé** doo pe *toe*
defeituoso/defeituosa ⓜ/①
de-fay-too-*o*-zoo/de-fay-too-*o*-za *faulty*
deficiente de-fee-see-*eng*-te *disabled*
deitar-se day-*taar*-se *lie (not stand)*
demais de-*maish* *too (much)*
democracia ① de-moo-kra-*see*-a
democracy
de noite de *noy*-te *overnight*
dente ⓜ *deng*-te *tooth*
dentes ⓜ pl *deng*-tesh *teeth*
dentista ⓜ&① deng-*teesh*-ta *dentist*
dentro *deng*-troo *inside*
dentro de *deng*-troo de *within (time)*
depois de-*poysh* *after*
— **de amanhã** de aa-ma-*nyang*
day after tomorrow
depósito ⓜ de-*po*-zee-too *deposit (bank)*
— **de bagagens** de-*po*-zee-too de
ba-*gaa*-zhengsh *luggage locker*
depressa de-*pre*-sa *fast* adv
descansar desh-kang-*saar* *rest*
descer desh-*ser* *get off (bus, train)*
desconfortável desh-kong-foor-*taa*-vel
uncomfortable
desconto ⓜ desh-*kong*-too *discount*
desde *dezh*-de *since (time)*
desejar de-ze-*zhaar* *wish*
desempregado/desempregada ⓜ/①
de-zeng-pre-*gaa*-doo/de-zeng-pre-*gaa*-da
unemployed
deserto ⓜ de-*zer*-too *desert*
desistir de-zeesh-*teer* *quit*
desligado/desligada ⓜ/①
desh-lee-*gaa*-doo/desh-lee-*gaa*-da
off (power)
desodorizante ⓜ de-zo-doo-ree-*zang*-te
deodorant

despertador ⓜ desh·per·ta·dor *alarm clock*
desportista ⓜ&ⓕ desh·poor·teesh·ta *sportsperson*
desporto ⓜ desh·por·too *sport*
destino ⓜ desh·tee·noo *destination*
detalhes ⓜ pl de·taa·lyesh *details*
Deus ⓜ de·oosh *God (general)*
devagar de·va·gaar *slow (down)* v
dever de·ver *owe*
dia ⓜ dee·a *day*
— de Ano Novo de a·noo no·voo *New Year's Day*
— de Natal de na·taal *Christmas Day*
diabetes ① dee·a·be·tesh *diabetes*
diafragma ⓜ dee·a·fraa·ge·ma *diaphragm*
diapositivo ⓜ dee·a·po·zee·tee·voo *slide (transparency)*
diário ⓜ dee·aa·ryoo *diary*
diário/diária ⓜ/① dee·aa·ryoo/dee·aa·rya *daily*
dicionário ⓜ dee·syoo·naa·ryoo *dictionary*
dieta ① dee·e·ta *diet*
diferença horária ① dee·fe·reng·sa o·raa·rya *time difference*
diferente dee·fe·reng·te *different*
difícil dee·fee·seel *difficult*
dinheiro ⓜ dee·nyay·roo *money*
direcção ① dee·re·sowng *direction*
directo/directa ⓜ/① dee·re·too/dee·re·ta *direct · straight*
director/directora ⓜ/① dee·re·tor/dee·re·to·ra *director*
(à) direita (aa) dee·ray·ta *right (direction)*
Direito ⓜ dee·ray·too *law (profession)*
direitos ⓜ pl dee·ray·toosh *rights*
— civis see·veesh *civil rights*
— humanos oo·ma·noosh *human rights*
discoteca ① deesh·koo·te·ka *nightclub*
discriminação ① deesh·kree·mee·na·sowng *discrimination*
discutir deesh·koo·teer *argue*
disponível deesh·po·nee·vel *available*
DIU ⓜ de·ee·oo *IUD*
divertido/divertida ⓜ/① dee·ver·tee·doo/dee·ver·tee·da *fun*
divertir-se dee·ver·teer·se *enjoy (oneself)*
divorciado/divorciada ⓜ/① dee·vor·see·aa·doo/dee·vor·see·aa·da *divorced*
dizer dee·zer *say · tell*
doce do·se *sweet*

documentário ⓜ doo·koo·meng·taa·ryoo *documentary*
doença ① doo·eng·sa *disease*
— venérea ve·ne·ree·a *venereal disease*
doente doo·eng·te *sick*
doloroso/dolorosa ⓜ/① doo·loo·ro·zoo/doo·loo·ro·za *painful*
dona de casa ① do·na de kaa·za *homemaker*
dono/dona ⓜ/① do·noo/do·na *owner*
dor ① dor *pain*
— de cabeça de ka·be·sa *headache*
— de dentes de deng·tesh *toothache*
— de estômago de shto·ma·goo *stomachache*
— menstrual meng·shtroo·aal *period pain*
dorido/dorida ⓜ/① doo·ree·doo/doo·ree·da *sore*
dormir door·meer *sleep*
dose excessiva ① do·ze she·see·va *overdose*
droga ① dro·ga *drug*
drogado/drogada ⓜ/① droo·gaa·doo/droo·gaa·da *stoned (drugged)*
duas vezes doo·ash ve·zesh *twice*
duplo/dupla ⓜ/① doo·ploo/doo·pla *double*
duro/dura ⓜ/① doo·roo/doo·ra *hard (not soft)*

E

e e *and*
educação ① e·doo·ka·sowng *education*
egoísta e·goo·eesh·ta *selfish*
ela e·la *she*
ele e·le *he*
electricidade ① ee·le·tree·see·daa·de *electricity*
eléctrico ⓜ ee·le·tree·koo *tram*
eleição ① e·lay·sowng *election*
eles/elas e·lesh/e·lash *they*
elevador ⓜ ee·le·va·dor *lift (elevator)*
em eng at · in
— breve bre·ve *soon*
— frente freng·te *ahead*
— segunda mão se·goong·da mowng *second-hand*
embaixada ① eng·bai·shaa·da *embassy*

embaixador/embaixatriz ⓜ/ⓕ
eng-bai-sha-*dor*/eng-bai-sha-*treesh*
ambassador

embraiagem ⓕ eng-brai-*aa*-zheng
clutch (car)

embrulho ⓜ eng-*broo*-lyoo *package*

ementa ⓕ ee-*meng*-ta *menu*

emergência ⓕ ee-mer-*zheng*-sya
emergency

empregado/empregada ⓜ/ⓕ
eng-pre-*gaa*-doo/eng-pre-*gaa*-da
employee

　—de escritório de shkree-*to*-ryoo
office worker

　— por conta própria poor *kong*-ta
pro-pree-a *self-employed person*

emprego ⓜ eng-*pre*-goo *job*

empresa ⓕ eng-*pre*-za *company (firm)*

empurrar eng-poo-*rraar* *push*

encher eng-*sher* *fill*

encomenda ⓕ eng-koo-*meng*-da *parcel*

encontrar eng-kong-*traar* *find • meet*

encontro ⓜ eng-*kong*-troo *date
(appointment)*

endereço ⓜ eng-de-*re*-soo *address*

enevoado/enevoada ⓜ/ⓕ
e-ne-vo-*aa*-doo/e-ne-voo-*aa*-da *foggy*

enfermeiro/enfermeira ⓜ/ⓕ
eng-fer-*may*-roo/eng-fer-*may*-ra *nurse*

engenharia ⓕ eng-zhe-nya-*ree*-a
engineering

engraçado/engraçada ⓜ/ⓕ
eng-gra-*saa*-doo/eng-gra-*saa*-da *funny*

enjoado/enjoada ⓜ/ⓕ
eng-zhoo-*aa*-doo/eng-zhoo-*aa*-da *seasick*

enjoo ⓜ eng-*zho*-oo *nausea*

　— de viagem de vee-*aa*-zheng
travel sickness

　— matinal ma-tee-*naal* *morning sickness*

enorme ee-*nor*-me *huge*

ensolarado/ensolarada ⓜ/ⓕ
eng-soo-la-*raa*-doo/eng-soo-la-*raa*-da
sunny

entorse ⓕ eng-*tor*-se *sprain*

entrada ⓕ eng-*traa*-da *admission • entry*

entrar eng-*traar* *enter*

entre *eng*-tre *between*

entregar eng-tre-*gaar* *deliver*

entrevista ⓕ eng-tre-*veesh*-ta *interview*

envergonhado/envergonhada ⓜ/ⓕ
en-ver-goo-*nyaa*-doo/en-ver-goo-*nyaa*-da
embarrassed

enviar eng-vee-*aar* *post • send*

enxaqueca ⓕ eng-sha-*ke*-ka *migraine*

equipa ⓕ e-*kee*-pa *team*

equipamento ⓜ e-kee-pa-*meng*-too
equipment

　— de mergulho de mer-*goo*-lyoo
diving equipment

errado/errada ⓜ/ⓕ e-*rraa*-doo/e-*rraa*-da
wrong

erro ⓜ e-*rroo* *mistake*

escadaria ⓕ shka-da-*ree*-a *stairway*

escada rolante ⓕ shkaa-da rroo-*lang*-te
escalator

escola ⓕ shko-la *school*

　— secundária se-koong-*daa*-ree-a
high school

escolher shkoo-*lyer* *choose*

escova ⓕ shko-va *hairbrush*

　— de dentes de *deng*-tesh *toothbrush*

escrever shkre-*ver* *write*

escritor/escritora ⓜ/ⓕ
shkree-*tor*/shkree-*to*-ra *writer*

escritório ⓜ shkree-*to*-ryoo *office*

　— de turismo de too-*reezh*-moo
tourist office

escultura ⓕ shkool-*too*-ra *sculpture*

escuro/escura ⓜ/ⓕ shkoo-roo/shkoo-ra
dark (colour/night)

escutar shkoo-*taar* *hear • listen*

esgotado/esgotada ⓜ/ⓕ
shgoo-*taa*-doo/shgoo-*taa*-da *booked out*

espaço ⓜ shpaa-soo *space (room)*

Espanha ⓕ shpa-nya *Spain*

espanhol ⓜ shpa-*nyol* *Spanish (language)*

especial shpe-see-*aal* *special*

especialista ⓜ&ⓕ shpe-see-a-*leesh*-ta
specialist

espectáculo ⓜ shpe-*taa*-koo-loo *show*

espelho ⓜ shpe-*lyoo* *mirror*

esperar shpe-*raar* *wait (for)*

esposa ⓕ shpo-za *wife*

esquadra da polícia ⓕ
shkwaa-dra da poo-*lee*-sya *police station*

esquecer shke-*ser* *forget*

esquerda ⓕ shker-da *left (direction)*

esqui ⓜ shkee *ski • skiing*

　— aquático a-*kwaa*-tee-koo
water-skiing

esquiar shkee-*aar* *ski*

esquina ⓕ shkee-na *corner*

estaca ⓕ shtaa-ka *tent peg*

estação ① shta-*sowng season* • *station*
— **de caminhos de ferro** de
ka-*mee*-nyoosh de *fe*-rroo *train station*
— **de metropolitano** de
me-troo-poo-lee-*ta*-noo *metro station*
estacionar shta-syoo-*naar park* (a car)
estádio ⓜ *shta*-dyoo *stadium*
estado civil ⓜ *shtaa*-doo see-*veel*
marital status
estar shtaar *be* (temporary)
— **constipado/constipada** ⓜ/①
kong-shtee-*paa*-doo/kong-shtee-*paa*-da
have a cold
estátua ① *shtaa*-too-a *statue*
este/esta ⓜ/① *esh*-te/*esh*-ta *this*
estendal da roupa ①
shteng-*daal* da *rroh*-pa *clothesline*
estéreo ⓜ *shte*-ree-oo *stereo*
estilo ⓜ *shtee*-loo *style*
estojo de primeiros socorros ⓜ
shto-zhoo de pree-*may*-roosh
so-*ko*-rroosh *first-aid kit*
estômago ⓜ *shto*-ma-goo *stomach*
estrada ① *shtraa*-da *road*
estrangeiro/estrangeira ⓜ/①
shtrang-*zhay*-roo/shtrang-*zhay*-ra *foreign*
estranho/estranha ⓜ/①
shtra-nyoo/*shtra*-nya *strange* • *stranger*
estrela ① *shtre*-la *star*
estudante ⓜ&① shtoo-*dang*-te *student*
estúdio ⓜ *shtoo*-dyoo *studio*
etiqueta de bagagem ①
e-tee-*ke*-ta de ba-*gaa*-zheng *luggage tag*
eu *e-oo I*
EUA ⓜ pl e-oo-*aa USA*
euro ⓜ *e-oo*-roo *euro*
Europa ① e-oo-*ro*-pa *Europe*
exactamente e-za-ta-*meng*-te *exactly*
exame papa nicolau ① e-*za*-me *paa*-pa
nee-koo-*low pap smear*
exaustor ⓜ ee-*zowsh*-tor *exhaust* (car)
excelente ay-she-*leng*-te *excellent*
excluído/excluída ⓜ/① aysh-kloo-ee-*doo*/
aysh-kloo-*ee*-da *excluded*
excursão ① shkoor-*sowng tour*
— **guiada** gee-*aa*-da *guided tour*
exemplo ⓜ e-*zeng*-ploo *example*
experiência ① shpe-ree-*eng*-sya *experience*
— **de trabalho** ① de tra-*baa*-lyoo
work experience
exploração ① shplo-ra-*sowng exploitation*
exposição ① shpoo-zee-*sowng exhibition*

expresso/expressa ⓜ/①
shpre-soo/esh-*pre*-sa *express*
extensão ① shteng-*sowng extension* (visa)

F

fábrica ① *faa*-bree-ka *factory*
faca ① *faa*-ka *knife*
fácil *faa*-seel *easy*
fado ⓜ *faa*-doo *fado* (music)
falar fa-*laar speak* • *talk*
falta ① *faal*-ta *foul* (soccer)
família ① fa-*mee*-lya *family*
faminto/faminta ⓜ/①
fa-*meeng*-too/fa-*meeng*-ta *hungry*
famoso/famosa ⓜ/①
fa-*mo*-zoo/fa-*mo*-za *famous*
farda ① *faar*-da *uniform*
farinha ① fa-*ree*-nya *flour*
farmacêutico/farmacêutica ⓜ/①
far-ma-se-oo-*tee*-koo/far-ma-se-oo-*tee*-ka
pharmacist
farmácia ① far-*maa*-sya *pharmacy*
faróis ⓜ pl fa-*roysh headlights*
fatia ① fa-*tee*-a *slice*
fato de banho ⓜ *faa*-too de *ba*-nyoo
swimsuit
fax ⓜ faaks *fax*
fazer fa-*zer do* • *make*
— **a barba** a *baar*-ba *shave*
— **a contagem** a kong-*taa*-zheng
score (keep)
— **compras** kong-*prash go shopping*
— **surf** sarf *surf*
febre ① *fe*-bre *fever*
— **dos fenos** doosh *fe*-noosh *hay fever*
— **glandular** glang-doo-*laar*
glandular fever
fechado/fechada ⓜ/①
fe-*shaa*-doo/fe-*shaa*-da *closed*
fechar fe-*shaar close*
fecho écler ⓜ *fe*-shoo e-*kler zip* (zipper)
feira ① *fay*-ra *fair* • *street market*
— **da ladra** da *laa*-dra *fleamarket*
feito/feita à mão ⓜ/①
fay-too/*fay*-ta aa mowng *handmade*
feliz fe-*leesh happy*
feminino/feminina ⓜ/①
fe-mee-nee-*noo*/fe-mee-nee-*na female*
feriado ⓜ fe-ree-*aa*-doo *holiday*
férias ① pl *fe*-ryash *vacation*

ferido/ferida ⓜ/ⓕ fe-*ree*-doo/fe-*ree*-da *injured*

ferimento ⓜ fe-ree-*meng*-too *injury*

ferro de engomar ⓜ fe-rroo de eng-goo-*maar* *iron (clothes)*

festa ⓕ *fesh*-ta *party (night out)*
— **na rua** na rroo-a *street party*

festival ⓜ *fesh*-tee-*vaal* *festival*

ficar fee-*kaar* *stay*

ficção ⓕ feek-*sowng* *fiction*

fígado ⓜ *fee*-ga-doo *liver*

fila ⓕ *fee*-la *queue*

filha ⓕ *fee*-lya *daughter*

filho ⓜ *fee*-lyoo *son*

filme ⓜ *feel*-me *movie • photographic film*
— **de diapositivos** de dee-a-po-zee-*tee*-voosh *slide film*

filtrado/filtrada ⓜ/ⓕ *feel*-*traa*-doo/*feel*-*traa*-da *filtered*

fim feeng *end*

fim-de-semana ⓜ feeng-de-se-*ma*-na *weekend*

fino/fina ⓜ/ⓕ *fee*-noo/*fee*-na *thin*

fio dental ⓜ *fee*-oo deng-*taal* *dental floss*

fixe *fee*-she *cool (exciting)*

flor ⓕ flor *flower*

floresta ⓕ floo-*resh*-ta *forest*

florista ⓕ floo-*reesh*-ta *florist (shop)*

fogão ⓜ foo-*gowng* *stove*

fogo ⓜ *fo*-goo *fire*

folha ⓕ *fo*-lya *leaf*

fora *fo*-ra *outside*

forças armadas ⓕ pl *for*-sash ar-*maa*-dash *military*

forma ⓕ *for*-ma *shape*

forno ⓜ *for*-noo *oven*

forte *for*-te *strong*

fósforos ⓜ pl *fosh*-foo-roosh *matches (for lighting)*

fotografar foo-too-gra-*faar* *photograph*

fotografia ⓕ foo-too-gra-*fee*-a *photography*

fotógrafo/fotógrafa ⓜ/ⓕ foo-*to*-gra-foo/foo-*to*-gra-fa *photographer*

fotómetro ⓜ foo-*to*-me-troo *light meter*

fraco/fraca ⓜ/ⓕ *fraa*-koo/*fraa*-ka *weak*

frágil *fraa*-zheel *fragile*

fralda ⓕ *fraal*-da *nappy (diaper)*

frequentemente fre-kweng-te-*meng*-te *often*

fresco/fresca ⓜ/ⓕ *fresh*-koo/*fresh*-ka *cool (cold) • fresh*

frigorífico ⓜ free-goo-*ree*-fee-koo *refrigerator*

frio/fria ⓜ/ⓕ *free*-oo/*free*-a *cold*

fronha ⓕ *fro*-nya *pillowcase*

fronteira ⓕ frong-*tay*-ra *border (country)*

fumar foo-*maar* *smoke*

fundo ⓕ *foong*-doo *bottom (position)*

funeral ⓜ foo-ne-*raal* *funeral*

furo ⓜ *foo*-roo *puncture*

futuro ⓜ foo-*too*-roo *future*

G

gabardina ⓕ gaa-baar-*dee*-na *raincoat*

gabinete de perdidos e achados ⓜ gaa-bee-*ne*-te de per-*dee*-doosh ee a-*shaa*-doosh *lost property office*

galeria de arte ⓕ ga-le-*ree*-a de *aar*-te *art gallery*

galinha ⓕ ga-*lee*-nya *chicken*

ganhar ga-*nyaar* *earn • win*

garagem ⓕ ga-*raa*-zheng *garage*

garantido/garantida ⓜ/ⓕ ga-rang-*tee*-doo/ga-rang-*tee*-da *guaranteed*

garfo ⓜ *gaar*-foo *fork*

garganta ⓕ gar-*gang*-ta *throat*

garrafa ⓕ ga-*rraa*-fa *bottle*

gás ⓜ gaash *gas (cooking)*

gasolina ⓕ ga-zoo-*lee*-na *gas (petrol)*

gastrenterite ⓕ gash-treng-te-*ree*-te *gastroenteritis*

gato/gata ⓜ/ⓕ *gaa*-too/*gaa*-ta *cat*

gaze ⓕ *gaa*-ze *gauze*

geada ⓕ zhee-*aa*-da *frost*

gelado/gelada ⓜ/ⓕ zhe-*laa*-doo/zhe-*laa*-da *frozen*

gelo ⓜ *zhe*-loo *ice*

gémeos/gémeas ⓜ/ⓕ *zhe*-mee-oosh/*zhe*-mee-ash *twins*

gerente zhe-*reng*-te *manager (business)*

gilete ⓕ zhee-*le*-te *razor*

ginásio ⓜ zhee-*naa*-zyoo *gym (place)*

golo ⓜ *go*-loo *goal (sport)*

gordo/gorda ⓜ/ⓕ *gor*-doo/*gor*-da *fat*

gorjeta ⓕ gor-*zhe*-ta *tip (gratuity)*

gostar goosh-*taar* *care (for someone) • like*

gostoso/gostosa ⓜ/ⓕ goosh-*to*-zoo/goosh-*to*-za *tasty*

governo ⓜ goo-*ver*-noo *government*

grama ⓜ *graa*-ma *gram*

grande *grang*-de big
grátis *graa*-teesh complimentary (free)
grato/grata ⓜ/ⓕ *graa*-too/*graa*-ta grateful
graus ⓜ pl growsh degrees (temperature)
gravação ⓕ gra-va-*sowng* recording
gravador de vídeo ⓜ
   gra-va-dor de vee-dee-oo video recorder
gravar gra-*vaar* record
grávida *graa*-vee-da pregnant
greve ⓕ *gre*-ve strike
gripe ⓕ *gree*-pe influenza
gritar gree-*taar* shout
grosso/grossa ⓜ/ⓕ *gro*-soo/*gro*-sa thick
grupo ⓜ *groo*-poo band (music) • group
   — **sanguíneo** sang-*gwee*-nee-oo
   blood type
guarda-chuva ⓜ gwar-da-*shoo*-va
   umbrella
guardanapo ⓜ gwar-da-*naa*-poo napkin
guarda-redes gwaar-da-*rre*-desh
   goalkeeper
guarda-roupa ⓜ gwaar-da-*rroh*-pa
   wardrobe
guerra ⓕ *ge*-rra war
guia ⓜ *gee*-a guide (person)
   — **auditivo** ow-dee-*tee*-voo audio guide
   — **de espectáculos** de
   shpe-*taa*-koo-loosh entertainment guide
   — **de viagem** de vee-*aa*-zheng
   guidebook

H

há (três dias) aa (tresh *dee*-ash)
   (three days) ago
hepatite ⓕ e-pa-*tee*-te hepatitis
hidratante ⓜ ee-dra-*tang*-te moisturiser
hindu ⓜ&ⓕ eeng-*doo* Hindu n&a
hipismo ⓜ ee-*peezh*-moo horseriding
história ⓕ *shto*-rya history • story
hoje *o*-zhe today
   — **à noite** aa *noy*-te tonight
homem ⓜ *o*-meng man
   — **de negócios** de ne-*go*-syoosh
   businessman
homosexual ⓜ&ⓕ o-mo-sek-soo-*aal*
   homosexual n&a
hóquei ⓜ *o*-kay hockey
   — **sobre o gelo** so-bre oo *zhe*-loo
   ice hockey
hora ⓕ *o*-ra hour

horário ⓜ o-*raa*-ryoo timetable
   — **de expediente** de shpe-dee-*eng*-te
   opening hours
horóscopo ⓜ o-*rosh*-koo-poo horoscope
horrível o-*rree*-vel awful
hospedagem ⓕ osh-pe-*daa*-zheng
   accommodation
hospital ⓜ osh-pee-*taal* hospital
hospitalidade ⓕ osh-pee-ta-lee-*daa*-de
   hospitality
hotel ⓜ o-*tel* hotel

I

idade ⓕ ee-*daa*-de age
ida e volta ee-da ee *vol*-ta return (ticket)
identificação ⓕ
   ee-deng-tee-fee-ka-*sowng*
   identification
igreja ⓕ ee-*gre*-zha church
igualdade ⓕ ee-gwal-*daa*-de equality
   — **de oportunidades**
   de o-poor-too-nee-*daa*-desh
   equal opportunity
ilha ⓕ *ee*-lya island
imigração ⓕ ee-mee-gra-*sowng*
   immigration
importante eeng-por-*tang*-te important
impossível eeng-po-*see*-vel impossible
imposto ⓜ eeng-*posh*-too tax
   — **de rendimentos**
   de rreng-dee-*meng*-toosh income tax
impressora ⓕ eeng-pre-*so*-ra
   printer (computer)
inchaço ⓜ eeng-*shaa*-soo swelling
incluído/incluída ⓜ/ⓕ eeng-kloo-ee-doo/
   eeng-kloo-ee-da included
indigestão ⓕ eeng-dee-zhesh-*towng*
   indigestion
indústria ⓕ eeng-*doosh*-trya industry
infantário ⓜ eeng-fang-*taa*-ree-oo crèche
infecção ⓕ eeng-fe-*sowng* infection
   — **urinária** oo-ree-*naa*-rya
   urinary infection
inflamação ⓕ eeng-fla-ma-*sowng*
   inflammation
informação ⓕ eeng-for-ma-*sowng*
   information
informática ⓕ eeng-for-*maa*-tee-ka IT
Inglaterra ⓕ eeng-gla-*te*-rra England
inglês ⓜ eeng-*glesh* English (language)

ingrediente ⓜ eeng-gre-dee-*eng*-te *ingredient*

íngreme *eeng*-gre-me *steep*

injecção ⓕ eeng-zhe-*sowng* *injection*

injectar eeng-zhe-*taar inject*

injusto/injusta ⓜ/ⓕ eeng-*zhoosh*-too/eeng-*zhoosh*-ta *unfair*

inocente ee-noo-*seng*-te *innocent*

inseguro/insegura ⓜ/ⓕ eeng-se-*goo*-roo/eeng-se-*goo*-ra *unsafe*

insolação ⓕ eeng-soo-la-*sowng sunstroke*

instrutor/instrutora ⓜ/ⓕ eeng-shtroo-*tor*/eeng-shtroo-*to*-ra *instructor*

interessante eeng-te-re-*sang*-te *interesting*

interior do país ⓜ eeng-te-*ree*-or doo pa-*eesh countryside*

internacional eeng-ter-naa-syoo-*naal international*

internet ⓕ eeng-ter-*net Internet*

intervalo ⓜ eeng-ter-*vaa*-loo *intermission*

inundação ⓕ ee-noong-da-*sowng flood*

inverno ⓜ eeng-*ver*-noo *winter*

invulgar eeng-vool-*gaar unusual*

ir eer *go*

irmã ⓕ eer-*mang sister*

irmão ⓜ eer-*mowng brother*

irritação da pele ⓕ ee-rree-ta-*sowng* da *pe*-le *rash*

irritação por causa da fralda ⓕ ee-rree-ta-*sowng* poor *kow*-sa da *fraal*-da *nappy rash*

isqueiro ⓜ eesh-*kay*-roo *cigarette lighter*

itinerário ⓜ ee-tee-ne-*raa*-ryoo *itinerary*

IVA ⓜ *ee*-va *sales tax*

J

já zhaa *already*

janela ⓕ zha-*ne*-la *window*

jantar ⓜ zhang-*taar dinner*

jardim ⓜ zhar-*deeng garden*
  — botânico boo-*ta*-nee-koo *botanic garden*
  — de infância de eeng-*fang*-sya *kindergarten*
  — zoológico zoo-oo-*lo*-zhee-koo *zoo*

jardinagem ⓕ zhar-dee-*naa*-zheng *gardening*

jardins públicos ⓜ pl zhar-*deengzh poo*-blee-koosh *public gardens*

jipe ⓜ *zhee*-pe *jeep*

joelho ⓜ zhoo-e-*lyoo knee*

jogar zhoo-*gaar play (cards, etc)*

jogo ⓜ *zho*-goo *game (sport)*
  — de computador de kong-poo-ta-*dor computer game*

jornal ⓜ zhor-*naal newspaper*

jornalista ⓜ&ⓕ zhor-na-*leesh*-ta *journalist*

jovem *zho*-veng *young*

Judeu/Judia ⓜ/ⓕ zhoo-*de*-oo/zhoo-*dee*-a *Jewish*

juiz/juiza ⓜ/ⓕ zhoo-*eesh*/zhoo-ee-za *judge • referee*

junto/junta ⓜ/ⓕ *zhoong*-too/*zhoong*-ta *together*

L

lá laa *there (where neither of us is)*

lã ⓕ lang *wool*

lábios ⓜ pl *laa*-byoosh *lips*

lado ⓜ *laa*-doo *side*

ladrão/ladra ⓜ/ⓕ la-*drowng*/*laa*-dra *thief*

lagarto ⓜ la-*gaar*-too *lizard*

lago ⓜ *laa*-goo *lake*

lama ⓕ *laa*-ma *mud*

lâmina de barbear ⓕ *laa*-mee-na de bar-bee-*aar razor blade*

lâmpada ⓕ *lang*-pa-da *light bulb*

lanterna eléctrica ⓕ lang-*ter*-na ee-*le*-tree-ka *torch (flashlight)*

lápis ⓜ *laa*-peesh *pencil*

largo/larga ⓜ/ⓕ *laar*-goo/*laar*-ga *wide*

lata ⓕ *laa*-ta *tin (can)*

lavandaria ⓕ la-vang-da-*ree*-a *laundry (clothes/place)*

lavar la-*vaar wash*

lavar-se la-*vaar*-se *wash (oneself)*

laxante ⓜ la-*shang*-te *laxative*

legal le-*gaal legal*

legendas ⓕ pl le-*zheng*-dash *subtitles*

legislação ⓕ le-zheezh-la-*sowng legislation*

lei ⓕ lay *law (legislation)*

leitura ⓕ lay-*too*-ra *reading*

lembrança ⓕ leng-*brang*-sa *souvenir*

lenço ⓜ *leng*/soo *scarf*
  — de mão de mowng *handkerchief*
  — de papel de pa-*pel tissue*

lençóis e mantas ⓕ pl leng-*soysh* ee *mang*-tash *bedding*

lençol ⓜ leng-*sol sheet (bed)*

lenha ① *le*-nya *firewood*
lente ① *leng*-te *lens (camera)*
lentes de contacto ⓜ pl
leng-tesh de kong-*taak*-too *contact lenses*
ler ler *read*
lésbica ① *lezh*-bee-ka *lesbian*
levantar (um cheque) le-vang-*taar*
(oong she-ke) *cash (a cheque)*
levar le-*vaar* *take*
leve *le*-ve *light (weight)*
libra ① *lee*-bra *pound (weight)*
licença ① lee-*seng*-sa *licence • permission*
— **de trabalho** de tra-*baa*-lyoo
work permit
ligação ① lee-ga-*sowng* *connection*
— **a cobrar** a koo-*braar* *collect call*
— **directa** dee-*re*-ta *direct-dial*
ligado/ligada ⓜ/①
lee-*gaa*-doo/lee-*gaa*-da *on (power)*
ligadura ① lee-ga-*doo*-ra *bandage*
limite de peso ⓜ lee-*mee*-te de *pe*-zoo
baggage allowance
limite de velocidade ⓜ lee-*mee*-te de
ve-loo-see-*daa*-de *speed limit*
limpar leeng-*paar* *clean*
limpeza ① leeng-*pe*-za *cleaning*
limpo/limpa ⓜ/①
leeng-poo/*leeng*-pa *clean*
língua ① *leeng*-gwa *language*
liquidação ① lee-kee-da-*sowng* *sale*
lista telefónica ① *leesh*-ta te-le-*fo*-nee-ka
phone book
livraria ① lee-vra-*ree*-a *book shop*
livre *lee*-vre *free (not bound)*
livro ⓜ *lee*-vroo *book*
— **de frases** de *fraa*-zesh *phrasebook*
lixo ⓜ *lee*-shoo *garbage • rubbish*
local ⓜ loo-*kaal* *venue*
— **de nascimento** de nash-see-*meng*-too
place of birth
local ⓜ&① loo-*kaal* *local*
loja ① *lo*-zha *shop*
— **de aparelhos eléctricos**
de a-pa-re-*lyoosh* ee-*le*-tree-koosh
electrical store
— **de bebidas** de be-*bee*-dash
liquor store
— **de brinquedos** de breeng-*ke*-doosh
toy shop
— **de campismo** de kang-*peezh*-moo
camping store

— **de ciclismo** de see-*kleesh*-moo
bike shop
— **de conveniência** de
kong-ve-*nyeng*-sya *convenience store*
— **de desporto** de desh-*por*-too
sports store
— **de equipamentos fotográficos**
de e-kee-pa-*meng*-toosh
foo-too-*graa*-fee-koosh *camera shop*
— **de ferramentas** de fe-rra-*meng*-tash
hardware store
— **de lembranças** de leng-*brang*-sash
souvenir shop
— **de música** de *moo*-zee-ka *music shop*
— **de roupas** de *rroh*-pash *clothing store*
— **de segunda mão**
de se-*goon*-da mowng *second-hand shop*
lombrigas ① pl long-*bree*-gash
worms (intestinal)
longe *long*-zhe *far*
longo/longa ⓜ/① *long*-goo/*long*-ga *long*
louco/louca ⓜ/① *loh*-koo/*loh*-ka *crazy*
lua ① *loo*-a *moon*
— **de mel** de mel *honeymoon*
lubrificante ⓜ loo-bree-fee-*kang*-te
lubricant
lucro ⓜ *loo*-kroo *profit*
lugar ⓜ loo-*gaar* *place*
luta ① *loo*-ta *fight*
luvas ① pl *loo*-vash *gloves*
— **de borracha** de boo-*rraa*-sha
gloves (latex)
luxo ⓜ *loo*-shoo *luxury*
luz ① loosh *light*
— **do flash** doo flaash *flashlight (torch)*

M

machado de gelo ⓜ
ma-*shaa*-doo de *zhe*-loo *ice axe*
machismo ⓜ ma-*sheezh*-moo *sexism*
madeira ① ma-*day*-ra *wood*
madrugada ① ma-droo-*gaa*-da *dawn*
mãe ① maing *mother*
maior may-*or* *bigger*
mais maish *more*
— **tarde** *tar*-de *later*
mala de mão ① *maa*-la de mowng
handbag
mala de viagem ①
maa-la de vee-*aa*-zheng *suitcase*

manhã ① ma-*nyang* morning
manifestação ① ma-nee-fesh-ta-*sowng*
    demonstration • protest
Manuelino/Manuelina ⓜ/①
    man-wel-*ee*-noo/man-wel-*ee*-na
    Manueline (art)
mão ① mowng *hand*
mapa ① *maa*-pa *map*
    — de estradas de *shtraa*-dash *road map*
maquilhagem ① ma-kee-*lyaa*-zheng
    make-up
máquina ① *maa*-kee-na *machine*
    — de lavar roupa de la-*vaar* rroh-pa
    washing machine
    — de vender bilhetes de veng-*der*
    bee-*lye*-tesh *ticket machine*
    — fotográfica foo-too-*graa*-fee-ka
    camera
mar ⓜ maar *sea*
maravilhoso/maravilhosa ⓜ/①
    ma-ra-vee-*lyo*-zoo/ma-ra-vee-*lyo*-za
    wonderful
marcar mar-*kaar* score (a goal)
maré ① ma-*re* tide
marido ⓜ ma-*ree*-doo husband
marijuana ① ma-ree-zhoo-*a*-na marijuana
martelo ⓜ mar-*te*-loo hammer
mas mash but
massagem ① ma-*saa*-zheng massage
matar ma-*taar* kill
mau/má ⓜ/① ma-oo/maa bad
maxilar ⓜ maak-see-*laar* jaw (human)
mecânico/mecânica ⓜ/①
    me-*ka*-nee-koo/me-*ka*-nee-ka mechanic
medicamentos ⓜ pl
    me-dee-ka-*meng*-toosh medication
medicina ① me-dee-*see*-na
    medicine (profession)
médico/médica ⓜ/①
    me-dee-koo/*me*-dee-ka doctor
meditação ① me-dee-ta-*sowng* meditation
meia ① *may*-a sock
meia-noite ① *may*-a-*noy*-te midnight
meias de vidro ① pl *may*-ash de *vee*-droo
    stockings
meio-dia ⓜ *may*-oo-dee-a midday
meio tempo *may*-oo teng-poo part-time
melhor me-*lyor* better
melodia ① me-loo-*dee*-a tune
membro ⓜ&① *meng*-broo member
memória ① me-*mo*-ree-a memory card
menina ① me-*nee*-na girl

Menina me-*nee*-na Miss (title)
menino ⓜ me-*nee*-noo boy
menor me-*nor* smaller
menos *me*-noosh less
mensagem ① meng-*saa*-zheng message
menstruação ① meng-shtroo-a-*sowng*
    menstruation
mentir meng-*teer* lie (not tell the truth)
mentiroso/mentirosa ⓜ/①
    meng-tee-*ro*-zoo/meng-tee-*ro*-za liar
mercado ⓜ mer-*kaa*-doo market
mercearia ① mer-see-a-*ree*-a grocery
mergulho ⓜ mer-*goo*-lyoo diving
mês ⓜ mesh month
mesa ① *me*-za table
mesmo/mesma ⓜ/①
    mezh-moo/*mezh*-ma same
mesquita ① mesh-*kee*-ta mosque
metro ⓜ me-troo metre
metropolitano ⓜ me-troo-poo-lee-*ta*-no
    subway (train)
meu/minha ⓜ/① me-oo/mee-nya my
microondas ⓜ pl mee-kro-*ong*-dash
    microwave oven
milímetro ⓜ mee-*lee*-me-troo millimetre
mim ⓜ&① meeng me
mimado/mimada ⓜ/① mee-*maa*-doo/
    mee-*maa*-da spoiled (person)
minúsculo/minúscula ⓜ/①
    mee-*noosh*-koo-loo/mee-*noosh*-koo-la
    tiny
minuto ⓜ mee-*noo*-too minute
miradouro ⓜ mee-ra-*doh*-roo lookout
missa ① *mee*-sa mass (Catholic)
misturar meesh-too-*raar* mix
mochila ① moo-*shee*-la backpack
moda ① *mo*-da fashion
moderno/moderna ⓜ/①
    moo-*der*-noo/moo-*der*-na modern
moedas ① pl moo-e-dash coins
molas ① pl *mo*-lash spring (coil)
molhado/molhada ⓜ/①
    moo-*lyaa*-doo/moo-*lyaa*-da wet
montanha ① mong-*ta*-nya mountain
montanhismo ⓜ mong-ta-*nyeezh*-moo
    mountaineering
monumento ⓜ moo-noo-*meng*-too
    monument
morar moo-*raar* live (somewhere)
mordedura ① moor-de-*doo*-ra bite (dog)
mordida (por um insecto) ① mor-*dee*-da
    (poor oong eeng-*se*-too) bite (insect)

morno/morna ⓜ/ⓕ *mor·*noo/*mor·*na warm

morrer moo·*rrer* die

morto/morta ⓜ/ⓕ *mor·*too/*mor·*ta dead

mosquiteiro ⓜ moosh·kee·*tay·*roo mosquito net

mosquito ⓜ moosh·*kee·*too mosquito

mosteiro ⓜ moosh·*tay·*roo monastery

mostrador de velocidade ⓜ moosh·tra·*dor* de ve·loo·see·*daa·*de speedometer

mostrar moosh·*traar* show

mota ⓕ *mo·*ta motorbike

motor ⓜ moo·*tor* engine

mourisco/mourisca ⓜ/ⓕ moh·*reesh·*koo/moh·*reesh·*ka Moorish

móveis ⓜ pl *mo·*vaysh furniture

muçulmano/muçulmana ⓜ/ⓕ moo·sool·*ma·*noo/moo·sool·*ma·*na Muslim n&a

mudança ⓕ moo·*dang·*sa change

mudo/muda ⓜ/ⓕ *moo·*doo/*moo·*da mute

muito mweeng·too very

muito/muita ⓜ/ⓕ mweeng·too/mweeng·ta (a) lot

mulher ⓕ moo·*lyer* woman

— **de negócios** de ne·*go·*syoosh businesswoman

multa ⓕ *mool·*ta fine (payment)

mundo ⓜ *moong·*doo world

músculo ⓜ *moosh·*koo·loo muscle

museu ⓜ moo·ze·oo museum

música ⓕ *moo·*zee·ka music

— **popular** poo·poo·*laar* folk music

músico/música ⓜ/ⓕ *moo·*zee·koo/*moo·*zee·ka musician

N

na frente de na *freng·*te de in front of

nacionalidade ⓕ na·syoo·na·lee·*daa·*de nationality

nada ⓜ *naa·*da nothing

nadar na·*daar* swim

nádegas ⓕ pl *naa·*de·gash bottom (body)

namorada ⓕ na·moo·*raa·*da girlfriend

namorado ⓜ na·moo·*raa·*doo boyfriend

namorar na·moo·*raar* date (a person)

não nowng no • not

não-fumador nowng·foo·ma·*dor* nonsmoking

nariz ⓜ na·*reesh* nose

— **a pingar** a peeng·*gaar* runny nose

nascer do sol ⓜ *nash·*ser doo sol sunrise

natação ⓕ na·ta·*sowng* swimming

Natal ⓜ na·*taal* Christmas

natureza ⓕ na·too·*re·*za nature

navio ⓜ na·*vee·*oo ship

necessário/necessária ⓜ/ⓕ ne·se·*saa·*ryoo/ne·se·*saa·*rya necessary

negativos ⓜ pl ne·ga·*tee·*voosh negatives (photos)

negócios ⓜ pl ne·*go·*syoosh business

nenhum/nenhuma ⓜ/ⓕ neng·*yoong*/neng·*yoo·*ma neither • none

neto/neta ⓜ/ⓕ *ne·*too/*ne·*ta grandchild

neve ⓕ *ne·*ve snow

nódoa negra ⓕ *no·*doo·a *ne·*gra bruise

nódulo ⓜ *no·*doo·loo lump

no estrangeiro noo shtrang·*zhay·*roo abroad • overseas

no interior noo eeng·te·ree·*or* indoors

noite ⓕ *noy·*te night

Noite de Natal ⓕ *noy·*te de na·*taal* Christmas Eve

noivado ⓜ noy·*vaa·*doo engagement (to marry)

noivo/noiva ⓜ/ⓕ *noy·*voo/*noy·*va fiancé/fiancée

nome ⓜ *no·*me name

nós nosh we

nosso/nossa ⓜ/ⓕ *no·*soo/*no·*sa our (one thing)

nossos/nossas ⓜ/ⓕ *no·*soosh/*no·*sash our (more than one thing)

nota bancária ⓕ *no·*ta bang·*kaa·*rya banknote

notícias ⓕ pl noo·*tee·*syash news

novamente no·va·*meng·*te again

novo/nova ⓜ/ⓕ *no·*voo/*no·*va new

nublado/nublada ⓜ/ⓕ noo·*blaa·*doo/noo·*blaa·*da cloudy

número ⓜ *noo·*me·roo number

— **da matrícula** da ma·*tree·*koo·la license plate number (car)

— **do passaporte** doo paa·sa·*por·*te passport number

— **do quarto** doo *kwaar·*too room number

nunca *noong·*ka never

nuvem ⓕ noo·*veng* cloud

O

o/a maior ⓜ/ⓕ oo/a may-or *biggest*
o/a mais perto ⓜ/ⓕ oo/a maish *per*-too
  nearest
o/a melhor ⓜ/ⓕ oo/a me-*lyor* *best*
o/a menor ⓜ/ⓕ oo/a me-*nor* *smallest*
oceano ⓜ o-see-*a*-noo *ocean*
óculos ⓜ pl o-*koo*-loosh *glasses (eye)*
  — de esqui de shkee *goggles (skiing)*
  — de natação de na-ta-*sowng*
  goggles (swimming)
  — de sol de sol *sunglasses*
ocupado ⓜ o-koo-*paa*-doo
  engaged (phone)
ocupado/ocupada ⓜ/ⓕ
  o-koo-*paa*-doo/o-koo-*paa*-da *busy*
oficina ⓕ o-fe-*see*-na *workshop*
olhar oo-*lyaar* *look*
olho ⓜ o-*lyoo* *eye*
ombro ⓜ *ong*-broo *shoulder*
onda ⓕ *ong*-da *wave (ocean)*
onde *ong*-de *where*
ontem *ong*-teng *yesterday*
operário/operária ⓜ/ⓕ o-pe-*raa*-ryoo/
  o-pe-*raa*-rya *factory worker*
opinião ⓕ o-pee-nee-*owng* *opinion*
oportunidade ⓕ o-poor-too-nee-*daa*-de
  chance
oposto/oposta ⓜ/ⓕ o-*posh*-too/o-*posh*-ta
  opposite
óptimo/óptima ⓜ/ⓕ o-*tee*-moo/o-*tee*-ma
  great (fantastic)
oração ⓕ o-ra-*sowng* *prayer*
orçamento ⓜ or-sa-*meng*-too *budget*
orelha ⓕ o-*re*-lya *ear*
orgasmo ⓜ or-*gaazh*-moo *orgasm*
orquestra ⓕ or-*kesh*-tra *orchestra*
o senhor/a senhora ⓜ/ⓕ oo seng-*yor*/a
  seng-*yo*-ra *you* pol sg
os senhores/as senhoras ⓜ/ⓕ oosh
  seng-*yo*-resh/ash seng-*yo*-rash *you* pol pl
osso ⓜ o-soo *bone*
ou *or*
ourivesaria ⓕ oh-ree-ve-za-*ree*-a *jewellery*
ouro ⓜ *oh*-roo *gold*
outro/outra ⓜ/ⓕ *oh*-troo/*oh*-tra *other* n&a
ovário ⓜ o-*vaa*-ryoo *ovary*
ovelha ⓕ oo-*ve*-lya *sheep*
oxigénio ⓜ ok-see-*zhe*-nyoo *oxygen*

P

pacote ⓜ pa-*ko*-te *packet*
padre ⓜ *paa*-dre *priest*
pagamento ⓜ pa-ga-*meng*-too *payment*
pagar pa-*gaar* *pay*
página ⓕ *paa*-zhee-na *page*
pai ⓜ pai *father*
país ⓜ pa-*eesh* *country*
pais ⓜ pl paish *parents*
palácio ⓜ pa-*laa*-syoo *palace*
palavra ⓕ pa-*laa*-vra *word*
palito ⓜ pa-*lee*-too *toothpick*
panela ⓕ pa-*ne*-la *pan • pot (cooking)*
papeira ⓕ pa-*pay*-ra *mumps*
papel ⓜ pa-*pel* *paper*
  — higiénico ee-zhee-e-*nee*-koo
  toilet paper
papelada ⓕ pa-pe-*laa*-da *paperwork*
papelaria ⓕ pa-pe-la-*ree*-a *stationery shop*
para baixo *pa*-ra bai-shoo *downhill*
parabéns ⓜ pl pa-ra-*bengzh*
  congratulations
pára-brisas ⓜ pl pa-ra-*bree*-zash
  windscreen (windshield)
para cima *pa*-ra *see*-ma *up*
paragem de autocarros ⓕ pa-*raa*-zheng
  de ow-to-*kaa*-rroosh *bus station/stop*
parapeito ⓜ pa-ra-*pay*-too *ledge*
paraplégico/paraplégica ⓜ/ⓕ
  pa-ra-pe-*le*-zhee-koo/pa-ra-pe-*le*-zhee-ka
  paraplegic n&a
parar pa-*raar* *stop*
para sempre *pa*-ra *seng*-pre *forever*
parecido/parecida ⓜ/ⓕ
  pa-re-*see*-doo/pa-re-*see*-da *similar*
parede ⓕ pa-*re*-de *wall (outer)*
parlamento ⓜ par-la-*meng*-too *parliament*
parque ⓜ *paar*-ke *park*
  — de campismo
  de kang-*peezh*-moo *camp site*
  — de estacionamento
  de shta-syoo-na-*meng*-too *car park*
  — nacional na-syoo-*naal* *national park*
parte ⓕ *paar*-te *part (component)*
partida ⓕ par-*tee*-da
  departure • match (sport)
partidário/partidária ⓜ/ⓕ
  par-tee-*daa*-ryoo/par-tee-*daa*-rya
  supporter (politics)
partido ⓜ par-*tee*-doo *party (politics)*

partilhar par-tee-*lyaar* share (room, etc)
partir par-*teer* depart (leave)
Páscoa ① *paash*-kwa Easter
passado ⓜ pa-*saa*-doo past
passado/passada ⓜ/①
pa-*saa*-doo/pa-*saa*-da last (previous)
passageiro/passageira ⓜ/①
pa-sa-*zhay*-roo/pa-sa-*zhay*-ra passenger
passagem de ano ①
pa-*saa*-zheng de a-noo New Year's Eve
passar pa-*saar* pass (kick/throw)
— por poor pass (go by)
pássaro ⓜ *paa*-sa-roo bird
passo ⓜ *paa*-soo step
pasta ① *pash*-ta briefcase
pasta de dentes ① *paash*-ta de *deng*-tesh
toothpaste
patinar pa-tee-*naar* skate
patins em linha ⓜ pl
pa-*teengzh* eng *lee*-nya rollerblading
pato/pata ⓜ/① *paa*-too/*paa*-ta duck
patrão/patroa ⓜ/① pa-*trowng*/pa-*tro*-a
employer
paz ① *pash* peace
pé ⓜ pe foot (body)
peão ⓜ pee-*owng* pedestrian
peça ① *pe*-sa play (theatre)
pedaço ⓜ pe-*daa*-soo piece
pedido ⓜ pe-*dee*-doo order
pedinte ⓜ&① pe-*deeng*-te beggar
pedir pe-*deer* ask (for something) • order
— emprestado eng-presh-*taa*-doo
borrow
pedra ① *pe*-dra stone
peito ⓜ *pay*-too breast • chest (body)
peixe ⓜ *pay*-she fish
pele ① *pe*-le skin
penhasco ⓜ pe-*nyaash*-koo cliff
Península Ibérica ① pe-*neeng*-soo-la
ee-be-ree-ka Iberian Peninsula
pénis ⓜ *pe*-neesh penis
pensar peng-*saar* think
penso ⓜ *peng*-soo Band-Aid
— higiénico ee-zhee-e-nee-koo
panty liner • sanitary napkin
pente ⓜ *peng*-te comb
pequeno/pequena ⓜ/①
pe-*ke*-noo/pe-*ke*-na small
pequeno almoço ⓜ pe-*ke*-noo aal-*mo*-soo
breakfast
perder per-*der* lose • miss (lose/overlook)

perdido/perdida ⓜ/① per-*dee*-doo/
per-*dee*-da lost
perdidos e achados ⓜ pl per-*dee*-doosh
ee aa-*shaa*-doosh left luggage
perdoar per-doo-*aar* forgive
perfeito/perfeita ⓜ/①
per-*fay*-too/per-*fay*-ta perfect
perfume ⓜ per-*foo*-me perfume
pergunta ① per-*goong*-ta question
perguntar per-goong-*taar* ask (a question)
perigoso/perigosa ⓜ/①
pe-ree-go-zoo/pe-ree-go-za dangerous
perna ① *per*-na leg (body)
perto *per*-too close • near
pesado/pesada ⓜ/①
pe-*zaa*-doo/pe-*zaa*-da heavy (weight)
pesca ① *pesh*-ka fishing
pescoço ⓜ pesh-ko-soo neck
peso ⓜ pe-zoo weight
pessoa ① pe-*so*-a person
pessoas ① pl pe-*so*-ash people
petróleo ⓜ pe-*tro*-lyoo petrol (gas)
piada ① pee-*aa*-da joke
picareta ① pee-ka-re-ta pickaxe
pico ⓜ pee-koo mountain peak
pilar ⓜ pee-*laar* pillory (stone column)
pilha ① pee-lya battery
pílula ① pee-loo-la the pill
— para dormir pa-ra door-meer
sleeping pills
pinça ① *peeng*-sa tweezers
pintor/pintora ⓜ/①
peeng-*tor*/peeng-*to*-ra painter
pintura ① peeng-*too*-ra painting
piolhos ⓜ pl pee-o-lyoosh lice
piscina ① pesh-see-na swimming pool
pista ① *peesh*-ta track (sport)
pistola ① peesh-to-la gun
placar ⓜ pla-*kaar* scoreboard
planalto ⓜ pla-*naal*-too plateau
plano/plana ⓜ/① *pla*-noo/*pla*-na flat
planta ① *plang*-ta plant
plástico/plástica ⓜ/①
plash-tee-koo/*plash*-tee-ka plastic
plataforma ① pla-ta-for-ma platform
pneu ⓜ pe-ne-oo tyre (tire)
pó ⓜ po powder
— de talco de taal-koo baby powder
pobre po-bre poor (wealth)
pobreza ① poo-*bre*-za poverty
poder ⓜ poo-*der* power
poder poo-*der* can

poesia ① po-ee-zee-a *poetry*
pólen ⓜ po-leng *pollen*
polícia ① poo-lee-sya *police • police officer*
política ① poo-lee-tee-ka *policy • politics*
político/política ⓜ/①
poo-lee-tee-koo/poo-lee-tee-ka *politician*
poluição ① poo-loo-ee-sowng *pollution*
ponte ① pong-te *bridge (structure)*
ponto ⓜ pong-too *point*
— **de controle** de kong-tro-le
checkpoint
popular poo-poo-laar *popular*
por poor *per (day)*
— **cento** seng-too *per cent*
— **cima de** see-ma de *above*
— **perto** per-too *nearby*
pôr do sol ⓜ por doo sol *sunset*
porco/porca ⓜ/① por-koo/por-ka *pig*
porquê poor-ke *why*
porta de partida ① por-ta de par-tee-da
departure gate
portão/porta ⓜ/① por-towng/por-ta
gate (airport)
porto ⓜ por-too *harbour • port*
Portugal ⓜ poor-too-gaal *Portugal*
português ⓜ poor-too-gesh
Portuguese (language)
positivo/positiva ⓜ/①
poo-zee-tee-voo/poo-zee-tee-vaa *positive*
possível poo-see-vel *possible*
pouco/pouca ⓜ/① poh-koo/poh-ka
little (quantity)
pousada de juventude ① poh-zaa-da de
zhoo-veng-too-de *youth hostel*
praça ① praa-sa *square (town)*
— **de táxis** de taak-seesh *taxi stand*
— **de touros** de toh-roosh *bullring*
praia ① prai-a *beach*
prancha de surf ① prang-sha de sarf
surfboard
prata ① praa-ta *silver*
prateleira ① pra-te-lay-ra *shelf*
prato ⓜ praa-too *dish • plate*
precisar pre-see-zaar *need*
preço ⓜ pre-soo *price*
— **da passagem** da pa-saa-zheng *fare*
prédio ⓜ pre-dyoo *building*
preferir pre-fe-reer *prefer*
preguiçoso/preguiçosa ⓜ/①
pre-gee-so-zoo/pre-gee-so-za *lazy*
prender preng-der *arrest*

preocupado/preocupada ⓜ/①
pree-o-koo-paa-doo/pree-o-koo-paa-da
worried
preparar pre-pa-raar *prepare*
presente ⓜ pre-zeng-te *gift • present (time)*
preservativo ⓜ pre-zer-va-tee-voo *condom*
presidente ⓜ&①
pre-zee-deng-te *president*
— **da câmara** da ka-ma-ra *mayor*
pressão ① pre-sowng *pressure (tyre)*
preto/preta ⓜ/① pre-too/pre-ta *black*
preto e branco pre-too e brang-koo
B&W (film)
primeiro/primeira ⓜ/①
pree-may-roo/pree-may-ra *first*
primeiro ministro/primeira ministra
ⓜ/① pree-may-roo mee-nee-shtroo/
pree-may-ra mee-nee-shtra *prime minister*
primeiro nome ⓜ pree-may-roo no-me
Christian name
principal preeng-see-paal *main*
prisão ① pree-zowng *jail (prison)*
— **de ventre** pree-zowng de ven-tre
constipation
prisioneiro/prisioneira pree-zyoo-nay-roo/
pree-zyoo-nay-ra *prisoner*
privado/privada ⓜ/① pree-vaa-doo/
pree-vaa-da *private*
problema de coração ⓜ proo-ble-ma de
koo-ra-sowng *heart condition*
procurar pro-koo-raar *look for*
produzir proo-doo-zeer *produce*
professor/professora ⓜ/①
proo-fe-sor/proo-fe-so-ra *lecturer • teacher*
profundo/profunda ⓜ/①
proo-foong-doo/proo-foong-da *deep*
programa ⓜ proo-gra-ma *program*
projector ⓜ proo-zhe-tor *projector*
prometer proo-me-ter *promise*
pronto/pronta ⓜ/①
prong-too/prong-ta *ready*
prostituto/prostituta ⓜ/①
proosh-tee-too-too/proosh-tee-too-ta
prostitute
protecção anti-solar ①
proo-te-sowng an-tee-soo-laar *sunblock*
protector de borracha ⓜ
proo-te-tor de boo-rraa-sha *dental dam*
proteger proo-te-zher *protect*
protegido/protegida ⓜ/①
proo-te-zhee-doo/proo-te-zhee-da
protected (species)

protestar proo-tesh-*taar* protest
provisões ① pl proo-vee-*zoyngsh* provisions
próximo/próxima ⓜ/① pro-see-moo/pro-see-ma nearby • next
pulga ① pool-ga flea
pulmão ⓜ pool-*mowng* lung
pulso ⓜ pool-soo wrist
puro/pura ⓜ/① poo-roo/poo-ra pure
puxar poo-*shaar* pull

Q

quadraplégico/quadraplégica ⓜ/①
kwa-dra-*ple*-zhee-koo/kwa-dra-*ple*-zhee-ka
quadriplegic n&a
qual kwaal which
qualidade ① kwa-lee-*daa*-de quality
qualificações ① pl kwa-lee-fee-ka-*soyngsh* qualifications
qualquer kwaal-*ker* any
quando kwang-doo when
quarentena ① kwa-reng-*te*-na quarantine
quarto ⓜ kwaar-too bedroom • room
    — de casal de ka-*zaal* double room
    — de solteiro de sol-*tay*-roo single room
quase kwaa-ze almost
que ke what
quebrado/quebrada ⓜ/①
ke-*braa*-doo/ke-*braa*-da broken
quebrar ke-*braar* break
queimadura ① kay-ma-*doo*-ra burn
quem keng who
quente keng-te hot
querer ke-*rer* want
quilograma ① kee-loo-*graa*-ma kilogram
quilómetro ⓜ kee-*lo*-me-troo kilometre
quinta ① keeng-ta farm
quinzena ① keeng-ze-na fortnight
quiosque ① kee-*osh*-ke kiosk • newsstand
quiroprático/quiroprática ⓜ/①
kee-roo-*praa*-tee-koo/kee-roo-*praa*-tee-ka chiropractor

R

racismo ⓜ rra-*seezh*-moo racism
radiador ⓜ rra-dee-a-*dor* radiator
rádio rraa-dyoo radio
rainha ① rra-*ee*-nya queen

raio de roda ⓜ rraa-yoo de *rro*-da spoke (wheel)
rápido/rápida ⓜ/① rraa-pee-doo/ rraa-pee-da fast
raquete ① rra-*ke*-te racquet
raro/rara ⓜ/① rraa-roo/rraa-ra rare (uncommon)
ratazana ⓜ&① rra-ta-*za*-na rat
rato ⓜ rraa-too mouse
rave ① rrayv rave (party)
razão ① rra-*zowng* reason
razoável rra-zoo-*aa*-vel sensible
realista rre-a-*leesh*-ta realistic
recarregador de bateria ⓜ
rre-ka-rre-ga-*dor* de ba-te-*ree*-a jumper leads
receber rre-se-*ber* welcome
receita médica ① rre-*say*-ta me-dee-ka prescription
recentemente rre-seng-te-*meng*-te recently
recibo ⓜ rre-*see*-boo receipt
reciclar rre-see-*klaar* recycle
reciclável rre-see-*klaa*-vel recyclable
reclamação ① rre-kla-ma-*sowng* complaint
reclamar rre-kla-*maar* complain
recomendar rre-koo-meng-*daar* recommend
recursos humanos ⓜ pl rre-*koor*-soosh oo-*ma*-noosh human resources
recusar rre-koo-*zaar* refuse
rede ① rre-de net • network (phone)
redondo/redonda ⓜ/① rre-dong-doo/rre-dong-da round
reembolso ⓜ rre-eng-*bol*-soo refund
refeição ① rre-fay-*sowng* meal
    — ligeira lee-*zhay*-ra snack
referência ① rre-fe-*reng*-sya reference
refrigerante ① rre-free-zhe-*rang*-te soft drink
refugiado/refugiada ⓜ/①
rre-foo-zhee-*aa*-doo/rre-foo-zhee-*aa*-da refugee
regional rre-zhyoo-*naal* regional
registo automóvel ⓜ rre-*zheesh*-too ow-too-*mo*-vel car registration
regra ① rre-gra rule
regressar rre-gre-*saar* return
rei ⓜ rray king
relacionamento ⓜ
rre-la-syoo-na-*meng*-too relationship
relações públicas ① pl rre-la-*soyngsh* poo-blee-kash public relations

relaxar rre-laa-*shaar* relax

religião ① rre-lee-zhee-*owng* religion

religioso/religiosa ⓜ/①
rre-lee-zhee-o-zoo/rre-lee-zhee-o-za
religious

relíquia ① rre-*lee*-kya relic

relógio ⓜ rre-*lo*-zhyoo clock • watch

relva ① *rrel*-va grass (lawn)

remoto/remota ⓜ/① rre-*mo*-too/rre-*mo*-ta
remote

renda ① *rreng*-da lace

repelente ⓜ rre-pe-*leng*-te insect repellant
— **em espiral** eng shpee-*raal*
mosquito coil

reserva ① rre-*zer*-va reservation

reservar rre-zer-*vaar* book (reserve)

respirar rresh-pee-*raar* breathe

resposta ① rresh-*posh*-ta answer

restaurante ⓜ resh-tow-*rang*-te
restaurant

reverenciar rre-ve-reng-see-*aar* worship

revisão ① rre-vee-*zowng* review

revista ① rre-*veesh*-ta magazine

ribeiro ⓜ rree-*bay*-roo stream

rico/rica ⓜ/① *rree*-koo/*rree*-ka wealthy

rim ⓜ rreeng kidney

rio ⓜ *rree*-oo river

rir rreer laugh

risco ⓜ *rreesh*-koo risk

ritmo ⓜ *rreet*-moo rhythm

roda ① *rro*-da wheel

romântico/romântica ⓜ/①
rroo-*maang*-tee-koo/rroo-*maang*-tee-ka
romantic

rosto ⓜ *rrosh*-too face

rota ① *rro*-ta route
— **de caminhada** de ka-mee-*nyaa*-da
hiking route

rotunda ① rroo-*toong*-da roundabout

roubado/roubada ⓜ/①
rroh-*baa*-doo/rroh-*baa*-da stolen

roubar rroh-*baar* steal

roubo ⓜ *rroh*-boo rip-off

roupa interior ① *rroh*-pa eeng-te-ree-*or*
underwear

roupas ① pl *rroh*-pash clothing

roxo/roxa ⓜ/① *rro*-shoo/*rro*-sha purple

rua ① *rroo*-a street
— **principal** preeng-see-*paal* main road

rubéola ① rroo-*be*-o-la rubella

ruínas ① pl rroo-*ee*-nash ruins

S

saber sa-*ber* know

sabonete ⓜ sa-boo-*ne*-te soap

saca-rolhas ⓜ *saa*-ka-rro-lyash
bottle opener • corkscrew

saco ⓜ *saa*-koo bag
— **de dormir** de dor-*meer* sleeping bag
— **saco de fatos** de *faa*-toosh suit bag

saia ① *sai*-a skirt

saída ① saa-*ee*-da exit
— **à noite** aa *noy*-te night out

sair sa-*eer* go out

sais de hidratação ⓜ pl
saish de ee-dra-ta-*sowng* rehydration salts

sala ① *saa*-la room
— **de espera** de *shpe*-ra waiting room
— **de estar** de shtaar foyer
— **de provas** de pro-vash change room
— **de trânsito** de trang-zee-too
transit lounge

salão de beleza ⓜ sa-*lowng* de be-*le*-za
beauty salon

saldo ⓜ *saal*-doo balance (account)

saltar saal-*taar* jump

sandália ① sang-*daa*-lya sandal

sangue ⓜ *sang*-ge blood

santo/santa ⓜ/① *sang*-too/*sang*-ta saint

santuário ⓜ sang-too-*aa*-ryoo shrine

sapato ⓜ sa-*paa*-too shoe

sarampo ⓜ sa-*rang*-poo measles

saúde ① sa-*oo*-de health

se se if

secar se-*kaar* dry

seco/seca ⓜ/① *se*-koo/*se*-ka
dried • dry • stale

seda ① *se*-da silk

sedento/sedenta ⓜ/①
se-*deng*-too/se-*deng*-ta thirsty

seguir se-*geer* follow

segundo ⓜ se-*goong*-doo second (time)

segundo/segunda ⓜ/①
se-*goong*-doo/se-*goong*-da second

seguro ⓜ se-*goo*-roo insurance
— **social** soo-see-*aal* welfare

seguro/segura ⓜ/① se-*goo*-roo/se-*goo*-ra safe

seios ⓜ pl *say*-oosh breasts

selo ⓜ *se*-loo stamp (postage)

sem seng without

semáforo ⓜ se-*maa*-foo-roo traffic light

semana ① se-*ma*-na week

sempre seng-pre always
Senhor se-nyor Mr
Senhora se-nyo-ra Mrs • Ms
senhoria se-nyoo-ree-a landlady
senhorio se-nyoo-ree-oo landlord
sensação ① seng-sa-sowng feeling (physical)
sensível seng-see-vel emotional
sensual seng-soo-aal sensual
sentar seng-taar sit
sentimentos ⓜ pl seng-tee-meng-toosh feelings
separado/separada ⓜ/① se-pa-raa-doo/se-pa-raa-da separate
ser ser be (ongoing)
seringa ① se-reeng-ga needle (syringe)
sério/séria ⓜ/① se-ryoo/se-rya serious
serviço ⓜ ser-vee-soo service
sexo ⓜ sek-soo sex
— protegido proo-te-zhee-doo safe sex
SIDA ① see-da AIDS
sim seeng yes
simpático/simpática ⓜ/① seeng-paa-tee-koo/seeng-paa-tee-ka nice
simples seeng-plesh simple
sinal ⓜ see-naal sign
— da linha telefónica da lee-nya te-le-fo-nee-ka dial tone
sintético/sintética ⓜ/① seeng-te-tee-koo/seeng-te-tee-ka synthetic
sobre so-bre on
sobremesa ① soo-bre-me-za dessert
sobretudo ⓜ soo-bre-too-doo overcoat
só de ida so de ee-da one-way (ticket)
sogra ① so-gra mother-in-law
sogro ⓜ so-groo father-in-law
sol ⓜ sol sun
solteiro/solteira ⓜ/① sol-tay-roo/sol-tay-ra single (person)
solto/solta ⓜ/① sol-too/sol-ta loose
sombra ① song-bra shadow
somente so-meng-te only
sonho ⓜ so-nyoo dream
sonolento/sonolenta ⓜ/① soo-noo-leng-too/soo-noo-leng-ta sleepy
sorrir so-rreer smile
sorte ① sor-te luck
soutien ⓜ soo-tee-eng bra
sozinho/sozinha ⓜ/① so-zee-nyoo/so-zee-nya alone
subir soo-beer climb
— a bordo a bor-doo board

suborno ⓜ soo-bor-noo bribe
suficiente soo-fee-see-eng-te enough
sujo/suja ⓜ/① soo-zhoo/soo-zha dirty
superstição ① soo-persh-tee-sowng superstition
surdo/surda ⓜ/① soor-doo/soor-da deaf
surpresa ① soor-pre-za surprise

T

tabacaria ① ta-ba-ka-ree-a tobacconist
tabaco ① ta-baa-koo tobacco
Taça Mundial de Futebol ① taa-sa moong-dee-aal de foo-te-bol World Cup
talheres ⓜ pl ta-lye-resh cutlery
talvez tal-vesh maybe
tamanho ⓜ ta-ma-nyoo size
também tang-beng also
tampão ⓜ tang-powng plug (bath) • tampon
tampões para os ouvidos ⓜ pl tang-poyngsh pa-ra oosh oh-vee-doosh earplugs
tapete ⓜ ta-pe-te rug
tarde ① taar-de afternoon
tarifa postal ① ta-ree-fa poosh-taal postage
taxa ① taa-sha fee • tax
— de aeroporto de a-e-ro-por-too airport tax
— de câmbio de kang-byoo exchange rate
— de serviço de ser-vee-soo service charge
teatro ⓜ te-aa-troo theatre
tecido ⓜ te-see-doo fabric
teclado ⓜ te-klaa-doo keyboard
técnica ① tek-nee-ka technique
teimoso/teimosa ⓜ/① tay-mo-zoo/tay-mo-za stubborn
teleférico ⓜ te-le-fe-ree-koo chairlift (skiing)
telefonar te-le-foo-naar telephone
telefone ⓜ te-le-fo-ne telephone
— público poo-blee-koo public telephone
telemóvel ⓜ te-le-mo-vel cell/mobile phone
telescópio ⓜ te-lesh-ko-pyoo telescope
televisão ① te-le-vee-zowng television
temperatura ① teng-pe-ra-too-ra temperature (weather)
tempestade ① teng-pesh-taa-de storm

tempo ⓜ teng-poo *time • weather*
— **inteiro** eeng-tay-roo *full-time*
tenda ⓕ teng-da *tent*
ténis ⓜ te-neesh *tennis*
— **de mesa** de me-za *table tennis*
tensão arterial ⓕ teng-sowng ar-te-ree-aal *blood pressure*
tensão pré-menstrual ⓕ teng-sowng pre-meng-shtroo-aal *premenstrual tension*
tentar teng-taar *try (attempt)*
ter ter *have*
— **saudades** sow-daa-desh *miss (feel absence of)*
terminar ter-mee-naar *finish*
terra ⓕ te-rra *land*
terramoto ⓜ te-rra-mo-too *earthquake*
terrível te-rree-vel *terrible*
terrorismo ⓜ te-rroo-reezh-moo *terrorism*
tesoura ⓕ sg te-zoh-ra *scissors*
teste ⓜ tesh-te *test*
— **de gravidez** de gra-vee-desh *pregnancy test kit*
— **nuclear** noo-klee-aar *nuclear testing*
teu/tua ⓜ/ⓕ te-oo/too-a *your (one thing)* inf sg
teus/tuas ⓜ/ⓕ te-oosh/too-ash *your (more than one thing)* inf sg
tia ⓕ tee-a *aunt*
tigela ⓕ tee-zhe-la *bowl*
tímido/tímida ⓜ/ⓕ tee-mee-doo/tee-mee-da *shy*
típico/típica ⓜ/ⓕ tee-pee-koo/tee-pee-ka *typical*
tipo ⓜ tee-poo *type*
título de registo do automóvel ⓜ tee-too-loo de rre-zheesh-too doo ow-too-mo-vel *car owner's title*
toalha ⓕ twaa-lya *towel*
— **de mesa** de me-za *tablecloth*
— **de rosto** de rrosh-too *face cloth*
tocar too-kaar *feel (touch) • play (guitar, etc) • touch*
todo/toda ⓜ/ⓕ to-doo/to-da *all • every*
todos/todas ⓜ/ⓕ to-doosh/to-dash *everyone*
tomada ⓕ too-maa-da *plug (electricity)*
tonto/tonta ⓜ/ⓕ tong-too/tong-ta *dizzy*
torneira ⓕ toor-nay-ra *faucet • tap (sink)*
tornozelo ⓜ toor-noo-ze-loo *ankle*
torre ⓕ to-rre *tower*
tossir too-seer *cough*

tourada ⓕ toh-raa-da *bullfight*
touro ⓜ toh-roo *bull*
toxicodependente tok-see-ko-de-peng-deng-te *drug user*
trabalhador/trabalhadora ⓜ/ⓕ tra-ba-lya-dor/tra-ba-lya-do-ra *labourer*
trabalhar tra-ba-lyaar *work*
trabalho ⓜ tra-baa-lyoo *work*
— **num bar** noong baar *bar work*
— **doméstico** doo-mesh-tee-koo *housework*
— **temporário** teng-poo-raa-ryoo *casual work*
traduzir tra-doo-zeer *translate*
tráfico ⓜ traa-fee-koo *traffic*
— **de drogas** de dro-gash *drug trafficking*
traição ⓕ tra-ee-sowng *cheat*
tranca ⓕ trang-ka *lock*
trancado/trancada ⓜ/ⓕ trang-kaa-doo/trang-kaa-da *locked*
traseiro/traseira ⓜ/ⓕ tra-zay-roo/tra-zay-ra *rear (location)*
travão ⓜ tra-vowng *brake (car)*
trazer tra-zer *bring*
treinador/treinadora ⓜ/ⓕ tray-na-dor/tray-na-do-ra *coach • manager (sport)*
treinamento ⓜ tre-na-meng-too *workout*
tribunal ⓜ tree-boo-naal *court (legal)*
trilho de montanha ⓜ tree-lyoo de mong-ta-nya *mountain path*
triste treesh-te *sad*
trocar troo-kaar *change (money) • exchange*
trocos ⓜ pl tro-koosh *loose change*
trombose ⓕ trong-bo-ze *stroke (health)*
trovoada ⓕ troo-voo-aa-da *thunderstorm*
tu too *you* inf sg
tudo ⓜ too-doo *everything*
tumor ⓜ too-mor *tumour*
túmulo ⓜ too-moo-loo *grave*
tuna ⓜ too-na *(university) music group*
turista ⓜ&ⓕ too-reesh-ta *tourist*

U

último/última ⓜ/ⓕ ool-tee-moo/ool-tee-ma *last (final)*
ultrasom ⓜ ool-tra-song *ultrasound*
uma vez oo-ma vezh *once*

um outro/uma outra ⓜ/ⓕ
oong oh·troo/oo·ma oh·tra *another*
universidade ⓕ oo·nee·ver·see·*daa*·de
college · university
universo ⓜ oo·nee·*ver*·soo *universe*
urgente oor·*zheng*·te *urgent*
usar oo·*zaar* *wear*
útil *oo*·teel *useful*

V

vaca ⓕ *vaa*·ka *cow*
vacina ⓕ va·*see*·na *vaccination*
vaga ⓕ *vaa*·ga *vacancy*
vagão cama ⓜ va·*gowng ka*·ma
sleeping car
vagão restaurante ⓜ va·*gowng*
rresh·tow·*rang*·te *dining car*
vagarosamente va·ga·ro·za·*meng*·te *slowly*
vagina ⓕ va·*zhee*·na *vagina*
vago/vaga ⓜ/ⓕ *vaa*·goo/*vaa*·ga *vacant*
validar va·lee·*daar* *validate*
valioso/valiosa ⓜ/ⓕ
va·lee·*o*·zoo/va·lee·*o*·za *valuable*
valor ⓜ va·*lor* *value*
varanda ⓕ va·*rang*·da *balcony*
vários/várias ⓜ/ⓕ *vaa*·ryoosh/*vaa*·ryash
many · several
vazio/vazia ⓜ/ⓕ va·*zee*·oo/va·*zee*·a *empty*
vegetariano/vegetariana ⓜ/ⓕ
ve·zhe·ta·ree·*a*·noo/ve·zhe·ta·ree·*a*·na
vegetarian n&a
veia ⓕ *vey*·a *vein*
vela ⓕ *ve*·la *candle*
velho/velha ⓜ/ⓕ *ve*·lyoo/*ve*·lya *old (age)*
velocidade ⓕ ve·loo·see·*daa*·de
speed (velocity)
— **do filme** doo *feel*·me *film speed*
vencedor/vencedora ⓜ/ⓕ
veng·se·*dor*/veng·se·*do*·ra *winner*
vender veng·*der* *sell*
venenoso/venenosa ⓜ/ⓕ
ve·ne·*no*·zoo/ve·ne·*no*·za *poisonous*
vento ⓜ *veng*·too *wind*
ventoínha ⓕ veng·too·ee·nya
fan (machine)
ver ver *see · watch (television)*
verão ⓜ ve·*rowng* *summer*

verde *ver*·de *green*
verificar ve·ree·fee·*kaar* *check*
vermelho/vermelha ⓜ/ⓕ
ver·me·*lyoo*/ver·me·*lya* *red*
vestido ⓜ vesh·*tee*·doo *dress*
via aérea ⓕ *vee*·a a·e·ree·a *airmail*
viagem ⓕ vee·*aa*·zheng *journey*
— **de negócios** de ne·*go*·syoosh
business trip
viajar vee·a·*zhaar* *travel*
vício ⓜ *vee*·syoo *addiction*
— **da droga** da *dro*·ga *drug addiction*
vida ⓕ *vee*·da *life*
vigiar vee·zhee·*aar* *watch (look after)*
VIH ⓜ ve ee a·*gaa* *HIV*
vinha ⓕ *vee*·nya *vineyard*
vinho ⓜ *vee*·nyoo *wine*
violação ⓕ vee·oo·la·*sowng* *rape*
vir veer *come*
virar vee·*raar* *turn*
vírus ⓜ *vee*·roosh *virus*
visitar vee·zee·*taar* *visit*
vista ⓕ *veesh*·ta *view*
visto ⓜ *veesh*·too *visa*
vitamina ⓕ vee·ta·*mee*·na *vitamin*
voar voo·*aar* *fly*
vocês vo·*sesh* *you* inf pl
vóleibol ⓜ *vo*·lay·bol *volleyball (sport)*
— **de praia** de *prai*·a *beach volleyball*
voltar vol·*taar* *return*
voo ⓜ *vo*·oo *flight*
vosso/vossa ⓜ/ⓕ *vo*·soo/*vo*·sa
your (one thing) inf pl
vossos/vossas ⓜ/ⓕ *vo*·soosh/*vo*·sash
your (more than one thing) inf pl
votar voo·*taar* *vote*
voz ⓕ vosh *voice*

X

xadrez ⓜ sha·*dresh* *chess*

Z

zangado/zangada ⓜ/ⓕ
zang·*gaa*·doo/zang·*gaa*·da *angry*
zona ⓕ *zo*·na *shingles (illness)*

FINDER

The topics covered in this book are listed below in Portuguese. Show this page to your Portuguese friends if you're having trouble understanding them.

don't just stand there, say something!

What kind of traveller are you?

A. You're eating chicken for dinner *again* because it's the only word you know.

B. When no one understands what you say, you step closer and shout louder.

C. When the barman doesn't understand your order, you point frantically at the beer.

D. You're surrounded by locals, swapping jokes, email addresses and experiences – other travellers want to borrow your phrasebook or audio guide.

If you answered A, B, or C, you NEED Lonely Planet's language products ...

- **Lonely Planet Phrasebooks** – for every phrase you need in every language you want
- **Lonely Planet Language & Culture** – get behind the scenes of English as it's spoken around the world – learn and laugh
- **Lonely Planet Fast Talk & Fast Talk Audio** – essential phrases for short trips and weekends away – read, listen and talk like a local
- **Lonely Planet Small Talk** – 10 essential languages for city breaks
- **Lonely Planet Real Talk** – downloadable language audio guides from lonelyplanet.com to your MP3 player

... and this is why

- **Talk to everyone everywhere**
  Over 120 languages, more than any other publisher
- **The right words at the right time**
  Quick-reference colour sections, two-way dictionary, easy pronunciation, every possible subject – and audio to support it

Lonely Planet Offices

Australia
90 Maribyrnong St, Footscray,
Victoria 3011
☎ 03 8379 8000
fax 03 8379 8111
✉ talk2us@lonelyplanet.com.au

USA
150 Linden St, Oakland,
CA 94607
☎ 510 250 6400
fax 510 893 8572
✉ info@lonelyplanet.com

UK
2nd floor, 186 City Rd
London EC1V 2NT
☎ 020 7106 2100
fax 020 7106 2101
✉ go@lonelyplanet.co.uk

lonelyplanet.com